Instant Pot for Two Cookbook

600 Quick & Easy Instant Pot Recipes

Susan Green

Warning-Disclaimer

The purpose of this book is to educate and entertain. The author or publisher does not guarantee that anyone following the techniques, suggestions, tips, ideas, or strategies will become successful. The author and publisher shall have neither liability or responsibility to anyone with respect to any loss or damage caused, or alleged to be caused, directly or indirectly by the information contained in this book.

CONTENTS

MEAT RECIPES............................36

SOUPS & SAUCES 71

INTRODUCTION

Hello! Welcome to my book of recipes for the Instant Pot.

My recipes are simply too delicious to keep to myself. And it's the only cookbook you'll need to make the most delicious Instant Pot recipes you've ever tasted!

If there's one kitchen appliance I can't live without, it's my Instant Pot. This gadget has changed my life completely in the kitchen! Gone are the days when I spent hours each week, prepping and then cooking meals. And so many times those meals were tasteless, with leftovers that no one wanted to eat.

Then along came my Instant Pot Pressure Cooker… and now I make delectable meals every day. Quick cooking, tasty recipes - and I have leftovers my family fights and squabbles over! Like the juiciest pork shoulders and spicy rice dishes. In my book, you'll find a collection of mouth watering and flavorsome recipes from every cuisine.

One of the biggest appealing features of the Instant Pot is that it makes fresh and fast homey meals in no time. Whether you're vegetarian or love your meat and chicken, my book has the best recipes for making amazing, healthy meals. And make sure you make an extravagant cheat recipe on those days when you're not counting Cal and fat! Those are the best recipes of all.

In this book, I share my favorite recipes with you, and I'll help you get familiar with the Instant Pot, so you know exactly how to use one. Breakfasts, appetizers, Sunday dinners, and delightfully sweet desserts! I have just the recipe for you.

So now, let's learn all about the Instant Pot so you can start cooking!

WHAT IS AN INSTANT POT PRESSURE COOKER?

Now that you know how much I love my Instant Pot, you'll want to know just what an electric Pressure cooker is. The Instant Pot is an appliance that's a combination of Pressure cooker, slow cooker, rice cooker, and yogurt maker – all in one handy kitchen device.

What parts makes up the Instant Cooker? There's an outer pot, which is the base and heat source of the Pressure cooker. Inside of this outer pot goes the inner pot, which is made from durable stainless steel. This inner pot is where all the cooking happens. There's a lid that goes on top of the inner pot, which has a Silicone ring that Seals tightly to keep food, liquids, and Pressure securely in the pot.

On top of the lid are the Pressure release and the float valve. The Pressure release does just that – it releases Pressure from inside the Instant Pot. The float valve on the lid pops up when the Instant Pot is Pressurized and lowers back down when it's not. You'll know it's safe to open the lid when the float valve is down.

The Instant Pot has a condensation collector on the side of the base unit that can be Removed. Its purpose is to collect condensation, usually when the Instant Pot is being used as a slow cooker.

Depending on the model of Instant Pot you have, it may come with some useful accessories – a steaming rack, measuring cup, and a set of spoons.

Not a complex appliance at all, right?

Get to know your brand of Instant Pot by taking a few minutes to read the instruction manual. Even though all electric pressure cookers have pretty much the same functions and settings, every brand comes with some unique features.

BENEFITS OF COOKING WITH THE INSTANT POT

Nutritious meals

Pressure cooking, slow cooking, and steaming foods keep in flavor and nutrients and create delicious and moist dishes. The recipes in my book use all of these functions.

Save time and energy

Using the Instant Pot saves you a lot of time. You can eat healthy at home, without spending the time you don't have, prepping and then cooking your meals. And fast cooking = energy saving. Cooking with your Instant pot is fast and efficient, cutting down your electricity bill by cooking in less time than you would on the stovetop or in the oven.

Pick your size

Most Instant Pots models come in three convenient sizes: 3, 6, and 8-quart. For most families, the 6-quart is the right size. The 3-quart mini Instant Pot is perfect for when you want to cook a small meal or a small amount of pasta or rice. And the 8-quart works for large families, or if you just like to make extra meals for another time. I've included recipes in my book that you can double so you can freeze mouth watering meals for lunches and dinner.

No more mad-rush cooking

How often have you had no time at all to even think about what you're making for dinner? Those days of panic are over. Your Instant Pot is there for you! There are some fast and easy meals included in the recipe book that in just minutes help you get a fantastic dinner on the table.

Hot breakfast!

Tired of waking up to cold cereal as your only breakfast option? Your Instant Pot can make hot oatmeal in minutes. Or make breakfast in your Instant Pot the night before and just Heat up in the morning.

Cook perfect rice every time!

Make rice in your electric pressure cooker, and you'll never go back to making it stove-top again. White, Brown, or basmati – some people would say the Instant Pot was made for rice.

Time your meals

Because of the Instant Pot cooks so fast, use the Delay Start function to time your meals, so they're ready when you get home. Many of my recipes let you prep your food the night before and then put them in the Instant Pot on the timer, cooking them to perfection every time.

MY TOP 5 INSTANT POT TIPS AND TRICKS TO MAKE PERFECTLY AMAZING FOOD FOR TWO!

1. The Friendly, Dried Bean

Using canned beans can get pricey if you're using a lot of them in soups and stews. The Instant Pot can cook dried beans in less than an hour, much faster than the 3 to 4 hours it takes to cook them on the stove. Using your electric pressure cooker, you can buy a variety of dried beans and have them on hand to make many of the delicious meals in my cookbook.

2. Creamy, Rich Yogurt

Eat a lot of yogurts? The Instant Pot is perfect for making low fat or creamy, rich yogurt. You'll save a lot of money by making your own. It's much tastier than store bought yogurt! And you can use it in my recipes.

3. Don't Forget the Sauté Function!

An often-over-looked function of your electric pressure cooker is the Sauté Function. Use this setting to Brown, Sauté, and simmer meat and other ingredients, such as onions. Sautéing gives recipes a richness that infuses your meals with flavor.

4. Avoid Messy Clean sup

Use the Natural Release, or as I call it the "do nothing release", to avoid messy clean up in your kitchen. Dishes that have a lot of liquid, such as soups, can move around a lot in the pot if you use the quick release, resulting in spills. Using the Natural Release means there less movement of liquid in the pot, so less clean up. And more time for you to read through my book for your next recipe!

5. Buy a Second Instant Pot!

Buy an Instant Pot for yourself… and an extra one as a gift. Because when your family and friends taste the great meals that come out of your kitchen, they're going to want to know how you're doing it. And when you share with them that it's my recipe book behind your delicious dinners, they'll want an Instant Pot of their own.

POULTRY RECIPES

Lemon-Peppered Chicken

Serves: 2 | Ready in about: 30 minutes

Ingredients

½ lb bone-in, skin-on chicken thighs
1 tbsp tamari sauce
1 tsp lemon pepper seasoning
3 tbsp agave nectar
1 lemon, juiced and zested
1 tbsp olive oil
2 cloves garlic, peeled and minced
½ cup water

Directions

Rub chicken with lemon pepper seasoning. Set your Instant Pot to Sauté and heat olive oil. Place in chicken and cook for 4-5 minutes on all sides until lightly browned. Add in the garlic and cook for 1 minute, stirring often.

In a bowl, combine lemon juice, lemon zest, agave nectar, water, and tamari sauce. Pour over the chicken. Seal the lid, select Poultry, and set the cooking time to 15 minutes. When done, perform a quick pressure release. Serve hot.

Buttered Chicken with Artichokes

Serves: 2 | Ready in about: 35 minutes

Ingredients

½ lb chicken breasts, chopped
2 artichokes, trimmed, halved
2 tbsp butter, melted
1 tbsp olive oil
1 lemon, juiced
Pink salt and black pepper to taste

Directions

Heat oil your Instant Pot on Sauté and cook the chicken for 2 minutes per side until slightly golden. Pour in 1 cup of water, seal the lid, and cook on High pressure for 13 minutes. Do a quick release. Set aside the chicken.

Place the trivet and pour 1 cup of water. Rub the artichoke halves with half of the lemon juice, and arrange on top of the trivet. Seal the lid and cook on Steam for 3 minutes on High. Do a quick release. Combine artichoke and chicken in a large bowl. Stir in salt, pepper, and lemon juice. Drizzle butter over.

Barbecued Chicken with Carrots

Serves: 2 | Ready in about: 20 minutes

Ingredients

½ lb boneless skinless chicken breasts
¼ tsp salt
½ cup barbecue sauce
½ small onion, minced
⅓ cup carrots, chopped
1 garlic clove, minced

Directions

Rub salt onto chicken and place inside the pot. Add onion, carrots, garlic, and barbeque sauce. Toss to coat. Seal the lid, press Poultry, and cook on High for 15 minutes. Do a quick release. Use 2 forks to shred chicken and stir into the sauce.

Asian-Style Chicken

Serves: 2 | Ready in about: 30 minutes

Ingredients

1 tbsp butter
½ onion, minced
⅓ tbsp grated fresh ginger
⅓ tbsp minced fresh garlic
¼ tsp ground turmeric
⅓ tbsp Kashmiri red chili powder
5 oz canned coconut milk, refrigerated
1 lb boneless, skinless chicken legs
1 tomato, pureed in a blender
2 tbsp chopped fresh cilantro, divided
⅓ tbsp Indian curry paste
1 tbsp dried fenugreek
⅓ tsp garam masala
Salt to taste

Directions

Melt butter on Sauté. Add in 1 teaspoon salt and onion. Cook for 2 to 3 minutes until fragrant. Stir in ginger, turmeric, garlic, and red chili powder to coat; cook for 2 more minutes. Place water and coconut cream into separate bowls. Stir the water from the coconut milk can, pureed tomatoes, and chicken with the onion mixture. Seal lid and cook on High for 8 minutes.

Release the pressure quickly. Stir coconut cream, fenugreek, curry paste, and garam masala through the chicken mixture; season with salt. Cook for 10 minutes until the sauce thickens on Sauté. Garnish with the cilantro before serving.

Cheesy Chicken Quinoa

Serves: 2-4 | Ready in about: 15 minutes

Ingredients

2 tbsp butter
2 leeks, sliced
3 garlic cloves, minced
1 ½ cups quick-cooking quinoa
1 tbsp chopped rosemary

2 ¾ cups chicken broth
2 chicken breasts, cubed
1 tsp dried basil
Salt and black pepper to taste
1 ½ cups frozen green peas, thawed

1 cup ricotta cheese
1 lemon, 2 tbsp zest, and juice
¼ cup fresh parsley, chopped
1 cup grated Parmesan cheese

Directions

Set your Instant Pot to Sauté. Melt butter in inner pot and sauté leeks until bright green and softened, 3 minutes. Mix in garlic and sauté until fragrant, 2 minutes. Add quinoa, rosemary, chicken broth, chicken, basil, salt, and pepper; give ingredients a good stir. Seal the lid, select Manual on High, and cook for 1 minute. Perform a quick pressure release and unlock the lid.

Stir in ricotta cheese, green peas, lemon zest, lemon juice, half of parsley, and Parmesan cheese. Press Sauté and continue cooking until cheese melts and chicken cooks through, 6 minutes. Adjust the taste. Garnish with remaining parsley to serve.

Chicken with Garlic Sauce

Serves: 2-4 | Ready in about: 30 minutes

Ingredients

2 tbsp olive oil
4 chicken breasts, skinless and boneless
Salt and black pepper to taste
3 tbsp butter

1 white onion, finely chopped
2 garlic cloves, minced
1 cup milk
½ cup chicken broth

½ lemon, juiced
1 lemon, sliced
2 tbsp chopped parsley

Directions

Set your Instant Pot to Sauté. Heat olive oil in inner pot, season chicken with salt and pepper, and fry in oil until golden brown on both sides, 4 minutes. Set aside. Melt butter in the pot and sauté onion and garlic until softened, 3 minutes. Stir in milk, chicken broth, and place chicken in sauce. Seal the lid, select Manual on High, and set cooking time to 4 minutes.

After cooking, perform a natural pressure release for 10 minutes. Stir in lemon juice and simmer on Sauté for 2 minutes. Adjust the taste. Dish chicken with sauce into serving bowls, garnish with parsley and lemon slices, and serve warm.

Spicy Chicken with Button Mushrooms

Serves: 2 | Ready in about: 25 minutes

Ingredients

½ lb chicken breasts, cubed
1 cup button mushrooms, chopped
2 cups chicken broth

2 tbsp flour
½ tsp ground cayenne pepper
Salt and black pepper to taste

1 tbsp olive oil
1 garlic clove, chopped

Directions

Grease the inner pot with oil. Add garlic and meat, Season with salt, and stir-fry for 3 minutes. Add mushrooms and pour the chicken broth. Seal the lid. Cook on High pressure for 8 minutes. Release the steam naturally for 10 minutes and tir in flour, cayenne and black peppers. Stir-fry for 5 more minutes, on Sauté. Serve warm.

Mediterranean Chicken Thighs with Mushrooms

Serves: 2 | Ready in about: 30 minutes

Ingredients

2 chicken thighs, boneless and skinless
6 oz button mushrooms
3 tbsp olive oil

1 tsp fresh rosemary, finely chopped
2 garlic cloves, crushed
½ tsp salt

1 tbsp butter
1 tbsp Italian seasoning mix

Directions

Heat a tablespoon of olive oil on Sauté. Add chicken thighs and sear for 5 minutes. Set aside. Pour in the remaining oil, and add mushrooms, rosemary, and Italian seasoning mix. Stir-fry for 5 minutes.

Add in butter, chicken, and 2 cups of water. Seal the lid and cook on Pressure Cook for 13 minutes on High. Do a quick release. Remove the chicken and mushrooms from the cooker and serve with onions.

Chicken Wrapped in Lettuce

Serves: 2 | Ready in about: 50 minutes

Ingredients

1 tbsp canola oil
½ lb chicken thighs, boneless, skinless
⅓ cup pineapple juice
2 tbsp water

2 tbsp soy sauce
1 tbsp maple syrup
⅓ tbsp rice vinegar
⅓ tsp chili-garlic sauce

1 tbsp cornstarch
Salt and black pepper to taste
4 large lettuce leaves
½ cup canned pinto beans, rinsed

Directions

Warm oil on Sauté. In batches, sear the chicken in the oil for 5 minutes until browned. Set aside in a bowl. Into the pot, mix chili-garlic sauce, pineapple juice, soy sauce, vinegar, maple syrup, and water; Stir in chicken to coat.

Seal the lid and cook on High pressure for 7 minutes. Release pressure naturally for 10 minutes. Shred the chicken with two forks. Take ¼ cup liquid from the pot to a bowl; Stir in cornstarch to dissolve.

Mix the cornstarch mixture with the mixture in the pot and return the chicken. Select Sauté and cook for 5 minutes until the sauce thickens; add pepper and salt for seasoning. Transfer beans into lettuce leaves, top with chicken carnitas, and serve.

Country Chicken Thighs with Vegetables

Serves: 2-4 | Ready in about: 35 minutes

Ingredients

2 tbsp olive oil
1 lb chicken thighs
Salt and black pepper to taste
½ lb asparagus, stems removed

2 large carrots, chopped
½ lb baby russet potatoes, quartered
½ lb radishes, halved
1 cup chicken broth

2 tbsp smoked paprika
1 tsp garlic powder
1 tsp onion powder
3 fresh rosemary sprigs

Directions

Set your Instant Pot to Sauté. Heat olive oil in the inner pot, season the chicken with salt and black pepper, and fry in oil until golden brown on both sides, 6 minutes. Set aside. Sweat asparagus and carrots in the pot for 1 minute and add potatoes, radishes, chicken broth, paprika, garlic powder, onion powder, rosemary sprigs, and return the chicken.

Seal the lid, select Manual on High, and set time to 4 minutes. After cooking, perform natural pressure release for 10 minutes. Discard rosemary sprigs, stir, and adjust the taste with salt and pepper. Spoon chicken and vegetables onto serving plates. Select Sauté and cook the remaining sauce until thickened, 2 minutes. Drizzle sauce over chicken and vegetables and serve.

Parsley & Lemon Chicken

Serves: 2 | Ready in about: 20 minutes

Ingredients

1 lb chicken breasts, sliced
1 cup olive oil
1 cup chicken broth

½ cup freshly squeezed lemon juice
½ cup parsley leaves, chopped
3 garlic cloves, crushed

1 tbsp cayenne pepper
½ tsp salt

Directions

In a bowl, mix olive oil, lemon juice, parsley, garlic, cayenne, and salt. Submerge fillets in the mixture. Chill for 30 minutes. Then place all inside the Instant Pot. Add in the broth. Seal the lid and cook on High pressure for 7 minutes. Release the pressure naturally for 10 minutes and serve immediately.

Saucy Chicken Wings

Serves: 2 | Ready in about: 40 minutes

Ingredients

2 chicken wings, bones and skin on
⅓ cups chicken broth
⅓ tsp fresh ginger, grated

¼ tbsp honey
1 tbsp oil
1 tbsp Worcestershire sauce

½ spring onion, chopped
1 garlic clove, crushed
1 tsp salt

Directions

Add the meat to the pot and pour in broth. Seal the lid and cook on Poultry for 15 minutes on High. Do a quick release. Remove chicken and broth, and wipe the pot clean. Heat oil in your Instant Pot on Sauté and stir-fry onion and garlic for 2-3 minutes. Add Worcestershire sauce, honey, and ginger. Cook for 1 minute and return the wings. Cook for 2 minutes. Serve.

One-Pot Chicken with Noodles

Serves: 2-4 | Ready in about: 20 minutes

Ingredients

2 tbsp butter
1 lb chicken breasts, sliced into strips
Salt and black pepper to taste
1 small onion, chopped

1 garlic clove, minced
16 oz bag frozen mixed vegetables
12 oz frozen egg noodles
4 cups chicken stock

1 tsp chicken seasoning
½ tsp dried thyme
1 tbsp cornstarch
1 tsp dried parsley

Directions

Set your Instant Pot to Sauté. Melt butter in inner pot, season chicken with salt and black pepper, and fry in oil until golden brown, 4 minutes. Add onion and garlic and cook for 3 minutes. Pour in mixed vegetables, top with noodles, chicken stock, chicken seasoning, and thyme; stir. Seal the lid, select Manual on High, and set the cooking time to 3 minutes.

After cooking, perform a quick pressure release, and unlock the lid. Stir in cornstarch, select Sauté, and allow the sauce to thicken for 1 minute. Adjust the taste with salt and pepper. Spoon into bowls, garnish with parsley and serve warm.

African Chicken with Pomegranate

Serves: 2-4 | Ready in about: 45 minutes

Ingredients

2 tbsp olive oil
4 chicken thighs, bone-in
Salt and black pepper to taste
2 large carrots, peeled and chopped
1 large onion, chopped
1 tsp fresh ginger puree

3 garlic cloves, minced
15 oz canned diced tomatoes with juice
1 tbsp balsamic vinegar
2 tbsp ras el hanout
1 tsp smoked paprika
1 tsp cumin powder

½ tsp cinnamon powder
1 cup chicken broth
½ lemon, juiced
½ cup frozen peas
1 tbsp fresh parsley leaves to garnish
1 tbsp pomegranate to garnish

Directions

Set your Instant Pot to Sauté. Heat olive oil in the inner pot, season chicken with salt and pepper, and cook until brown on both sides, 6 minutes; set aside. Stir-fry carrots, ginger, garlic, and onion in the pot until softened, 3-4 minutes. Mix in tomatoes, vinegar, ras el hanout, paprika, cumin, and cinnamon and cook until tomatoes begin to soften 3 minutes.

Add chicken broth, lemon juice, salt, black pepper, and the chicken. Seal the lid, select Manual on High, and cook for 10 minutes. After cooking, perform natural pressure release for 10 minutes. Stir in peas and parsley and adjust the taste. Cook on Sauté to warm the peas, 2 minutes. Garnish with pomegranate and serve warm with pita bread.

Sweet & Herbed Chicken

Serves: 2-4 | Ready in about: 45 minutes

Ingredients

4 chicken breasts
¼ cup olive oil
1 cup onion, chopped

¼ cup celery stalks, chopped
3 apricots, cut into chunks
½ tsp dried thyme

½ tsp dried sage
1 cup cider
2 cups chicken stock

Directions

Heat oil on Sauté, and stir-fry the onions for 2-3 minutes, until soft. Add celery stalks and apricots, and cook for 5 minutes, stirring occasionally. Rub the meat with thyme and sage. Add it in the pot along with cider and stock. Seal the lid and cook on High pressure for 35 minutes. Do a quick release.

Chicken in Garlic-Mustard Sauce

Serves: 2 | Ready in about: 35 minutes

Ingredients

1 lb chicken breasts
¼ cup apple cider vinegar

1 tsp garlic powder
2 tbsp Dijon mustard

2 tbsp olive oil
2 cups chicken stock

Directions

Place the chicken in the Instant Pot and pour in the stock. Seal the lid and cook on Poultry for 20 minutes on High. Do a quick release and remove the meat along with the stock. In the pot, mix olive oil, mustard, and apple cider. Press Sauté. Add in the chicken and cook for 10 minutes, turning once. When done, remove from the pot and drizzle with the sauce to serve.

Drumsticks in Adobo Sauce

Serves: 2-4 | Ready in about: 35 min + marinating time

Ingredients

1 lb chicken drumsticks
½ cup plain vinegar
½ cup soy sauce
1 bay leaf
2 tbsp olive oil

10 Ancho dried chilies, seeds removed
5 Guajillo dried chilies, seeds removed
8 garlic cloves, peeled
½ tsp Mexican oregano
½ tsp cumin powder

A pinch clove powder
Salt and black pepper to taste
¼ cup apple cider vinegar
½ cup water
2 tbsp chopped cilantro to garnish

Directions

In a medium bowl, combine chicken, vinegar, soy sauce, and bay leaf. Cover the bowl with a plastic wrap and marinate the chicken in the fridge for 1 hour. Set your Instant Pot to Sauté. Remove chicken from marinade, and fry in olive oil on both sides until golden brown, 6 minutes. Transfer to a paper towel-lined plate and set aside.

In a blender, grind chilies, garlic, oregano, cumin powder, and clove powder until smooth paste forms. Pour mixture into the oil in inner pot and stir-fry until fragrant, 3 minutes. Add salt, pepper, vinegar, and water; stir and place chicken in the sauce.

Seal the lid, select Manual on High, and set cooking time to 4 minutes. After cooking, perform natural pressure release for 10 minutes. Spoon chicken with sauce into serving bowls and garnish with cilantro. Serve warm with rice.

Hot Citrus Chicken

Serves: 2 | Ready in about: 30 minutes

Ingredients

1 tbsp olive oil
2 chicken breasts, cubed
2 tbsp soy sauce

½ tbsp lemon juice
⅓ tbsp garlic powder
⅓ tsp chili sauce

⅓ cup orange juice
Salt and black pepper to taste
1 cup cooked gnocchi

Directions

Warm oil in your Instant Pot on Sauté. Sear the chicken for 5 minutes until browned. Add in orange juice, 1 cup water, chili sauce, garlic, vinegar, and soy sauce. Stir to coat. Seal the lid and cook on High for 7 minutes. Release the pressure quickly.

Take ¼ cup liquid from the pot to a bowl; stir in cornstarch to dissolve; mix into the sauce in the pot until the color is consistent. Press Sauté. Cook for 5 minutes until thickened. Season with pepper and salt and serve with gnocchi.

Greek-Style Cheesy Chicken

Serves: 2 | Ready in about: 30 minutes

Ingredients

½ lb boneless skinless chicken drumsticks

½ cup hot tomato salsa
½ onion, chopped

⅓ cup feta cheese, crumbled

Directions

Sprinkle salt over the chicken and set in the Instant Pot. Stir in salsa to coat the chicken. Seal the lid and cook for 15 minutes on High pressure. Do a quick pressure release. Press Sauté and cook for 5 minutes as you stir until excess liquid has evaporated. Top with feta cheese and serve.

Juicy Chicken

Serves: 2-4 | Ready in about: 25 minutes

Ingredients

2 tbsp olive oil
4 chicken thighs, bone-in
Salt and black pepper to taste

3 tbsp Dijon mustard
1 tbsp tamarind sauce
1 tbsp honey

½ cup chicken broth
3 garlic cloves, minced
1 tbsp chopped parsley

Directions

Set your Instant Pot to Sauté and heat olive oil. Season chicken with salt and pepper and sear in oil until golden brown on both sides, 6 minutes. In a bowl, combine mustard, tamarind sauce, honey, chicken broth, and garlic and pour into the pot.

Seal the lid, select Manual on High, and set cooking time to 2 minutes. After cooking, do a natural pressure release for 10 minutes, then a quick pressure release to let out the remaining steam. Unlock the lid, stir in parsley, and adjust the taste with salt and black pepper. Dish chicken with sauce and serve.

Asiago Chicken

Serves: 2-4 | Ready in about: 35 minutes

Ingredients

2 tbsp olive oil
4 chicken breasts, boneless and skinless
Salt and black pepper to taste

1 small white onion, diced
2 tbsp all-purpose flour
1 ½ cups chicken broth

2 tsp chopped thyme leaves
½ cup grated Asiago cheese

Directions

Set your Instant Pot to Sauté and heat olive oil. Season chicken with salt and black pepper, and sear in oil until golden brown, 4 minutes. Place on a plate and set aside. Add onion to oil and sauté until softened, 3 minutes. Stir in flour until light brown and mix in chicken broth and thyme. Allow reduction by one-third and stir in cheese to melt.

Place chicken in sauce and turn over 3 to 4 times until chicken is well-coated. Seal the lid, select Manual on High, and set the cooking time to 3 minutes. After cooking, perform natural pressure release for 10 minutes. Place the chicken on serving plates. Spoon sauce all over and serve with mashed potatoes.

Chicken Gruyere with Bell Peppers

Serves: 2-4 | Ready in about: 40 minutes

Ingredients

1 tbsp olive oil
1 onion, chopped
2 red bell peppers, chopped
2 green bell peppers, chopped
Salt and black pepper to taste

2 garlic cloves, minced
¾ cup marinara sauce
2 tbsp basil pesto
4 chicken breasts
1 cup chicken broth

1 cup sliced baby Bella mushrooms
1 cup grated Gruyere cheese
4 flatbreads, warmed for serving
2 tbsp chopped parsley

Directions

Set your Instant Pot to Sauté. Heat olive oil in the inner pot and sauté onion, bell peppers, salt, and pepper until softened, 3 minutes. Stir in garlic and cook until fragrant, 30 seconds. Add marinara sauce, basil pesto, chicken, and chicken broth. Seal the lid, select Manual on High, and set cooking time to 12 minutes.

After cooking, perform a natural pressure release for 10 minutes. Remove chicken onto a plate and shred into strands. Fetch out a two-thirds cup of liquid in inner pot, making sure to leave in vegetables. Select Sauté and mix in mushrooms. Cook for 3 minutes. Stir in chicken, adjust taste with salt, pepper, and mix in Gruyere cheese to melt. Garnish with parsley and serve.

Balsamic & Thyme Chicken

Serves: 2-4 | Ready in about: 40 minutes

Ingredients

¼ cup balsamic vinegar
2 tbsp maple syrup
1 tbsp Dijon mustard

½ cup chicken broth
1 medium brown onion, chopped
2 garlic cloves, minced

½ tsp dried thyme
4 chicken breasts

Directions

In inner pot, mix balsamic vinegar, maple syrup, Dijon mustard, chicken broth, onion, garlic, thyme, and chicken. Seal the lid, select Manual on High, and set cooking time to 12 minutes.

After cooking, perform a natural pressure release for 10 minutes. Unlock the lid and remove chicken onto a plate and select Sauté. Shred chicken with two forks and return to sauce. Cook until sauce thickens, 5 minutes. Serve immediately.

Tasty Chicken with White Sauce

Serves: 2 | Ready in about: 42 minutes

Ingredients

4 chicken wings
1 tbsp olive oil

1 cup chicken broth
¼ cup sour cream

⅓ cup yogurt
1 garlic clove, peeled and crushed

Directions

Heat oil in your Instant Pot on Sauté. Brown the wings for 6-8 minutes, turning once. Pour in the broth and seal the lid. Cook on Poultry for 15 minutes on High pressure. Do a natural release for about 10 minutes. In a bowl, mix sour cream, yogurt, and garlic. Chill the wings for a while and drizzle with yogurt sauce. Serve.

Spicy Chicken Manchurian

Serves: 2-4 | Ready in about: 35 minutes

Ingredients

½ cup olive oil
4 tbsp cornstarch, divided
2 eggs, beaten
2 tbsp soy sauce, divided
Salt and black pepper to taste

4 chicken breasts, cubed
2 tbsp sesame oil
1 tbsp fresh garlic paste
1 tbsp fresh ginger paste
1 red chili, sliced

2 tbsp hot sauce
½ tsp honey
½ cup chicken broth
2 scallions, sliced for garnishing

Directions

Set your Instant Pot to Sauté. Heat olive oil in the inner pot. In a medium bowl, whisk cornstarch, eggs, soy sauce, salt, and black pepper. Pour chicken into mixture and stir to coat well. Fry coated chicken in oil until cooked through and golden brown on all sides, 6 to 8 minutes. Transfer to a paper towel-lined plate to drain grease.

Empty inner pot, wipe clean with a paper towel and return to base. Heat in sesame oil and sauté garlic, ginger, and red chili until fragrant and chili softened, 1 minute. Stir in hot sauce, honey, chicken broth, and arrange chicken in sauce.

Seal the lid, select Manual on High, and set cooking time to 3 minutes. After cooking, perform natural pressure release for 10 minutes. Unlock the lid, stir, and adjust the taste with salt and black pepper. Garnish with scallions. Serve warm with rice.

Chicken with Kale & Rice

Serves: 2-4 | Ready in about: 35 minutes

Ingredients

2 tbsp olive oil
4 chicken breasts
Salt and black pepper to taste
1 medium white onion, chopped

1 cup sliced white button mushrooms
¼ tsp ginger paste
½ cup short-grain rice
15 oz can diced tomatoes

½ cup chicken broth
1 tbsp Italian seasoning
¼ cup grated Parmesan cheese
2 cups kale, steamed

Directions

Set your Instant Pot to Sauté. Heat olive oil in the inner pot, season chicken with salt and black pepper, and sear in oil on both sides until golden brown, 4 minutes; set aside. Add onion and mushrooms to the pot and cook until softened, 4 minutes.

Add ginger and let release of fragrance, 1 minute. Stir in rice, tomatoes, chicken broth, and Italian seasoning. Adjust the taste and return the chicken. Seal the lid, select Manual on High, and cook for 10 minutes. After cooking, perform natural pressure release for 10 minutes. Spoon chicken over a bed of steamed kale. Top with Parmesan cheese and serve warm.

Party BBQ Chicken

Serves: 2-4 | Ready in about: 40 minutes

Ingredients

1 ½ cups chopped sweet pineapple
¼ cup chicken broth

¼ tsp salt
¾ cup BBQ sauce

4 chicken breasts, cut into 1-inch cubes

Directions

In your Instant Pot, combine pineapples, chicken broth, salt, BBQ sauce, and chicken. Seal the lid, select Manual on High, and set cooking time to 12 minutes. After cooking, perform a natural pressure release for 10 minutes. Unlock the lid. Remove chicken onto a plate and select Sauté. Cook sauce until boiled down by half, 4 minutes, and stir in chicken. Serve.

Chicken with Brussels Sprouts

Serves: 2-4 | Ready in about: 40 minutes

Ingredients

1 tbsp honey
1 cup teriyaki sauce

¼ cup chicken broth
4 chicken breasts, skinless and boneless

1 cup Brussels sprouts, halved
2 tbsp chopped scallions

Directions

In inner pot, mix honey and teriyaki sauce until evenly combined. Stir in chicken broth and place in chicken. Seal the lid, select Manual on High, and set cooking time to 12 minutes. After cooking, perform a natural pressure release for 10 minutes. Remove chicken onto a plate and shred into strands. Fetch out two-thirds of cooking liquid and return chicken with Brussels sprouts to inner pot. Select Sauté and cook until Brussels sprouts soften, 5 minutes. Stir in scallions and serve warm.

Spicy Mango-Glazed Chicken

Serves: 2-4 | Ready in about: 25 minutes

Ingredients

1 tbsp butter
1 lb chicken breasts, halved
Salt and black pepper to taste

1 medium mango, chopped
1 small red chili, minced
2 tbsp spicy mango chutney

½ cup chicken broth
2 scallions, thinly sliced

Directions

Set Instant Pot to Sauté and melt butter. Season chicken with salt and pepper, and cook for 8 minutes. Set aside. To the pot, add mango, red chili, mango chutney, and broth. Seal the lid, select Manual on High, and set cooking time to 1 minute.

After cooking, perform natural pressure release for 10 minutes, and then quick pressure release to let out the remaining steam. Unlock the lid, stir sauce, and season to taste. Spoon sauce over chicken, garnish with scallions and serve.

Ginger Chicken Drumsticks

Serves: 2-4 | Ready in about: 30 minutes

Ingredients

1 tbsp olive oil
4 chicken drumsticks
Salt and black pepper to taste

¼ cup honey
3 limes, juiced
¼ cup soy sauce

2 garlic cloves, minced
1 tsp freshly grated ginger
2 scallions, thinly sliced to garnish

Directions

Set your Instant Pot to Sauté. Heat olive oil in the inner pot, season chicken with salt and black pepper, and sear chicken on both sides until golden brown, 6 minutes; set aside. Pour honey, lime juice, soy sauce, garlic, ½ cup water, and ginger into inner pot and place chicken in sauce. Seal the lid, select Manual on High, and set cooking time to 5 minutes.

After cooking, perform natural pressure release for 10 minutes, then quick pressure release to let out the remaining steam. Unlock the lid, baste the chicken with sauce, and plate. Garnish with scallions and serve over a bed of rice.

Orange Chicken

Serves: 2-4 | Ready in about: 45 minutes

Ingredients

2 tbsp olive oil
4 chicken breasts, cut into 1-inch cubes
Salt and black pepper to taste
1 cup orange juice
6 garlic cloves, minced
2 tbsp ginger puree

1 tbsp dry white wine
¼ cup honey
¼ cup brown sugar
¼ cup coconut aminos
1 tbsp hot sauce
¼ cup chicken broth

1 orange, zested
2 tbsp cornstarch
2 tbsp orange juice
4 scallions, chopped
1 tbsp sesame seeds

Directions

Set your Instant Pot to Sauté. Heat olive oil in inner pot, season chicken with salt, black pepper, and sear in oil until golden, 5 minutes. In a bowl, mix orange juice, garlic, ginger, white wine, honey, brown sugar, coconut aminos, hot sauce, chicken broth, and orange zest. Pour mixture onto chicken and stir. Seal the lid, select Manual on High, and cook for 12 minutes.

After cooking, perform a natural pressure release for 10 minutes. Mix in cornstarch with orange juice and pour in the pot. Cook on Sauté until syrupy, 3 minutes. Dish food onto serving plates, garnish with scallions and sesame seeds, and serve.

Ranch Chicken

Serves: 2-4 | Ready in about: 40 minutes

Ingredients

2 bacon slices, chopped
1 oz pack ranch seasoning

1 cup chicken broth
4 chicken breasts

4 oz light cream cheese, softened
2 tbsp chopped scallions

Directions

Set your Instant Pot to Sauté. Add bacon and cook until crispy and brown, 5 minutes. Stir in ranch seasoning, broth, and chicken. Seal the lid, select Manual on High, and set cooking time to 12 minutes. After cooking, perform a natural pressure release for 10 minutes. Remove chicken onto a plate and select Sauté. Shred chicken with two forks and return to sauce. Stir in cream cheese until melted and mix in scallions. Dish and serve.

Chicken Pozole

Serves: 2-4 | Ready in about: 40 minutes

Ingredients

2 tbsp olive oil

1 onion, chopped

2 garlic cloves, minced

1 tbsp tomato paste

2 green chilis, minced

2 tsp cumin powder

1 tbsp chili powder

2 tsp dried oregano

½ tsp chipotle paste

Salt and black pepper to taste

2 chicken thighs, skinless and boneless

4 cups chicken broth

3 cups cooked hominy

1 lime, juiced

½ cup shredded red cabbage

1 cup sour cream

1 large avocado, pitted and sliced

½ cup grated cheddar cheese

Directions

Set your Instant Pot to Sauté. Heat olive oil in inner pot and sauté onion, garlic, tomato paste, and green chilies. Cook until softened, 3 minutes. Mix in cumin powder, chili powder, oregano, chipotle paste, salt, and black pepper; cook until fragrant, 30 seconds. Add chicken, broth, and hominy. Seal the lid, select Manual on High, and set cooking time to 12 minutes.

After cooking, perform a natural pressure release for 10 minutes and unlock the lid. Remove chicken onto a plate, shred into strands, return to sauce, and stir in lime juice. Adjust the taste with salt and black pepper. Dish soup into serving bowls and top with cabbage, sour cream, avocado, and cheddar cheese. Serve.

Onion Chicken with Salsa Verde

Serves: 2-4 | Ready in about: 35 minutes

Ingredients

1 large yellow onion, chopped

1 cup salsa verde

½ cup chicken broth

Salt and black pepper to taste

4 chicken breasts, cut into 1-inch cubes

Directions

In inner pot, combine onion, salsa verde, chicken broth, salt, black pepper, and chicken. Seal the lid, select Manual on High, and set cooking time to 12 minutes. After cooking, perform a natural pressure release for 10 minutes. Unlock the lid and remove chicken onto a plate and serve warm over salad.

Chicken Piccata

Serves: 2-4 | Ready in about: 25 minutes

Ingredients

4 chicken breasts, boneless and skinless

Salt and black pepper to taste

3 tbsp butter, room temperature

½ cup + 2 tbsp flour

2 tbsp olive oil

¼ cup dry white wine

¼ cup chicken broth

2 lemons, juiced

¼ cup drained capers

Directions

Place chicken between two plastic wraps and using a meat pounder, lightly pound chicken until about ¼-inch thickness. Take off the plastic wrap and season chicken with salt and pepper. Set your Instant Pot to Sauté and heat the olive oil. Dip chicken in the remaining flour and fry in oil until golden brown on both sides, about 8 minutes; reserve.

In a bowl, combine 1 tbsp butter with 2 tbsp flour until smooth. Pour white wine, chicken broth, and lemon juice into inner pot, allow boiling, and stir in butter mixture. Stir in capers, remaining butter, parsley, and cook until sauce thickens, 2 minutes. Adjust taste with salt and black pepper. Plate chicken and spoon sauce all over. Serve warm with mashed potatoes.

Hunter's Chicken

Serves: 2-4 | Ready in about: 30 minutes

Ingredients

2 cups tomato sauce

4 chicken breasts, cubed

1 onion, sliced

3 red bell peppers, chopped

½ tsp cayenne pepper

Salt and black pepper to taste

½ cup chicken broth

1 cup sliced oyster mushrooms

1 cup Kalamata olives, pitted

Directions

In your Instant Pot, add tomato sauce, chicken, onion, bell peppers, cayenne pepper, salt, black pepper, chicken broth, and mushrooms. Seal the lid, select Manual on High, and set time to 10 minutes. After cooking, perform a natural pressure release for 10 minutes. Unlock the lid, stir in olives, and adjust the taste. Serve warm.

Dijon Chicken with Broccoli

Serves: 2-4 | Ready in about: 17 minutes

Ingredients

1 lb chicken breasts, cubed
2 cups broccoli florets
½ cup bourbon
½ cup teriyaki sauce

2 tbsp honey
1 tsp Dijon mustard
1 tsp garlic powder
2 tsp onion powder

1/8 tsp ginger powder
½ cup brown sugar
1 tbsp cornstarch
1 tbsp water

Directions

Pour chicken and broccoli into inner pot of your Instant Pot. In a medium bowl, mix bourbon, teriyaki sauce, honey, mustard, garlic powder, onion powder, ginger powder, and brown sugar. Pour mixture all over the chicken and broccoli and stir. Seal the lid, select Manual on High, and set cooking time to 6 minutes. Perform a quick pressure release to let out all the steam.

Combine cornstarch and water in a small bow. On the Instant Pot, select Sauté, and pour cornstarch mixture over chicken. Stir and allow thickening for a minute. Spoon chicken over rice and serve warm.

Cheddar Chicken Taco Bowls

Serves: 2-4 | Ready in about: 45 minutes

Ingredients

2 tbsp olive oil
4 chicken breasts, cut into 1-inch cubes
1 tbsp taco seasoning
1 ½ cups salsa

½ cup sweet corn kernels, drained
1 (15 oz) can black beans, rinsed
1 cup basmati rice, rinsed
2 cups chicken broth

½ cup grated cheddar cheese
2 scallions, chopped
1 large avocado, pitted and chopped
1 cup sour cream

Directions

Set Instant Pot to Sauté and heat the olive oil. Season chicken breasts with taco seasoning and sear on both sides until golden, 5 minutes. Mix in salsa, corn kernels, black beans, rice, and chicken broth. Seal the lid, select Manual on High, and cook for 8 minutes. Perform a quick pressure release. Top with cheddar cheese, scallions, avocado, and sour cream to serve.

Miso Chicken

Serves: 2-4 | Ready in about: 45 minutes

Ingredients

1 tbsp olive oil
1 small red onion, chopped
½ red bell pepper, chopped

1 cup peanut sauce
2 tsp soy sauce
½ tsp miso paste

½ cup chicken broth
4 chicken breasts
2 tbsp chopped cilantro

Directions

Set your Instant Pot to Sauté. Heat olive oil in the inner pot and sauté onion and bell pepper until softened, 3 minutes. Mix in peanut sauce, soy sauce, miso paste, and chicken broth. Boil for 1 minute and stir in chicken. Seal the lid, select Manual on High, and set cooking time to 12 minutes.

After cooking, perform a natural pressure release for 10 minutes, then a quick pressure release to let out the remaining steam, and unlock the lid. Remove chicken onto a plate and select Sauté. Shred chicken with two forks and return to sauce. Cook until sauce thickens, 5 minutes. Top with cilantro and serve chicken and sauce with rice.

Chili Drumsticks in Cilantro-Lime Sauce

Serves: 2-4 | Ready in about: 30 minutes

Ingredients

1 tbsp olive oil
4 chicken drumsticks
Salt and black pepper to taste

4 garlic cloves, minced
1 tsp chili powder
1 tsp red chili flakes

2 limes, juiced
¼ chopped cilantro
1 cup chicken broth

Directions

Set your Instant Pot to Sauté. Heat olive oil in the inner pot, season chicken with salt, black pepper, and sear in oil until golden on the outside, 5 minutes. Stir in garlic, chili powder, red chili flakes, lime juice, cilantro, and broth.

Seal the lid, select Manual on High, and set cooking time to 10 minutes. After cooking, perform a natural pressure release for 10 minutes. Unlock the lid, stir, and dish food onto serving plates. Serve warm.

Chicken Fajitas with Cucumber & Cherry Tomatoes

Serves: 2-4 | Ready in about: 30 minutes

Ingredients

1 can (10-oz) fire-roasted tomatoes, chopped

1 lb chicken breasts

8 corn tortilla shells, warm

1 cucumber, sliced

½ cup cherry tomatoes, halved

½ onion, chopped

1 garlic clove, minced

1 tbsp olive oil

½ cup chicken broth

½ tbsp chili powder

1 tbsp taco seasoning

Salt and black pepper to serve

¼ tsp ground coriander

Directions

Add the chicken to your Instant Pot. In a bowl, mix fire-roasted tomatoes, onion, garlic, olive oil, chicken broth, chili powder, taco seasoning, ground coriander, salt, and pepper. Pour the mixture over the chicken. Seal the lid, select Manual on High, and cook for 15 minutes. When done, perform a quick pressure release.

Remove the chicken to a cutting board and let it cool for a few minutes before shredding it. Then, return to the pot and stir to combine. To serve, divide the chicken mixture between the tortilla and top with cherry tomatoes and avocado.

French Chicken Cordon Bleu

Serves: 2-4 | Ready in about: 30 minutes

Ingredients

10 oz rotini pasta

2 ½ cups chicken broth

4 chicken breasts, cut into strips

1 lb ham, cubed

1 tbsp Dijon mustard

1 tsp garlic powder

Salt and black pepper to taste

¼ cup shredded Gouda cheese

¼ cup shredded Parmesan cheese

½ cup heavy cream

2 tbsp unsalted butter, melted

1 cup crushed pork rinds

Directions

In your Instant Pot, add rotini, chicken broth, and arrange chicken and ham on top. Top with Dijon mustard, garlic powder, salt, and black pepper. Seal the lid, select Manual on High, and cook for 10 minutes.

After cooking, perform a quick pressure release. Mix in cheeses and heavy cream. Cook on Sauté until cheeses melt, 5 minutes. Spoon cordon bleu onto plates. In a bowl, mix butter with pork rinds and drizzle on cordon bleu. Serve.

Garlic Chicken with Lemongrass

Serves: 2-4 | Ready in about: 40 minutes

Ingredients

2 lemongrass stalks, chopped

2 garlic cloves, minced

Salt and black pepper to taste

1 cup chicken broth

4 chicken breasts

1 lemon, juiced

Directions

In your Instant Pot, combine lemongrass, garlic, salt, pepper, broth, and chicken. Seal the lid, select Manual, and cook for 12 minutes. After cooking, do a natural pressure release for 10 minutes. Remove the chicken. Take out lemongrass and discard. Shred chicken into strands and return to sauce. Select Sauté and stir in lemon juice. Cook further for 5 minutes. Serve.

Cheesy Chicken Meatballs with Tomato Sauce

Serves: 2-4 | Ready in about: 25 minutes

Ingredients

1 lb ground chicken

3 tbsp breadcrumbs

2 ¼ tbsp whole milk

1 garlic clove, minced

1 egg, beaten

2 tbsp fresh basil, chopped

2 ¼ tbsp Parmesan cheese, grated

2 tbsp olive oil

2 tbsp white wine

½ can (14.5-oz) tomato sauce

Salt and black pepper to taste

Directions

In a bowl, mix chicken, breadcrumbs, garlic, black pepper, salt, egg, and Parmesan cheese with your hands. Shape the mixture into medium-size balls. Set your Instant Pot to Sauté and heat oil. Add in the meatballs and cook for 8 minutes; reserve.

Pour in the white wine to scrape up any browned bits from the bottom of the pot. Stir in the tomato sauce and meatballs. Seal the lid, select Manual, and set cooking time to 5 minutes. When done, perform a quick pressure release to let out the steam. Garnish with parsley and serve.

Sweet Chili Chicken

Serves: 2-4 | Ready in about: 40 minutes

Ingredients

4 chicken breasts
¼ cup soy sauce
2 tbsp teriyaki sauce
¼ cup ketchup

2 tbsp sweet chili sauce
2 ½ tbsp brown sugar
3 garlic cloves, minced
1 tbsp freshly grated ginger

½ tsp onion powder
1 ½ tbsp cornstarch
¼ cup chicken broth
Salt and black pepper to taste

Directions

Place chicken your Instant Pot. Add in soy sauce, teriyaki sauce, ketchup, chili sauce, brown sugar, garlic, ginger, onion powder, cornstarch, broth, salt, and pepper and stir well. Seal the lid, select Manual on High, and cook for 12 minutes.

After cooking, do a natural pressure release for 10 minutes. Remove chicken onto a plate and shred with two forks. Return it to the sauce, top with cornstarch mixture, and stir. Select Sauté and cook until sauce is syrupy. Dish food and serve warm.

Pecorino-Romano Chicken with Potatoes

Serves: 2-4 | Ready in about: 40 minutes

Ingredients

4 chicken breasts
1 lb baby russet potatoes, cleaned
3 tbsp olive oil
3 tbsp ranch seasoning

Salt and black pepper to taste
½ tsp dried basil
½ tsp dried oregano
1 tsp garlic powder

1 tsp dried rosemary
1 cup chicken broth
3 tbsp grated Pecorino Romano cheese

Directions

In a large bowl, add chicken, potatoes, olive oil, 2 tablespoons of ranch seasoning, salt, black pepper, basil, oregano, garlic powder, and rosemary. Toss well. Pour broth into inner pot, add potatoes, and place chicken on top.

Seal the lid, select Manual on High, and cook for 15 minutes. After cooking, perform a natural pressure release for 10 minutes. Plate chicken and potatoes, sprinkle with remaining ranch seasoning, and scatter Pecorino cheese on top. Serve.

Italian-Style Chicken

Serves: 2-4 | Ready in about: 55 minutes

Ingredients

1 lb chicken thighs, with the bone, skin removed

Salt and black pepper to taste
1 bay leaf
2 tbsp olive oil
2 red bell peppers, cut into strips

1 red onion, diced
1 garlic clove, minced
¼ cup dry white wine
1 ½ cups canned passata

½ cup chicken stock
2 tbsp black olives, pitted
½ tbsp capers, drained
½ tsp dried rosemary

Directions

Set your Instant Pot to Sauté and heat olive oil. Season chicken with salt and pepper. Add to the pot and cook for 8 minutes until golden brown. Remove to a plate. Pour in bell peppers, onion, and garlic. Cook for 6 minutes until the vegetables are softened. Pour in white wine, passata, chicken stock, bay leaf, and rosemary and cook for another 2 minutes.

Return the chicken to the pot. Seal the lid, select Manual, and cook for 15 minutes on High. When done, perform a natural pressure release for 10 minutes, then a quick pressure release to let out the remaining steam. Unlock the lid, remove and discard the bay leaf. Stir in olives and capers and adjust the seasoning. Serve.

White Wine Chicken with Herbs

Serves: 2-4 | Ready in about: 15 minutes

Ingredients

4 chicken breasts
½ tsp salt
1 cup water

¼ cup dry white wine
½ tsp rosemary
½ tsp mint

½ tsp marjoram
½ tsp sage

Directions

Sprinkle salt over the chicken and set in the pot. Mix in mint, rosemary, marjoram, and sage. Pour wine and water around the chicken. Seal the lid, and cook for 6 minutes on High pressure. Release the pressure naturally. Serve.

Jalapeno Chicken

Serves: 2-4 | Ready in about: 40 minutes

Ingredients

1 tbsp olive oil	Salt and black pepper to taste	1 (10 oz) can diced tomatoes
1 white onion, chopped	2 tsp cumin powder	1 cup chicken broth
1 red bell pepper, deseeded and chopped	½ tsp chili powder	4 chicken breasts, cut into 1-inch cubes
1 green bell pepper, chopped	2 jalapeño peppers, chopped	1 lemon, juiced

Directions

Set your Instant Pot to Sauté. Heat olive oil in inner pot and sauté onion, bell peppers, and season with salt until vegetables soften, 3 minutes. Mix in black pepper, cumin powder, chili powder, jalapeño peppers, tomatoes, broth, and chicken breasts. Seal the lid, select Manual on High, and set time to 12 minutes. After cooking, perform a natural pressure release for 10 minutes. Select Sauté and stir in lemon juice. Cook for 3 minutes and adjust taste with salt and pepper. Dish food and serve.

Smoked Paprika Chicken

Serves: 2-4 | Ready in about: 50 minutes

Ingredients

2 garlic cloves, minced	2 chicken breasts	1 lemon, zested and juiced
Salt and black pepper to taste	2 tbsp olive oil	1 cup chicken broth
½ tsp smoked paprika	4 tbsp balsamic vinegar	1 large white onion, diced

Directions

In a bowl, mix the garlic, salt, pepper, and paprika. Rub spice mixture all over the chicken breasts. Set your Instant Pot to Sauté. Heat olive oil in the inner pot and sear chicken until golden, 7 minutes. Remove to a plate. Pour balsamic vinegar, lemon zest, lemon juice, and chicken broth into the pot. Using a spatula, scrape the stuck bits at the bottom of the pot.

Place onion and then chicken in inner pot. Seal the lid, select Manual on High, and cook for 18 minutes. After cooking, perform a natural pressure release for 10 minutes. Serve warm.

Effortless Chicken Pot

Serves: 2-4 | Ready in about: 35 minutes

Ingredients

2 tbsp olive oil	2 medium red onions, chopped	2 tbsp coriander powder
4 chicken breasts	3 poblano peppers, thinly sliced	1 ½ cups orange juice
Salt and black pepper to taste	3 garlic cloves, minced	1 ½ cups chicken broth

Directions

Set your Instant Pot to Sauté and heat olive oil. Season chicken with salt and pepper, and sear chicken on both sides until golden brown, 6 minutes. Stir in onion, poblano peppers, garlic, coriander, orange juice, and chicken broth.

Seal the lid, select Manual on High, and set cooking time to 6 minutes. After cooking, perform natural pressure release for 10 minutes, then a quick pressure release, and unlock the lid. Stir and adjust the taste with salt and black pepper. Spoon food into serving bowls and serve with tortilla chips, salsa, and taco toppings.

Basil Chicken Breasts

Serves: 2-4 | Ready in about: 45 minutes

Ingredients

4 chicken breasts	3 garlic cloves, minced	¼ cup heavy cream
1 cup chicken broth	Salt and black pepper to taste	1 ½ tbsp cornstarch
1 tsp Italian seasoning	¼ cup chopped roasted red peppers	1 tbsp basil pesto

Directions

In inner pot, add chicken, broth, Italian seasoning, garlic, salt, black pepper, and roasted peppers; stir. Seal the lid, select Manual on High, and set cooking time to 10 minutes. After cooking, perform a natural pressure release for 10 minutes, then a quick pressure release to let out the remaining steam, and unlock the lid.

Select Sauté and remove chicken onto a plate. Into sauce, mix heavy cream, cornstarch, and pesto. Cook for 3 to 4 minutes or until sauce thickens. Return chicken to pot, coat with sauce, and cook for 2 minutes. Dish chicken and serve with sauce.

Veggie & Chicken with Rosemary

Serves: 2-4 | Ready in about: 40 minutes

Ingredients

4 skin-on, bone-in chicken legs
2 tbsp olive oil
Salt and black pepper to taste
4 cloves garlic, minced

1 tsp fresh chopped rosemary
½ cup dry white wine
1¼ cups chicken stock
1 cup carrots, chopped

1 cup parsnip, chopped
3 tomatoes, chopped
1 tbsp honey
4 slices lemon

Directions

Season the chicken with pepper and salt. Warm oil on Sauté in the Instant Pot. Cook the chicken legs for 3-5 minutes each side until browned; set aside. Sauté garlic in the chicken fat for 1 minute until soft and lightly golden. Add in wine to deglaze, scrape the pot's bottom to get rid of any brown bits of food. Simmer for 2- 3 minutes until slightly reduced in volume.

Add stock, carrots, parsnips, tomatoes, pepper, and salt into the pot. Lay steam rack onto veggies. Into the pressure cooker's steamer basket, arrange chicken legs. Set the steamer basket onto the rack. Drizzle the chicken with honey.

Top with lemon slices. Seal the lid and cook on High for 12 minutes. Release pressure naturally for 10 minutes. Place the chicken to a bowl. Drain the veggies and place around the chicken. Garnish with rosemary before serving.

Chicken Drumsticks with Potatoes

Serves: 2-4 | Ready in about: 40 minutes

Ingredients

4 potatoes, peeled and quartered
2 lemons, zested and juiced
1 tbsp olive oil
2 tsp fresh oregano
Salt and black pepper to taste

2 serrano peppers, chopped
4 boneless skinless chicken drumsticks
3 tbsp finely chopped parsley
1 cup packed watercress
1 cucumber, sliced

½ cup cherry tomatoes, quartered
¼ cup Kalamata olives, pitted
¼ cup hummus
¼ cup feta cheese, crumbled
Lemon wedges, for serving

Directions

In your Instant Pot, add potatoes and cover with water. Set trivet over them. In a baking bowl, mix lemon juice, olive oil, black pepper, oregano, zest, salt, and red pepper flakes. Add chicken drumsticks in the marinade and stir to coat. Set the bowl with chicken on the trivet in the inner pot. Seal the lid, select Poultry and cook on High for 15 minutes. Do a quick release.

Take out the bowl with chicken and the trivet from the pot. Drain potatoes and add parsley and salt. Divide the potatoes between four serving plates and top with watercress, cucumber slices, hummus, cherry tomatoes, chicken, olives, and feta cheese. Each bowl should be garnished with a lemon wedge.

Sweet Chicken Breasts

Serves: 2-4 | Ready in about: 30 minutes

Ingredients

4 chicken breasts, cut into chunks
1 onion, diced
4 garlic cloves, smashed

½ cup honey
3 tbsp soy sauce
2 tsp sesame oil

1 tsp rice vinegar
Salt and black pepper to taste
1 tbsp cornstarch

Directions

Mix garlic, onion, and chicken in your Instant Pot. In a bowl, combine honey, sesame oil, soy sauce, and rice vinegar; pour over the chicken. Seal the lid and cook on High pressure for 15 minutes. Release the pressure quickly. Mix 2 tbsp water and cornstarch until well dissolved; stir into the sauce. Press Sauté. Simmer the sauce for 2 to 3 minutes as you stir until thickened.

Fast & Fun Chicken Breasts

Serves: 2-4 | Ready in about: 30 minutes

Ingredients

2 lb chicken breasts, cubed
2 lb Swiss chard, chopped

2 cups chicken broth
2 tbsp butter, unsalted

2 tbsp olive oil
1 tsp sea salt

Directions

Add the meat, oil and broth to the pot. Season with salt, seal the lid, and cook on Manual for 13 minutes on High. Do a quick release, open the lid, and add Swiss chard and butter. Stir for 2 minutes until the chard is wilted. Serve warm.

Creole Chicken with Rice & Vegetables

Serves: 2-4 | Ready in about: 40 minutes

Ingredients

1 tbsp olive oil
4 chicken breasts, cut into 1-inch cubes
1 tbsp Creole seasoning

1 small white onion, chopped
3 garlic cloves, minced
1 tbsp tomato paste

1 cup basmati rice
1 ¼ cups chicken broth
1 cup frozen mixed vegetables, thawed

Directions

Set Instant Pot to Sauté and heat olive oil. Season chicken with Cajun seasoning and sear in oil until golden on the outside, 5 minutes. Mix in onion, garlic, and cook for 3 minutes or until fragrant. Stir in tomato paste, rice, and cook for 1 minute.

Stir in broth. Seal the lid, select Manual on High, and set cooking time to 5 minutes. Once ready, perform a quick pressure release. Select Sauté and mix in vegetables; cook until warmed through. Serve.

Bombay Chicken Tikka Masala

Serves: 2-4 | Ready in about: 40 minutes

Ingredients

4 chicken thighs, boneless and cut into bite-size pieces
1 (14 oz) can diced tomatoes
2 tsp ginger puree
1 tsp turmeric powder
½ tsp cayenne powder

1 tsp sweet paprika
Salt to taste
1 tsp garam masala
1 tsp cumin powder

2 tbsp butter
½ cup chicken broth
2 tbsp coconut milk
¼ chopped cilantro

Directions

In your Instant Pot, add tomatoes, ginger, turmeric powder, cayenne powder, sweet paprika, salt, garam masala, cumin powder, chicken, butter, broth, and coconut milk. Seal the lid, select Manual on High, and cook for 12 minutes.

After cooking, perform a natural pressure release for 10 minutes. Unlock the lid and stir and adjust the taste with salt. Ladle into serving bowls, garnish with cilantro and serve warm.

Chicken with Mushrooms

Serves: 2-4 | Ready in about: 40 minutes

Ingredients

1 (10-oz) can condensed cream of mushroom soup
2 pancetta slices, chopped
¼ cup flour
1 lb bone-in, skinless chicken thighs

2 tbsp olive oil
1 cup mushrooms, sliced
1 leek, white part only, chopped

2 garlic cloves, minced
1 cup chicken broth
1 cup tomato sauce

Directions

Rub chicken thighs with some olive oil. Roll them in flour until evenly coated. Set your Instant Pot to Sauté, heat the remaining oil, and brown chicken for 3 minutes per side. Add in pancetta, mushrooms, leek, and garlic.

Cook for 5 minutes. Stir in broth and tomato sauce. Seal the lid, select Manual on High, and cook 15 minutes. When done, do a natural pressure release for 10 minutes. Select Sauté. Add in the cream of mushroom soup and cook for 3 minutes. Serve.

Bean & Sriracha Chicken

Serves: 2-4 | Ready in about: 25 minutes

Ingredients

½ cup soy sauce
½ cup chicken broth
3 tbsp honey
2 tbsp tomato paste

1 tbsp sriracha
1 (1 inch) piece fresh ginger, grated
3 garlic cloves, grated
4 boneless, skinless chicken drumsticks

1 tbsp cornstarch
1 tbsp sesame oil
2 cups canned black beans
2 green onions, chopped

Directions

In the cooker, mix the soy sauce, honey, ginger, tomato paste, chicken broth, sriracha, and garlic. Stir well until smooth; toss in the chicken to coat. Seal the lid and cook for 3 minutes on High. Release the pressure quickly. Press Sauté.

In a bowl, mix 2 tbsp water and cornstarch until no lumps remain. Stir into the sauce and cook for 5 minutes until thickened. Stir in sesame oil. Garnish with green onions. Serve with black beans.

Chicken with Peach Sauce

Serves: 2-4 | Ready in about: 40 minutes

Ingredients

15 oz canned peach chunks
4 boneless, skinless chicken thighs
14 oz canned diced tomatoes

2 cloves garlic, minced
½ tsp cumin
½ tsp salt

2 tbsp cheddar cheese, shredded
Fresh chopped mint leaves

Directions

Strain canned peach chunks. Reserve the juice and set aside. In the Instant Pot, add chicken, tomatoes, cumin, garlic, peach juice, and salt. Seal the lid, press Poultry, and cook on High for 15 minutes. Do a quick pressure release.

Shred chicken with the use of two forks. Transfer to a serving plate. Add peach chunks to the cooking juices and mix until well combined. Pour the peach salsa over the chicken, top with mint leaves and cheddar cheese. Serve immediately.

Avocado Chicken Carnitas

Serves: 2-4 | Ready in about: 30 minutes

Ingredients

4 chicken breasts, boneless and skinless
1 tsp taco seasoning
1 tbsp olive oil
1 (24-oz) can diced tomatoes

3 bell peppers, julienned
1 shallot, chopped
4 garlic cloves, minced
Juice from 1 lemon

Salt and black pepper to taste
4 flour tortillas
2 tbsp cilantro, chopped
1 avocado, chopped

Directions

In a bowl, mix taco seasoning and chicken until evenly coated. Warm oil on Sauté. Sear chicken for 2 minutes per side until browned. Add in tomatoes, shallot, lemon juice, garlic, and bell peppers; season. Seal the lid, press Poultry, and cook for 4 minutes on High. Release the pressure quickly. Move the bell peppers and chicken to the tortillas. Add avocado slices and serve.

Homemade Tandoori Chicken with Cilantro Sauce

Serves: 2-4 | Ready in about: 40 minutes + cooling time

Ingredients

4 chicken thighs, skinless
½ cup Greek yogurt
1 tbsp vegetable oil
1 tbsp red chili powder
1 tsp garam masala

½ tbsp grated fresh ginger
½ tbsp garlic powder
A handful of fresh cilantro leaves
1 tsp cumin seeds
½ jalapeno pepper

2-3 garlic cloves
2 tsp honey
2 tsp lemon juice
¾ cup olive oil
Salt to taste

Directions

In a bowl, mix yogurt, garam masala, garlic powder, red chili powder, vegetable oil, salt, and ginger. Place the thighs into a resealable plastic bag. Add in yogurt mixture and seal. Massage bag to ensure the marinade coats the chicken completely and place in the refrigerator for 12 hours. Take out of the fridge and set aside for 30 minutes before cooking.

Add 1 cup water into your Instant Pot. Place a trivet over the water. Remove chicken from marinade and arrange on the trivet. Seal the lid and cook for 15 minutes on High pressure. Release the pressure quickly.

In a food processor, blend cilantro, cumin seeds, jalapeño pepper, garlic, honey, lemon juice, olive oil, and salt with a little water until smooth. Over the chicken, drizzle sauce, and serve.

Simple Chicken Thighs

Serves: 2-4 | Ready in about: 50 minutes

Ingredients

1 lb chicken thighs
2 tbsp oil
4 cups chicken broth

1 tsp salt
2 tsp lime zest
1 tsp chili powder

½ cup tomato puree
1 tbsp sugar

Directions

Season the chicken with salt and chili powder. Warm oil in your Instant Pot on Sauté and add the thighs. Briefly brown on both sides; set aside. Add the tomato puree, sugar, and lime zest. Cook for 10 minutes to obtain a thick sauce. Add the chicken thighs and pour in the broth. Seal the lid and cook on Poultry for 20 minutes on High. When done, do a quick release. Serve.

Chili Chicken Wings

Serves: 2-4 | Ready in about: 40 minutes

Ingredients

2 tbsp olive oil
8 chicken wings
½ tsp chili powder

½ tsp onion powder
½ dried oregano
½ tsp cayenne pepper

Sea salt and black pepper to taste
½ cup chicken broth
2 lemons, juiced

Directions

Coat the chicken with olive oil. Season with chili powder, onion powder, salt, oregano, cayenne and black peppers. In the pot, add the wings and broth. Seal the lid and cook on High pressure for 4 minutes. Do a quick pressure release.

Preheat oven to 360 F. Onto a greased baking sheet, place the wings in a single layer and drizzle over the lemon juice. Bake for 5 minutes until the skin is crispy.

Tomato Chicken with Capers

Serves: 2-4 | Ready in about: 45 minutes

Ingredients

4 chicken legs
Sea salt and black pepper to taste
2 tbsp olive oil

1 onion, diced
2 garlic cloves, minced
⅓ cup red wine

2 cups diced tomatoes
⅓ cup capers
2 pickles, chopped

Directions

Sprinkle pepper and salt over the chicken. Warm oil in your Instant Pot on Sauté. Add in onion and sauté for 3 minutes. Add in garlic and cook for 30 seconds until softened. Mix the chicken with vegetables and cook for 6 minutes until browned.

Add red wine to the pan to deglaze, scraping the pan's bottom to get rid of any browned bits of food; Stir in tomatoes. Seal the lid and cook on High pressure for 12 minutes. Release the pressure quickly. To the chicken mixture, add capers and pickles. Serve the chicken in plates covered with the tomato mixture.

Honey Garlic Chicken with Hoisin Sauce

Serves: 2-4 | Ready in about: 30 minutes

Ingredients

2 chicken breasts, cubed
½ cup honey
½ cup orange juice
⅓ cup soy sauce

⅓ cup chicken stock
⅓ cup hoisin sauce
1 garlic clove, minced
2 tsp cornstarch

2 tsp water
1 cup diced orange
3 cups hot cooked quinoa

Directions

Arrange the chicken at the bottom of the pot. In a bowl, mix honey, soy sauce, garlic, hoisin sauce, chicken stock, and orange juice until the honey is dissolved. Pour the mixture over the chicken. Seal the lid and cook on High pressure for 7 minutes. Release the pressure quickly. Take the chicken from the pot and set it to a bowl. Press Sauté.

In a small bowl, mix water with cornstarch. Pour into the liquid within the pot and cook for 3 minutes until thick. Stir diced orange and chicken into the sauce until well coated. Serve with quinoa.

Pancetta & Cabbage Chicken Thighs

Serves: 2-4 | Ready in about: 35 minutes

Ingredients

1 tbsp lard
4 slices pancetta, diced
4 chicken thighs, boneless skinless

Salt and black pepper to taste
1 cup chicken broth
1 tbsp Dijon mustard

1 lb green cabbage, shredded
2 tbsp fresh parsley, chopped

Directions

Warm lard in your Instant Pot on Sauté. Fry pancetta for 5 minutes until crisp. Set aside. Season chicken with pepper and salt. Sear in the pressure cooker for 2 minutes each side until browned. In a bowl, mix mustard and chicken broth.

In your pressure cooker, add pancetta and chicken broth mixture. Seal the lid and cook on High pressure for 6 minutes. Release the pressure quickly. Mix in green cabbage, seal the lid again, and cook on High pressure for 2 minutes. Release the pressure quickly. Serve with sprinkled parsley.

Herbed Chicken Cacciatore

Serves: 2-4 | Ready in about: 40 minutes

Ingredients

2 tsp olive oil
1 lb chicken drumsticks, boneless, skinless
Salt and black pepper to taste
1 carrot, chopped
1 red bell pepper, chopped

1 yellow bell pepper, chopped
1 onion, chopped
2 garlic cloves, minced
½ tsp dried oregano
½ tsp dried basil
½ tsp dried parsley

½ red pepper flakes
1 (14-oz) can diced tomatoes
½ cup dry red wine
¾ cup chicken stock
1 cup black olives, pitted and chopped
2 bay leaves

Directions

Warm the oil in your Instant Pot on Sauté. Season the drumsticks with pepper and salt. In batches, sear the chicken for 5-6 minutes until golden brown. Set aside on a plate. Drain the pot and remain with 1 tablespoon of fat.

In the hot oil, Sauté onion, garlic, and bell peppers for 4 minutes until softened; add red pepper flakes, basil, parsley, and oregano, and cook for 30 more seconds. Season with salt and pepper. Stir in tomatoes, olives, chicken stock, red wine and bay leaves. Return chicken to the pot. Seal the lid and cook on High pressure for 15 minutes. Release the pressure quickly. Divide chicken into four serving bowls; top with tomato mixture before serving.

Primavera Chicken Stew

Serves: 2-4 | Ready in about: 55 minutes

Ingredients

4 green onions, chopped
3 garlic cloves, crushed
3 potatoes, chopped

8 baby carrots, chopped
4 oz can tomato sauce
1 tsp salt

8 oz chicken breasts, cubed
2 cups chicken broth
2 tbsp olive oil

Directions

Place the veggies in the Instant Pot and pour water to cover. Seal the lid and cook on Manual for 15 minutes on High. Do a quick release. Remove the vegetables along with the liquid. Heat oil on Sauté and stir-fry the chicken for 5 minutes. Add the remaining ingredients and seal the lid. Set on Poultry and cook for 15 minutes on High. Do a natural release for 10 minutes.

Mama's Chicken with Salsa Verde

Serves: 2-4 | Ready in about: 50 minutes

Ingredients

1 jalapeño pepper, chopped
½ cup capers
2 tbsp parsley, chopped

1 lime, juiced
1 tsp salt
¼ cup extra virgin olive oil

4 boneless skinless chicken breasts
2 cups water
1 cup quinoa, rinsed

Directions

In a blender, mix olive oil, salt, lime juice, jalapeño pepper, capers, and parsley and blend until smooth. Arrange chicken breasts on the bottom of the cooker. Over the chicken, add salsa verde mixture.

In a bowl that can fit in the cooker, mix quinoa and water. Set a steamer rack onto chicken and sauce. Set the bowl onto the rack. Seal the lid and cook on High pressure for 20 minutes. Release the pressure quickly. Using two forks, shred chicken into the sauce; stir to coat. Divide the quinoa between plates. Top with chicken and salsa verde before serving.

Potato & Ginger Chicken

Serves: 2-4 | Ready in about: 30 minutes

Ingredients

4 chicken thighs, boneless
3 large potatoes, wedged
1 tbsp lemon juice

2 garlic cloves, crushed
1 tsp ginger, ground
1 tbsp cayenne pepper

1 tsp fresh mint, finely chopped
¼ cup olive oil
½ tsp salt

Directions

In a bowl, combine olive oil, lemon juice, garlic, ginger, mint, cayenne, and salt. Brush each chicken piece with some of the mixture. Spread the remaining mixture on your Instant Pot. Place the potatoes and top with chicken. Add 1 cup water and seal the lid. Cook on Manual for 15 minutes on High. When done, release the pressure naturally for 10 minutes. Serve.

Lemon Saucy Chicken with Herbs

Serves: 2-4 | Ready in about: 40 minutes

Ingredients

1 (3 ½ lb) young whole chicken
4 garlic cloves, minced
2 tsp olive oil
4 fresh thyme, minced
3 fresh rosemary, minced

2 lemons, zested and quartered
Salt and black pepper to taste
2 tbsp olive oil
8 oz asparagus, trimmed and chopped
1 onion, chopped

1 cup chicken stock
1 tbsp soy sauce
1 fresh thyme sprig
1 tbsp flour
2 tbsp chopped parsley

Directions

Rub all sides of the chicken with garlic, rosemary, black pepper, lemon zest, thyme, and salt. Into the chicken cavity, insert lemon wedges. Warm the oil in your Instant Pot on Sauté. Add in onion and asparagus and sauté for 5 minutes until softened. Mix in chicken stock, 1 thyme sprig, and soy sauce.

Into the pot, set trivet over asparagus mixture. On top of the trivet, place the chicken with breast-side up. Seal the lid, select Poultry, and cook for 20 minutes on High. Do a quick release. Remove the chicken to a serving platter.

In the inner pot, sprinkle flour over asparagus mixture and blend it with an immersion blender until desired consistency. Top the chicken with asparagus sauce and garnish with parsley.

Homemade Meatballs in Tomato Sauce

Serves: 2-4 | Ready in about: 35 minutes

Ingredients

1 lb ground chicken
3 tbsp red hot sauce
1 egg
⅓ cup crumbled blue cheese

¼ cup bread crumbs
¼ cup Pecorino Romano cheese, grated
1 tbsp ranch dressing
1 tsp dried basil

Salt and black pepper to taste
15 oz canned tomato sauce
1 cup chicken broth
2 tbsp olive oil

Directions

In a bowl, mix chicken, egg, pecorino, basil, pepper, salt, ranch dressing, blue cheese, 3 tbsp hot sauce, and bread crumbs; shape the mixture into meatballs. Warm oil on Sauté. Add in meatballs and cook for 2 to 3 minutes until browned on all sides. Add in tomato sauce and broth. Seal the lid and cook on High pressure for 7 minutes. Release the pressure quickly. Remove meatballs carefully and place them on a serving plate. Serve.

Stuffed Chicken with Pesto

Serves: 2-4 | Ready in about: 20 minutes

Ingredients

4 chicken breasts
1 tbsp butter
1 tbsp olive oil
¼ cup dry white wine

¾ cup chicken stock
1 cup green beans, trimmed and chopped
1 cup fresh basil

1 garlic clove, smashed
2 tbsp pine nuts
¼ cup Parmesan cheese, grated
¼ cup extra virgin olive oil

Directions

In a food processor, mix fresh basil, pine nuts, garlic, salt, pepper, and Parmesan cheese. Add in oil and process until the desired consistency is attained. Apply a thin layer of pesto to one side of each chicken breast; tightly roll into a cylinder and fasten closed with small skewers.

Press Sauté on your Instant Pot. Heat olive oil and butter. Cook chicken rolls for 1 to 2 minutes per side until browned. Add in wine and cook until the wine has evaporated, 3 minutes. Add stock and top the chicken with green beans. Seal the lid, press Manual, and cook for 5 minutes. Release the pressure quickly. Serve chicken rolls with cooking liquid and green beans.

Easy Chicken in Tropical Gravy

Serves: 2-4 | Ready in about: 25 minutes

Ingredients

1 tbsp olive oil
4 boneless, skinless chicken thighs,
¼ cup pineapple juice

2 tbsp ketchup
2 tbsp Worcestershire sauce
1 garlic clove, minced

1 tsp cornstarch
2 tsp water
1 tbsp fresh cilantro, chopped

Directions

Warm oil on Sauté in your Instant Pot. Sear chicken 3 minutes until golden brown; set aside. Add pineapple juice, Worcestershire sauce, garlic, and ketchup to the pot to deglaze, scrape the bottom to get rid of any browned bits of food. Place the chicken into the sauce and stir well to coat. Seal the lid cook for 5 minutes on High pressure. Release the pressure quickly.

In a small bowl, mix water and cornstarch until well dissolved. Press Cancel and set to Sauté. Stir the cornstarch slurry into the sauce; cook for 2 minutes until the sauce is well thickened. Set in serving bowls and cilantro to serve.

Bell Pepper & Carrot Chicken Stew

Serves: 2-4 | Ready in about: 35 minutes

Ingredients

½ lb chicken breasts, cut into pieces	1 carrot, chopped	2 tbsp olive oil
1 potato, peeled, chopped	2 cups chicken broth	1 tsp chili pepper powder
2 green bell peppers, chopped	1 tomato, roughly chopped	1 tsp salt

Directions

Warm the olive oil in your Instant Pot on Sauté. Stir-fry the bell peppers and carrot for 3 minutes. Add potato and tomato. Sprinkle with chili pepper and salt and stir well. Add in the chicken and broth and seal the lid. Cook on High pressure for 13 minutes. When ready, do a quick pressure release. Serve hot.

Tuscan Chicken Stew

Serves: 2-4 | Ready in about: 20 minutes

Ingredients

1 lb chicken wings	2 garlic cloves, chopped	2 tbsp fresh parsley, chopped
2 peeled potatoes, cut into chunks	2 tbsp olive oil	Salt and black pepper to taste
2 fire-roasted tomatoes, chopped	1 tsp smoked paprika, ground	1 cup spinach, chopped
1 carrot, cut into chunks	2 cups chicken broth	

Directions

Rub the chicken with salt, pepper, and paprika, and place in the pot. Add in all remaining ingredients and seal the lid. Cook on High pressure for 8 minutes. When ready, do a quick release. Serve hot.

Vegetable Chicken Legs

Serves: 2-4 | Ready in about: 50 minutes

Ingredients

1 lb chicken legs, boneless and skinless	2 tomatoes, roughly chopped	1 small onion, peeled and chopped
1 cup chicken stock	½ lb Brussels sprouts	3 tbsp olive oil
½ cauliflower head, roughly chopped	2 zucchinis, chopped	1 tsp salt

Directions

Heat oil in your Instant Pot and stir-fry onions for 2 minutes on Sauté. Add vegetables and stir-fry for 5 minutes. Add the remaining ingredients and seal the lid. Cook on Poultry for 15 minutes on High. Do a quick release.

Delicious Herbed Chicken

Serves: 2-4 | Ready in about: 1 hour 30 minutes

Ingredients

4 chicken thighs	3 garlic cloves, crushed	1 tbsp fresh rosemary, chopped
1 cup chicken broth	½ cup freshly squeezed lemon juice	1 tsp cayenne pepper
1 cup olive oil	1 tbsp fresh basil, chopped	1 tsp salt
¼ cup apple cider vinegar	2 tbsp fresh thyme, chopped	

Directions

In a bowl, add oil, vinegar, garlic, juice, basil, thyme, rosemary, salt, and cayenne. Submerge thighs into this mixture and refrigerate for one hour. Remove from the fridge and pat dry with kitchen paper. Pour broth in the pot.

Set a trivet and place the chicken on it. Seal the lid and cook on Steam for 15 minutes. Do a quick release and remove the chicken and broth; wipe clean. Press Sauté, warm oil, and brown the thighs for 5 minutes, turning once until nice and golden.

Chicken Stew with Fire-Roasted Tomato

Serves: 2-4 | Ready in about: 50 minutes

Ingredients

2 lb chicken breasts
1 cup fire-roasted tomatoes, diced

1 tbsp chili powder
Salt and white pepper to taste

1 cup orange juice
2 cups chicken broth

Directions

Season the meat with salt and white pepper and place in your Instant Pot. Add the remaining ingredients, except for the orange juice and chicken broth, and cook on Sauté for 10 minutes, stirring occasionally. Pour in the broth and orange juice. Seal the lid and cook on Manual for 25 minutes on High. Release the pressure naturally for 10 minutes. Serve immediately.

Bean & Veggie Chicken Stew

Serves: 2-4 | Ready in about: 50 minutes

Ingredients

1 whole chicken, 3 lb
8 oz broccoli florets
6 oz cauliflower florets
1 onion, chopped

1 potato, peeled and chopped
1 carrot, chopped
1 tomato, peeled and chopped
A handful of whole yellow wax beans

2 tbsp fresh parsley, chopped
¼ cup extra virgin olive oil
Salt and black pepper to taste

Directions

Warm the olive oil in your Instant Pot on Sauté. Stir-fry the onion for 3-4 minutes. Add the carrot, and cook for 5 more minutes. Add the vegetables, salt, and pepper and top with chicken. Add 1 cup of water and seal the lid. Cook on High pressure for 30 minutes. Release the pressure naturally for about 10 minutes. Serve.

Traditional Chicken Tikka Masala

Serves: 2-4 | Ready in about: 40 minutes

Ingredients

2 lb boneless, skinless chicken thighs,
Salt and black pepper to taste
2 tbsp olive oil
½ onion, chopped
2 garlic cloves, minced
3 tbsp tomato puree

1 tsp fresh ginger, minced
1 tbsp garam masala
2 tsp curry powder
1 tsp ground coriander
½ tsp ground cumin
1 jalapeño pepper, seeded and chopped

29 oz canned tomato sauce
3 tomatoes, chopped
½ cup natural yogurt
1 lemon, juiced
¼ cup fresh chopped cilantro leaves
4 lemon wedges

Directions

Rub black pepper and salt onto chicken. Warm oil on Sauté. Add garlic and onion and cook for 3 minutes until soft. Stir in tomato puree, garam masala, cumin, curry powder, ginger, coriander, and jalapeño pepper and cook for 30 seconds until fragrant. Stir in tomato sauce, and tomatoes. Simmer the mixture as you scrape the bottom to get rid of any browned bits.

Stir in chicken. Seal the lid and cook on High pressure for 10 minutes. Release the pressure quickly. Press Sauté and simmer for 3 minutes until thickened. Stir lemon juice and yogurt through the sauce. Serve topped with lemon wedges and cilantro.

Sweet Saucy Chicken

Serves: 2-4 | Ready in about: 45 minutes

Ingredients

4 chicken breasts
Salt and black pepper to taste
2 tbsp olive oil
2 tbsp soy sauce

2 tbsp tomato paste
2 tbsp honey
2 tbsp minced garlic
½ cup chicken broth

1 tbsp cornstarch
1 tbsp water
½ cup chives, chopped

Directions

Season the chicken with pepper and salt. Warm oil on Sauté. Add in chicken and cook for 5 minutes until browned. In a small bowl, mix garlic, soy sauce, honey, and tomato paste. Pour the mixture over the chicken. Stir in ½ cup broth. Seal the lid and cook on High pressure for 12 minutes. Release the pressure quickly.

Set the chicken to a bowl. Mix water and cornstarch to create a slurry. Briskly stir the mixture into the sauce left in the pan for 2 minutes until thickened. Serve the chicken with sauce and chives.

Okra & Honey Garlic Chicken

Serves: 2-4 | Ready in about: 25 minutes

Ingredients

2 garlic cloves, minced
¼ cup tomato puree
½ cup soy sauce
⅓ cup honey

2 tbsp rice vinegar
2 tbsp olive oil
2 chicken breasts, chopped
½ cup rice, rinsed

2 cups frozen okra
1 tbsp cornstarch
2 tsp toasted sesame seeds
4 spring onions, chopped

Directions

In the pot, mix garlic, tomato puree, vinegar, soy sauce, ginger, honey, and oil; toss in chicken to coat. In a bowl that can fit in the Instant Pot, mix 1 cup water and rice. Set the steamer rack on top of chicken. Lower the bowl onto the rack. Seal the lid and cook on High pressure for 10 minutes. Release the pressure quickly. Use a fork to fluff the rice. Lay okra onto the rice. Allow the okra steam in the residual heat for 3 minutes. Take the trivet and bowl from the pot. Set the chicken to a plate. Press Sauté. In a bowl, mix well 1 tbsp water and cornstarch. Stir into the sauce and cook for 3 to 4 minutes until thickened. Divide the rice, chicken, and okra between 4 bowls. Drizzle sauce over each portion; garnish with spring onions and sesame seeds.

Basil & Coconut Chicken Stew

Serves: 2-4 | Ready in about: 55 minutes

Ingredients

2 cups fire-roasted tomatoes, diced
½ lb chicken breasts, chopped
1 tbsp fresh basil, chopped
1 cup coconut milk

1 cup chicken broth
Salt and black pepper to taste
1 tbsp tomato paste
1 celery stalk, chopped

1 carrot, chopped
2 tbsp coconut oil
1 onion, finely chopped
½ cup button mushrooms, sliced

Directions

Warm the coconut oil in your Instant Pot on Sauté. Add celery, onion, and carrot and cook for 5 minutes, stirring constantly. Stir in tomato paste and mushrooms. Continue to cook for 5 more minutes. Add the remaining ingredients except for the basil. Seal the lid and cook on Manual for 15 minutes on High. Do a quick release. Serve topped with basil.

Bell Pepper & Turkey Casserole

Serves: 2 | Ready in about: 55 minutes

Ingredients

½ tbsp olive oil
½ small onion, diced
1 garlic clove, minced
½ lb ground turkey
1 bell pepper, chopped

2 potatoes, peeled and chopped
⅓ cup carrots, chopped
⅓ cup corn kernels, roasted
⅓ cup tomato puree
1 cup diced tomatoes

⅓ cup chicken broth
⅓ tbsp ground cumin
⅓ tbsp chili powder
Salt and black pepper to taste

Directions

Warm oil on Sauté, and stir-fry onions and garlic until soft, for about 3 minutes. Stir in turkey and cook until thoroughly browned, about 5-6 minutes. Add the remaining ingredients, and stir to combine. Seal lid and cook for 25 minutes on High pressure. Do a quick release. Cook on Sauté uncovered for 15 minutes.

Spiced Turkey Breast

Serves: 2-4 | Ready in about: 45 minutes

Ingredients

1 tbsp olive oil
½ sweet onion, diced
3 cloves garlic, minced
1 jalapeno pepper, minced

1 lb turkey breast, cubed
2 (14-oz) cans fire-roasted tomatoes
1 cup salsa
2 bell peppers, cut into thick strips

2 tsp chili powder
1 tsp ground cumin
Sea salt to taste
2 tbsp fresh oregano, chopped

Directions

Warm oil in your Instant Pot on Sauté. Add in garlic, onion, and jalapeño and cook for 5 minutes until fragrant. Stir turkey into the pot and cook for 5-6 minutes. Add in salsa, tomatoes, bell peppers, and 1 ½ cups water. Season with salt, cumin, and chili powder. Seal the lid, press Manual, and cook for 10 minutes. Release the pressure quickly. Top with oregano and serve.

Rosemary & Garlic Chicken

Serves: 2-4 | Ready in about: 30 minutes

Ingredients

½ lb chicken breasts

2 garlic cloves, crushed

1 tbsp fresh rosemary, chopped

1 tbsp olive oil

1 onion, finely chopped

Salt and white pepper to taste

Directions

Warm the olive oil in your Instant Pot on Sauté. Stir-fry the onion and garlic for 3 minutes until fragrant. Add the chicken and 1 cup water. Season with salt and white pepper. Seal the lid and cook on High pressure for 15 minutes. When ready, do a quick pressure release. Serve topped with fresh rosemary.

Turkey Stuffed Potatoes

Serves: 2-4 | Ready in about: 30 minutes

Ingredients

2 cups vegetable broth

1 tsp chili powder

1 tsp ground cumin

½ tsp onion powder

½ tsp garlic powder

1 lb turkey breasts

4 potatoes

2 tbsp fresh cilantro, chopped

1 Fresno chili pepper, chopped

Directions

In the pot, combine broth, cumin, garlic powder, onion powder, and chili. Toss in turkey to coat. Place a steamer rack over the turkey. On top of the rack, set the steamer basket. Use a fork to pierce the potatoes and set them into the steamer basket.

Seal the lid and cook for 20 minutes on High pressure. Release the pressure quickly. Remove rack and steamer basket from the cooker. Place the potatoes on a plate. Place turkey in a mixing bowl and use two forks to shred. Cut in half each potato lengthwise. Stuff with shredded turkey. Top with cilantro, onion, and chili pepper.

Homemade Turkey Burgers

Serves: 2-4 | Ready in about: 25 minutes

Ingredients

1 lb ground turkey

2 eggs

1 cup flour

1 onion, finely chopped

Salt and black pepper to taste

1 cup sour cream

Directions

In a bowl, add all ingredients and mix well with hands. Form patties out the mixture. Line parchment paper over a baking dish and arrange the patties. Pour 1 cup water in the pot. Lay the trivet and place the baking dish on top. Seal the lid. Cook on Pressure Cook for 15 minutes on High. Release the pressure naturally for 10 minutes. Serve with lettuce and tomatoes.

Garlic Roast Turkey

Serves: 2 | Ready in about: 50 minutes

Ingredients

½ lb boneless turkey breast, halved

1 garlic clove, crushed

⅓ tsp dried basil

⅓ tsp white pepper

1 whole clove

2 tbsp soy sauce

1 tbsp lemon juice

2 tbsp olive oil

1 cup chicken broth

Directions

Place the turkey in a Ziploc bag and add basil, clove, soy sauce, oil, and lemon juice. Pour in ½ cup of broth and seal. Shake and refrigerate for 30 minutes. Heat oil in your Instant Pot on Sauté. Cook garlic for 1 minute. Add in the turkey with 2 tbsp of the marinade and remaining broth. Seal the lid. Cook on Poultry for 25 minutes on High. Release the pressure naturally.

Fried Turkey Meatballs with Pasta

Serves: 2 | Ready in about: 40 minutes

Ingredients

2 tbsp canola oil

½ lb ground turkey

1 egg

¼ cup breadcrumbs

2 cloves garlic, minced

Salt and black pepper to taste

2 cups tomato sauce

8 oz rigatoni

2 tbsp Grana Padano cheese, grated

Directions

In a bowl, combine turkey, breadcrumbs, garlic, and egg. Season with salt and pepper. Form the mixture into meatballs with well-oiled hands. Warm the canola oil in your Instant Pot on Sauté. Cook the meatballs for 3 to 4 minutes until browned on all sides. Remove to a plate. Add rigatoni to the cooker and cover with tomato sauce. Pour enough water to cover the pasta. Stir well. Throw in the meatballs. Seal the lid and cook for 10 minutes on High pressure. Release the pressure quickly. Serve topped with Grana Padano cheese.

Zucchini Turkey Casserole

Serves: 2-4 | Ready in about: 45 minutes

Ingredients

1 lb turkey breast, chopped
1 tsp red pepper flakes
2 cups canned tomatoes, diced
3 cups chicken broth

1 tsp honey
2 cups zucchini, cubed
3 garlic cloves, chopped
1 cup onions, finely chopped

2 tbsp tomato paste
1 cup baby carrots, chopped
Salt and black pepper to taste
2 tbsp olive oil

Directions

Mix all ingredients in your Instant Pot. Seal the lid and cook on Meat/Stew for 25 minutes on High pressure. When ready, do a quick release and open the lid. Serve immediately.

Potato & Turkey Casserole

Serves: 2 | Ready in about: 40 minutes

Ingredients

1 lb turkey breast, boneless, chopped
2 tomatoes, pureed

1 onion, finely chopped
2 potatoes, peeled and chopped

1 tsp dried oregano
2 cups chicken broth

Directions

Combine all ingredients in the pot and seal the lid. Cook on Manual for 30 minutes on High. When done, press Cancel and release the steam naturally for 10 minutes. Serve warm.

Hazelnut Turkey with Cranberry Sauce

Serves: 2-4 | Ready in about: 40 minutes

Ingredients

1 lb turkey breast, sliced
3 tbsp butter, softened
2 cups fresh cranberries

1 cup toasted hazelnuts, chopped
1 cup red wine
1 tbsp fresh rosemary, chopped

2 tbsp oil
2 tbsp orange zest

Directions

Rub the meat with oil and sprinkle with orange zest and rosemary. Melt butter in the pot, and brown turkey breast for 5-6 minutes, on Sauté. Pour in wine, cranberries, and 1 cup of water. Seal the lid. Cook on High pressure for 25 minutes. Do a quick release. Serve with chopped hazelnuts.

Turkey Meatballs with Feta

Serves: 2 | Ready in about: 30 minutes

Ingredients

½ onion, minced
¼ cup plain breadcrumbs
2 tbsp feta cheese, crumbled

Salt and black pepper to taste
1 lb ground turkey
1 egg, lightly beaten

½ tbsp olive oil
⅓ carrot, minced
2 cups tomato puree

Directions

In a mixing bowl, combine half of the onion, turkey, salt, crumbs, pepper, and egg, and stir until everything is well incorporated. Heat oil in your Instant Pot on Sauté and cook remaining onion and carrot for 5 minutes until soft.

Pour in 1 cup water and tomato puree. Adjust the seasonings. Roll the mixture into meatballs, and drop into the sauce. Seal the lid. Press Meat/Stew and cook on High pressure for 5 minutes. Allow the cooker to cool and release the pressure naturally for 20 minutes. Serve topped with feta cheese.

MEAT RECIPES

Broccoli Pork Chops with Creamy Sauce

Serves: 2 | Ready in about: 45 minutes

Ingredients

⅓ tsp garlic powder

⅓ tsp onion powder

⅓ tsp red pepper flakes

2 boneless pork chops

⅓ broccoli head, broken into florets

⅓ cup chicken stock

2 tbsp butter, melted

2 tbsp heavy cream

Salt and black pepper to taste

Directions

Mix the garlic powder, pepper flakes, onion, salt, and pepper in a bowl. Rub the mixture onto the pork chops. Place butter, stock, and broccoli in your Instant Pot. Lay the pork chops on top. Seal the lid. Cook for 15 minutes on High. Release the pressure quickly.

Transfer the pork chops and broccoli to a plate. Press Sauté and simmer the liquid remaining in the pot. Mix in heavy cream and cook for 4-6 minutes until thickened and bubbly. Top the chops and broccoli with the gravy and serve.

Sunday Mustardy Ham

Serves: 2 | Ready in about: 30 minutes

Ingredients

½ lb smoked ham

2 tbsp apricot jam

1 tbsp brown sugar

Juice from ¼ lime

⅓ tsp mustard

1/8 tsp ground cardamom

Directions

Into the pot, add ½ cup water and ham. In a bowl, mix jam, lemon juice, cardamom, mustard, and sugar. Pour the mixture over the ham. Seal the lid and cook on High for 10 minutes. Release the pressure quickly. Let the ham sit for 10 minutes.

Press Sauté. Simmer the liquid and cook for 4 to 6 minutes until thickened into a sauce. Slice the ham and place it onto a serving bowl. Drizzle with sauce before serving.

Sweet Tropical Pork

Serves: 2 | Ready in about: 50 minutes + marinating time

Ingredients

2 tbsp orange juice

1 tbsp lime juice

1 tbsp canola oil

1 tbsp chopped fresh cilantro

¼ tsp red pepper flakes

2 cloves garlic, minced

¼ tsp ground cumin

Salt and black pepper to taste

½ lb pork shoulder

Directions

In a bowl, mix orange juice, canola oil, cumin, salt, pepper, lime juice, and garlic. Add into a large plastic bag alongside the pork. Seal and massage the bag to ensure the marinade covers the pork thoroughly. Place in the refrigerator for 2 hours.

In your Instant Pot, set your removed pork from the bag. Add the marinade on top. Seal the lid and cook on High for 30 minutes. Release pressure naturally for 15 minutes. Transfer the pork to a cutting board and use a fork to break into smaller pieces. Skim and get rid of the fat from liquid in the cooker. Serve the liquid with pork and sprinkle with cilantro.

Cabbage & Veggies Pork Dinner

Serves: 2 | Ready in about: 25 minutes

Ingredients

½ lb ground pork

⅓ cup cabbage, shredded

2 tbsp chopped celery

½ red onion, chopped

1 tomato, chopped

½ carrot, shredded

2 tbsp olive oil

1 red bell pepper, chopped

1/8 tsp cumin

¼ tsp red pepper flakes

Salt and black pepper to taste

1 tbsp fresh cilantro, chopped

Directions

Select Sauté on your Instant Pot and heat olive oil. Add the pork and cook until browned, about 6-8 minutes. Stir in the remaining ingredients, and pour the 1 cup of water. Seal the lid and set to Pressure Cook for 15 minutes on High. Do a quick pressure release. Sprinkle with freshly chopped cilantro and serve.

Cheddar & Corn Bundt Casserole

Serves: 2-4 | Ready in about: 50 minutes

Ingredients

8 bacon strips, chopped
2 eggs, beaten
1 cup shredded cheddar cheese

3 tbsp finely chopped habanero chilies
1 (15 oz) can corn, drained
1 (8.5 oz) pack corn muffin mix

1 (10.5 oz) cream of sweet corn
¼ cup salted butter, melted
¾ cup heavy cream

Directions

Set your Instant Pot to Sauté. Cook the bacon until crispy and brown, 5 minutes. Fetch bacon into a large bowl and clean inner pot. Return the pot to the base. In the bowl, add eggs, cheddar cheese, habanero chilies, corn, muffin mix, corn cream, butter, and heavy cream. Pour mixture into a greased bundt pan, safe for the Instant Pot, and cover with aluminum foil.

Pour 1 cup water into the inner pot, fit in a trivet, and sit bundt pan on top. Seal the lid, select Manual on High, and cook for 20 minutes. When done, perform natural pressure release for 10 minutes. Unlock the lid and carefully remove the bundt pan. Take off the foil and turn the casserole over onto a plate. Garnish with parsley, slice, and serve.

Shredded Pork in Corn Tortillas

Serves: 2 | Ready in about: 1 hour 15 minutes

Ingredients

1 tsp grapeseed oil
1 lb boneless pork shoulder
¼ onion, chopped
1 garlic clove, minced

½ orange, juiced
½ lime, juiced
½ tbsp sweet smoked paprika
⅓ tbsp dried oregano

Salt and black pepper to taste
½ jalapeño pepper, chopped
½ avocado, sliced
2 corn tortillas, warm

Directions

Warm the oil in your Instant Pot on Sauté. Add in pork and cook for 5 minutes until golden brown. Transfer to a plate. Add garlic and onion to the pot and cook for 3 minutes until soft. Add lime and orange juices into the pan to deglaze, scrape the bottom to get rid of any browned bits of food. Stir in pepper, paprika, salt, and oregano. Return the pork to pot. Stir to coat.

Seal the lid and cook for 35 minutes on High. Release the pressure quickly. Press Sauté. When the liquid starts to simmer, use 2 forks to shred the pork. Cook for 10 minutes until liquid is reduced by half. Serve in tortillas topped with jalapeños and avocado.

Cannellini & Sausage Stew

Serves: 2 | Ready in about: 45 minutes

Ingredients

½ tbsp olive oil
⅓ lb Italian sausages, halved
⅓ celery stalk, chopped
⅓ carrot, chopped

⅓ onion, chopped
⅓ sprig fresh sage
⅓ sprig fresh rosemary
½ bay leaf

½ cup Cannellini beans, soaked
3/4 cup vegetable stock
1 cup fresh spinach
⅓ tsp salt

Directions

Warm the oil in your Instant Pot on Sauté. Add in sausages and sear for 5 minutes until browned; set aside. To the pot, add celery, onion, bay leaf, sage, carrot, and rosemary; cook for 3 minutes to soften slightly. Stir in vegetable stock and beans.

Arrange sausage pieces on top of the beans. Seal the lid, press Bean/Chili, and cook on High for 10 minutes. Release pressure naturally for 20 minutes, do a quick release. Get rid of bay leaf, rosemary, and sage. Mix spinach into the mixture to serve.

Cilantro Pulled Pork

Serves: 2 | Ready in about: 45 minutes

Ingredients

bay lb pork shoulder
2 tbsp maple syrup
¼ cup sun-dried tomatoes, diced

1 cup beef stock
½ tbsp mustard powder
1 tbsp brown sugar

½ tbsp sea salt
⅓ cup fresh cilantro, chopped

Directions

Rub the meat with salt and sugar, and place it in the pot. Add the remaining ingredients except for the cilantro. Seal the lid and cook on High for 30 minutes. Allow the pressure to release naturally for 10 minutes and serve immediately. Shred the pork with two forks, transfer to a plate, and top with cilantro to serve.

Chickpea & Chili Pork Stew

Serves: 2 | Ready in about: 40 minutes

Ingredients

1 tbsp olive oil
½ lb boneless pork shoulder, cubed
⅓ white onion, chopped
5 oz canned chickpeas, drained

2 tbsp sweet paprika
Salt to taste
⅓ tbsp chili powder
½ bay leaf

1 red bell pepper, chopped
2 clove garlic, minced
⅓ tbsp cornstarch

Directions

Set your Instant Pot to Sauté, add pork and oil, and allow cooking for 5 minutes until browned. Add in the onion, paprika, bay leaf, salt, ½ cup water, chickpeas, and chili powder. Seal the lid and cook on High for 8 minutes. Do a quick release.

Discard bay leaf. Remove 1 cup of cooking liquid from the pot and add it to a blender alongside garlic, cornstarch, and red bell peppers. Pulse until smooth. Add the blended mixture into the stew and mix well. Serve.

Party Honey-Glazed Ham

Serves: 2 | Ready in about: 30 minutes

Ingredients

1 tbsp apple cider
1 tbsp honey
⅓ tbsp Dijon mustard

1 tbsp brown sugar
½ tbsp orange juice
½ tbsp pineapple juice

1/8 tsp grated nutmeg
1/8 tbsp ground cloves
½ lb ham, bone-in

Directions

Set your Instant pot to Sauté. Mix in apple cider, mustard, pineapple juice, cloves, sugar, honey, orange juice, and nutmeg; cook until the sauce becomes warm, and the sugar and spices are completely dissolved. Lay ham into the sauce. Seal the lid and cook on High for 10 minutes. Release the pressure quickly. Transfer the ham to a baking sheet.

Preheat the oven's broiler. On Sauté, cook the remaining liquid for 4 to 6 minutes until you have a thick and syrupy glaze. Brush the glaze onto the ham. Set the glazed ham in the preheated broiler and bake for 3 to 5 minutes until the glaze is caramelized. Place the ham on a cutting board and slice. Transfer to a serving bowl and drizzle glaze over the ham. Serve.

Italian-Style Sausages

Serves: 2 | Ready in about: 30 minutes

Ingredients

½ cup water
2 Italian sausages
½ tbsp olive oil

1 garlic clove, smashed
1 potato, peeled and cut into chunks
2 tbsp butter, melted

2 tbsp milk
Salt and black pepper to taste
½ tbsp chopped chives

Directions

Select Sauté on your Instant Pot and heat olive oil. Cook the sausages for 8-10 minutes, turning periodically until browned. Set aside. Add the water to the pot and set a steamer rack over water and steamer basket onto the rack. Place potato in the basket. Seal the lid and cook on High for 12 minutes. Release the pressure quickly. Remove basket and rack from the pot.

Drain water from the pot. Return potato to the pot. Add in salt, butter, pepper, garlic, and milk and mash until no large lumps remain. Transfer the mash to a serving plate. Top with sausages and scatter chopped chives over to serve.

Mushroom Saucy Pork Roast

Serves: 2 | Ready in about: 50 minutes

Ingredients

½ lb pork shoulder
½ cup button mushrooms, chopped
1 tbsp butter

⅓ tbsp balsamic vinegar
¼ tsp garlic powder
Salt to taste

1/8 cup soy sauce
⅓ cup beef broth
1 tsp cornstarch

Directions

Rinse the meat and rub with salt and garlic powder. Melt butter in your Instant Pot on Sauté. Brown the meat for 5 minutes on each side. Stir in soy sauce. Cook for 2 minutes before, add in beef broth and balsamic vinegar. Seal the lid.

Set to Meat/Stew. Cook for 30 minutes on High. Do a quick release and Stir in mushrooms. Cook until tender, about 5 minutes on Sauté. Stir in cornstarch and cook for 2 minutes. Serve warm.

Cinnamon & Orange Pork

Serves: 2 | Ready in about: 60 minutes

Ingredients

1 tbsp olive oil
½ lb pork shoulder
⅓ cinnamon stick
½ cup orange juice

⅓ tbsp cumin
1/8 tsp garlic powder
1/8 tsp onion powder
¼ onion, chopped

¼ Jalapeno pepper, diced
½ tsp thyme
¼ tsp oregano
1/8 tsp pepper

Directions

Place half of the oil in a small bowl. Add all of the spices and stir well to combine the mixture. Rub it all over the meat, making sure that the pork is well-coated. Heat the remaining oil on Sauté. Add the pork and sear it on all sides until browned. Transfer to a plate. Pour the orange juice into the pan and deglaze the bottom with a spatula.

Add the rest of the ingredients and stir to combine well. Return the pork to the pot. Seal the lid, select Pressure Cook, and cook for 40 minutes on High. When ready, allow natural pressure release for 10 minutes. Grab two forks and shred the pork inside the pot. Stir to combine with the juices and serve.

Jamaican Sweet Pulled Pork

Serves: 2 | Ready in about: 1 hour 15 minutes

Ingredients

½ tsp onion powder
Sea salt and black pepper to taste
⅓ tsp dried thyme
⅓ tsp cayenne pepper

⅓ tsp ground allspice
¼ tsp ground nutmeg
¼ tsp ground cinnamon
½ lb pork shoulder

½ mango, cut into chunks
½ tbsp olive oil
¼ cup water
1 tbsp fresh cilantro, minced

Directions

In a bowl, combine onion, thyme, allspice, cinnamon, sugar, pepper, sea salt, cayenne, and nutmeg. Coat the pork shoulder with olive oil. Season with seasoning mixture. Warm oil on Sauté. Add in the pork and cook for 5 minutes until browned completely. To the pot, add water and mango chunks. Seal the lid, press Meat/Stew, and cook on High for 45 minutes.

Release the pressure naturally for 15 minutes, then quickly release the remaining pressure. Transfer the pork to a cutting board to cool. To make the sauce, pour the cooking liquid in a food processor and pulse until smooth. Use two forks to shred the pork and arrange on a serving platter. Serve the pork topped with mango salsa and cilantro.

Garlicky-Buttery Pork Shoulder

Serves: 2 | Ready in about: 1 hour

Ingredients

½ lb pork shoulder, boneless
⅓ garlic head, divided into cloves
Salt and black pepper to taste

¼ tsp red pepper flakes
½ tbsp butter
½ tsp fresh ginger, grated

1 tbsp apple cider vinegar
1 tbsp soy sauce
⅓ tsp garlic powder

Directions

In a bowl, mix apple cider, soy sauce, garlic powder, and ginger. Brush the pork with the mixture. Melt butter in your Instant Pot on Sauté and brown the pork for 6 minutes. Add in 1 cup water and garlic. Seal the lid and cook on High for 35 minutes. Do a quick release. Season with salt, pepper, and red pepper flakes. Cook on Sauté until the liquid evaporates, 10 minutes.

Pork in Tomato Cream Sauce

Serves: 2 | Ready in about: 45 minutes

Ingredients

½ lb pork shoulder, cut into pieces
½ onion, chopped
½ cup sour cream

⅓ cup tomato puree
1/6 tbsp coriander
1/8 tsp cumin

1/8 tsp cayenne pepper
⅓ tsp garlic, minced
Salt and black pepper to taste

Directions

Coat your Instant Pot with cooking spray and add the pork. Cook for 6-8 minutes on Sauté until lightly browned. Add onion and garlic and cook for 1 minute until fragrant. Stir in the remaining ingredients and turn the vent clockwise to seal. Set to 30 minutes on Soup/Broth on High. When it beeps, let sit for 5 minutes before quickly release the pressure. Serve.

Pork Sausage with Potato Mash

Serves: 2-4 | Ready in about: 45 minutes

Ingredients

1 tbsp olive oil
½ pork sausages
1 onion, chopped
1 cup vegetable broth

4 potatoes, peeled and diced
1 cup celeriac, chopped
2 tbsp butter
¼ cup milk

Salt and black pepper to taste
1 tbsp heavy cream
1 tsp Dijon mustard
2 tbsp fresh parsley, chopped

Directions

Warm the oil in your Instant Pot on Sauté. Add in sausages and cook for 2 minutes for each side until browned; remove to a plate. To the same pot, add onion and sauté for 3 minutes until fragrant. Return the sausages and pour ½ cup water and broth over them. Place a trivet over onions and sausages. Put potatoes and celeriac in the steamer basket and transfer it to the trivet. Seal the lid and cook for 11 minutes on High. Release the pressure quickly. Transfer potatoes and celeriac to a bowl and set sausages on a plate and cover them with aluminum foil. Mash potatoes and celeriac with pepper, milk, salt, and butter.

Set the pot to Sauté. Add the onion mixture and bring to a boil. Cook for 5-10 minutes until the mixture is reduced and thickened. Into the gravy, stir in salt, pepper, mustard, and heavy cream. Place the mash in bowls in equal parts and top with sausages and gravy. Garnish with parsley and serve.

Pancetta Winter Minestrone

Serves: 2 | Ready in about: 40 minutes

Ingredients

1 tbsp olive oil
3 slices pancetta, chopped
⅓ onion, diced
⅓ parsnip, peeled and chopped
½ carrot, cut into rounds

½ celery stalk, chopped
1 garlic clove, minced
⅓ tbsp dried basil
2 cups chicken broth
1 cup green beans, trimmed and chopped

½ cup canned diced tomatoes
½ cup canned chickpeas, rinsed
½ cup small shaped pasta
Salt and black pepper to taste
¼ cup grated Parmesan cheese

Directions

Heat oil in your Instant Pot on Sauté. Add onion, carrot, garlic, pancetta, celery, and parsnip and cook for 5 minutes until they become soft. Stir in basil, green beans, broth, tomatoes, pepper, salt, chickpeas, and pasta. Seal the lid and cook for 6 minutes on High. Release pressure naturally for 10 minutes. Ladle soup into bowls and serve topped with Parmesan cheese.

Pork Cabbage Rolls

Serves: 2-4 | Ready in about: 70 minutes

Ingredients

½ head Savoy cabbage, leaves separated (scraps kept)
2 tbsp butter
½ sweet onion, finely chopped
2 garlic cloves, minced

½ lb ground pork
Salt and black pepper to taste
1 cup buckwheat groats

1 ¾ cups beef stock
2 tbsp chopped cilantro
1 (23 oz) canned chopped tomatoes

Directions

Set your Instant Pot to Sauté and melt butter. Sauté onion and garlic until slightly softened, 4 minutes. Stir in pork, season with salt and pepper, and cook until no longer pink, 5 minutes. Stir in buckwheat and beef stock. Seal the lid, select Manual on High, and set the cooking time to 6 minutes. After cooking, perform a quick pressure release. Add cilantro and stir. Spread large cabbage leaves on a clean flat surface and spoon 3-4 tbsp of mixture onto each leave center. Then, roll.

Clean the pot and spread in cabbage scrap. Pour in tomatoes with liquid and arrange cabbage rolls on top. Seal the lid, select Manual on Low pressure, and set the cooking time to 25 minutes. After, perform natural pressure release for 10 minutes. Using a slotted spoon, remove cabbage rolls onto serving plates and serve.

Green Pepper & Beer-Braised Hot Dogs

Serves: 2 | Ready in about: 15 minutes

Ingredients

1 tbsp olive oil
2 sausages pork sausage links

1 green bell pepper, chopped into strips
1 spring onion, chopped

½ cup beer
2 hot dog rolls

Directions

Warm oil on Sauté. Add in sausage links and sear for 5 minutes until browned; set aside on a plate. Into the Instant Pot, pile peppers. Lay the sausages on top. Add beer into the pot. Seal the lid and cook for on High 5 minutes. Release the pressure quickly. Serve sausages in buns topped with onions and peppers.

Tender Pork Ribs with Mushroom Gravy

Serves: 2-4 | Ready in about: 70 minutes

Ingredients

1 lb boneless pork short ribs, cut into 3-inch pieces

Salt and black pepper to taste	2 tbsp oil	1 carrot, sliced
½ onion, chopped	½ tbsp tomato paste	1 tbsp cornstarch
½ cup red wine	1 cup mushrooms, sliced	2 tbsp fresh parsley, chopped

Directions

Rub the ribs with salt and pepper. Heat the oil in your Instant Pot on Sauté and brown short ribs on all sides, 3-5 minutes per side. Remove to a plate. Add onions to the pot and cook for 3 minutes, until tender. Pour in wine and tomato paste to deglaze by scraping any browned bits from the bottom of the cooker. Cook for 2 minutes until the wine has reduced slightly.

Return ribs to the pot and cover with carrots. Pour in 1 cup of water. Hit Cancel to stop Sauté. Seal the lid, and select Meat/ Stew on High for 35 minutes. When ready, let pressure release naturally for 10 minutes. Transfer ribs and carrots to a plate. Discard vegetables and herbs. Stir in mushrooms. Press Sauté and cook until mushrooms are soft, 4 minutes.

In a bowl, add water and cornstarch and mix until smooth. Pour this slurry into the pot, stirring constantly, until it thickens slightly, 2 minutes. Season the gravy with salt and pepper. Pour over the ribs and garnish with parsley and serve.

Mac & Cheese with Chorizo

Serves: 2 | Ready in about: 30 minutes

Ingredients

⅓ lb macaroni	½ tbsp minced garlic	½ cup cheddar cheese, shredded
1 oz chorizo, chopped	½ cup milk	Salt to taste

Directions

Set your Instant Pot to Sauté and stir-fry chorizo until crispy, about 6 minutes. Set aside. Wipe the pot. Add in 1 cup water, macaroni, garlic, and salt to taste. Seal lid and cook on for 5 minutes on High. Release the pressure quickly. Stir in cheese and milk until the cheese melts. Divide the mac and cheese between serving bowls. Top with chorizo and serve.

Easy Pork Roast with Beer Sauce

Serves: 2 | Ready in about: 50 minutes

Ingredients

½ lb pork roast	3 oz root beer	¼ package dry onion soup
2 oz mushrooms, sliced	2.5 oz cream of mushroom soup	

Directions

In the pressure cooker, whisk mushroom soup, dry onion soup mix, and root beer. Add the mushrooms and pork. Seal the lid, and set to Meat/Stew for 40 minutes on High. When ready, let sit for 5 minutes before doing a quick pressure release.

Sweet Pork Meatballs

Serves: 2 | Ready in about: 30 minutes

Ingredients

½ lb ground pork	1/8 tbsp dried thyme	1/8 cup apple juice
2 tbsp tamari sauce	¼ cup diced onions	¼ cup breadcrumbs
½ garlic clove, minced	½ tsp honey	Salt and black pepper to taste

Directions

Whisk honey, tamari, apple juice, ½ cups water, and thyme in the cooker. Season with salt and pepper. Set to Sauté and cook for 15 minutes. Combine all the remaining ingredients in a bowl. Shape meatballs out of the mixture. Drop the meatballs into the sauce and seal the lid. Set to Pressure Cook for 15 minutes on High. Release the pressure naturally for 10 minutes. Serve.

Tasty Pork with Green Peas

Serves: 2 | Ready in about: 55 minutes

Ingredients

½ lb ground pork
½ onion, diced
5 oz canned diced tomatoes
⅓ cup green peas

1 garlic clove, crushed
1 tbsp butter
⅓ serrano pepper, chopped
⅓ cup vegetable broth

⅓ tsp ground ginger
½ tsp chopped cilantro
Salt and black pepper to taste
⅓ tsp cumin

Directions

Melt butter in your Instant Pot on Sauté. Add onions and cook for 3 minutes until soft. Stir in the spices and garlic and cook for 2 more minutes. Add in the pork and cook until browned. Pour broth and add serrano pepper, green peas, and tomatoes. Seal the lid and cook for 30 minutes on Meat/Stew on High. When ready, release the pressure naturally for 10 minutes.

Dijon-Apple Pork Roast

Serves: 2 | Ready in about: 60 minutes

Ingredients

1 lb pork roast
1 apple, peeled and sliced
1 tbsp Dijon mustard

⅓ tbsp dried rosemary
2 tbsp white wine
⅓ cup water

⅓ tbsp garlic, minced
½ tbsp olive oil
Salt and black pepper to taste

Directions

Brush the pork with mustard. Heat oil on Sauté and sear the pork on all sides for 5 minutes. Add apple and stir in the remaining ingredients. Seal the lid and cook for 40 minutes on Meat/Stew on High. When ready, release the pressure naturally for 10 minutes. Serve warm.

Party BBQ Ribs

Serves: 2 | Ready in about: 75 minutes

Ingredients

1 lb pork ribs
2 tbsp apple jelly
⅓ cup barbecue sauce

⅓ onion, diced
½ tbsp ground cloves
¼ cup water

⅓ tbsp brown sugar
⅓ tsp Worcestershire sauce
⅓ tsp ground cinnamon

Directions

Whisk together all ingredients in your pressure cooker, except the ribs. Place the ribs inside and seal the lid. Set the cooker to Meat/Stew and cook for 45-55 minutes on High. When ready, release the pressure naturally for 10 minutes.

Sweet Pork Loin

Serves: 2 | Ready in about: 30 minutes

Ingredients

½ lb pork loin, cut into 6 equal pieces
5 oz canned pineapple
⅓ cup vegetable broth
⅓ tbsp brown sugar

1 tbsp olive oil
2 tbsp tomato paste
⅓ cup sliced onions
1/8 tsp ginger, grated

Garlic salt and black pepper to taste
2 tbsp tamari
2 tbsp rice wine vinegar
¼ tbsp cornstarch

Directions

Heat oil in your Instant Pot on Sauté. Cook the onions for 3 minutes. Add in the pork and stir in the rest of the ingredients, except for the cornstarch. Seal the lid and cook for 20 minutes on Manual on High. Release the pressure quickly. In a bowl, mix cornstarch with 1 tbsp water until slurry. Add it to the cooker and cook for 2 minutes or until thickened on Sauté. Serve.

Onion & Bell Peppers Pork Sausages

Serves: 2 | Ready in about: 20 minutes

Ingredients

2 pork sausages
½ sweet onion, sliced

1 red bell pepper, cut into strips
½ tbsp olive oil

¼ cup beef broth
2 tbsp white wine

Directions

Set your Instant Pot to Sauté. Add in the sausages and brown for 3-4 minutes. Remove to a plate and discard the liquid. Press Cancel. Wipe clean the cooker and heat the oil on Sauté. Stir in onion and bell pepper. Stir-fry them for 5 minutes until soft.

Add in the garlic and cook for 1 minute. Pour in the sausages, broth, and wine. Seal the lid and cook for 5 minutes on High. Once done, do a quick pressure release. Serve warm.

Delicious Pork Soup with Mushrooms

Serves: 2 | Ready in about: 25 minutes

Ingredients

½ lb ground pork	1 potato, diced	½ carrot, chopped
⅓ onion, diced	2 button mushrooms, sliced	1 tbsp butter
½ lb Napa cabbage, chopped	1 scallion, sliced	1 ½ cups chicken broth

Directions

Melt butter in your Instant Pot on Sauté, and add the pork. Cook until it browned, breaking it with a spatula. Once browned, add onion and mushrooms, and cook for another 4-5 minutes. Pour in chicken broth and stir in the remaining ingredients. Seal the lid, cook on Pressure Cook for 6 minutes on High. Do a quick release. Ladle into bowls and serve.

Yummy Pork Fillets with Ginger

Serves: 2 | Ready in about: 30 minutes

Ingredients

⅓ lb pork loin filets	2 tbsp apple cider vinegar	⅓ tbsp brown sugar
5 oz canned peaches	1/8 tsp garlic, minced	1 tbsp olive oil
1/8 tsp ginger, finely chopped	Salt and black pepper to taste	⅓ cup tomato sauce
2 tbsp Worcestershire sauce	⅓ cup onions, sliced	⅓ tbsp arrowroot slurry

Directions

Heat the olive oil in your Instant Pot on Sauté. Cook onions until tender, about 4 minutes. Stir in the remaining ingredients, except for the arrowroot slurry. Seal the lid, Select Meat/Stew, and cook for 20 minutes on High. Do a quick pressure release. Stir in the arrowroot slurry and cook on Sauté until the sauce thickens, about 2-3 minutes. Serve.

Pancetta with Beans & Chickpeas

Serves: 2 | Ready in about: 30 minutes

Ingredients

½ oz onion soup mix	½ cup canned chickpeas, soaked	¼ onion, chopped
1 tbsp olive oil	½ tsp yellow mustard	¼ cup kale, chopped
¼ tbsp garlic, minced	3 pancetta slices, chopped	

Directions

Heat the oil in your Instant Pot and cook the onion, garlic, and pancetta for 5 minutes on Sauté. Add in 2 cups water and soup mix and cook for 5 minutes. Stir in the chickpeas, kale, and mustard. Seal the lid and cook for 15 minutes on Pressure Cook on High. Once cooking is completed, perform a quick pressure release. Serve immediately.

Apple Cider Pork Chops

Serves: 2-4 | Ready in about: 35 minutes

Ingredients

½ lb pork fillets	1 tbsp olive oil	Salt and black pepper to taste
1 apple, cut into wedges	¼ cup apple cider vinegar	½ tsp dry rosemary
1 leek, white part only, cut into rings	½ tsp chili pepper	½ tsp dry thyme

Directions

Heat the oil in your Instant Pot. Season the pork with salt, black and cayenne peppers. Brown the fillets for about 4 minutes per side. Set aside. Add the leek to the pot and sauté for about 4 minutes. Add in apple, rosemary, and thyme.

Place the pork among the apple cider vinegar. Seal the lid and cook for 20 minutes on Meat/Stew on High. Once cooking is complete, perform a quick pressure release. To serve, arrange the pork on a plate and pour the apple sauce all over.

Dinner BBQ Pork Butt

Serves: 2 | Ready in about: 55 minutes

Ingredients

1 tbsp olive oil
½ lb pork butt
1/8 tsp garlic powder

Salt and black pepper to taste
¼ cup barbecue sauce
¼ tsp cumin powder

1/8 tsp onion powder
1 cup beef broth
1 tbsp fresh parsley, chopped

Directions

In a bowl, combine the barbecue sauce and all of the spices and mix well. Brush the pork with the mixture. Heat oil in your Instant Pot on Sauté. Add in the pork and sear on all sides for 6-8 minutes. Pour in the beef broth. Seal the lid and cook for 40 minutes on Meat/Stew on High. When ready, wait 10 minutes before releasing the pressure quickly. Top with parsley to serve.

Honey Chili Pork with Rosemary

Serves: 2 | Ready in about: 45 minutes

Ingredients

1 lb sirloin pork roast
⅓ tbsp honey

⅓ tsp chili powder
⅓ tbsp rosemary

⅓ tbsp olive oil
½ tbsp lemon juice

Directions

Combine the spices in a bowl and rub them onto the pork. Heat oil in your Instant Pot on Sauté and sear the pork on all sides, about 8-10 minutes. Stir in the remaining ingredients and ¼ cup water. Seal the lid and cook for 30 minutes on Meat/Stew on High. Do a natural pressure release for 10 minutes. Serve warm.

Cauliflower Pork Sausage & Tater Tots

Serves: 2 | Ready in about: 20 minutes

Ingredients

½ lb pork sausages, sliced
⅓ lb tater tots

⅓ lb cauliflower florets
3 oz canned mushroom soup

3 oz canned cauliflower soup
Salt and black pepper to taste

Directions

Place roughly ¼ of the sausage slices in your pressure cooker. In a bowl, whisk together the canned soups and 1 cup water. Pour some of the mixtures over the sausages. Top the sausage slices with ¼ of the cauliflower followed by ¼ of the tater tots.

Pour some of the soup mixtures again. Repeat the layers until you use up all ingredients. Seal the lid and cook on Pressure Cook for 10 minutes on High. When ready, do a quick release. Serve.

Fruity Pork Tenderloin

Serves: 2-4 | Ready in about: 55 minutes

Ingredients

1 ¼ lb pork tenderloin
1 chopped celery stalk
2 cups apples, peeled and chopped

1 cup cherries, pitted
½ cup apple juice
½ cup water

¼ cup onions, chopped
Salt and black pepper to taste
2 tbsp olive oil

Directions

Heat the oil in your Instant Pot and cook the onion and celery for 5 minutes until soft. Season the pork with salt and pepper and add to the cooker. Brown for 2-3 minutes per side. Top with apples and cherries and pour in water and apple juice.

Seal the lid and cook on Meat/Stew for 40 minutes on High. Once ready, do a quick pressure release. Slice the pork tenderloin and arrange on a serving platter. Spoon the apple-cheery sauce over the pork slices and to serve.

Mushroom & Pork Stew

Serves: 2 | Ready in about: 50 minutes

Ingredients

2 pork chops, bones removed and cubed
1 cup crimini mushrooms, sliced
2 large carrots, chopped

½ tsp garlic powder
Salt and black pepper to taste
2 tbsp butter

1 cup beef broth
1 tbsp apple cider vinegar
2 tbsp cornstarch

Directions

Season the meat with salt and pepper. Melt butter in your Instant Pot on Sauté and brown the pork chops for 10 minutes, stirring occasionally. Add in the mushrooms and cook for 5 minutes. Stir in the remaining ingredients and seal the lid. Cook on High for 25 minutes. Do a quick release and serve hot.

Old-Fashioned Pork Belly with Tamari Sauce

Serves: 2 | Ready in about: 40 minutes

Ingredients

1 garlic clove, sliced	½ lb pork belly, sliced	2 tbsp tamari sauce
1 tbsp olive oil	1/8 cup white wine	⅓ tsp sugar maple syrup
⅓ tsp grated fresh ginger	¼ cup yellow onions, chopped	1 cup white rice, cooked, warm

Directions

Heat the oil in your Instant Pot and brown the pork belly for about 6 minutes per side. Add the remaining ingredients and ½ cup water. Seal the lid and cook for 25 minutes on Pressure Cook on High. Once ready, switch the pressure release valve to open and do a quick pressure release. Serve with rice.

Basmati Rice & Bacon Chowder

Serves: 2-4 | Ready in about: 20 minutes

Ingredients

2 cups basmati rice	½ cup green peas	1 tsp dried thyme
1 cup bacon, chopped	3 tbsp olive oil	1 tsp salt
1 medium onion, chopped	2 garlic cloves, chopped	4 cups beef broth

Directions

Heat oil in your Instant Pot on Sauté and stir-fry onions and garlic for 2-3 minutes or until translucent. Add all the remaining ingredients and seal the lid. Cook on High for 5 minutes. When ready, release the pressure naturally for 10 minutes. Serve.

Jalapeno Bacon with White Peas

Serves: 2-4 | Ready in about: 30 minutes

Ingredients

½ lb white peas	1 jalapeno pepper, chopped	1 tbsp cayenne pepper
4 slices bacon	2 tbsp flour	1 bay leaf
½ onion, chopped	2 tbsp butter	Salt and black pepper to taste

Directions

Melt butter in your Instant Pot on Sauté and stir-fry the onion for 2-3 minutes until translucent. Add in bacon, peas, jalapeno pepper, bay leaf, salt, and pepper. Stir in 2 tbsp of flour and add 3 cups of water. Seal the lid and cook on High for 15 minutes. Release the steam naturally for 10 minutes. Discard the bay leaf and serve warm.

Pork Meatloaf with Ketchup

Serves: 2-4 | Ready in about: 30 minutes

For the Meatloaf:

1 lb ground pork	Salt and black pepper to taste	¼ cup tomato paste
1 cup breadcrumbs	½ tsp turmeric powder	1 tsp garlic powder
1 egg	½ tsp dried oregano	½ tsp onion powder
1 cup milk	1 cup ketchup	½ tsp cayenne pepper
1 onion, finely chopped	1 tsp brown sugar	

Directions

Place a trivet in your Instant Pot and pour in 1 cup water. Combine pork, breadcrumbs, milk, onion, egg, salt, pepper, oregano, and turmeric in a bowl. Use your hands to mix thoroughly. Shape into a loaf and place onto a greased sheet pan.

In another bowl, mix the ketchup, brown sugar, tomato paste, onion powder, and cayenne pepper. Spread the topping over the meatloaf and lower the sheet pan onto the trivet. Seal the lid, select Pressure Cook, and cook for 24 minutes on High. Once ready, do a quick pressure release. Remove to a cutting board and slice before serving.

Crunchy Pork Fajitas

Serves: 2-4 | Ready in about: 1 hour 30 minutes

Ingredients

1 tbsp ground cumin
2 tsp dried oregano
1 tsp paprika
1 tsp onion powder
Salt and black pepper to taste

½ tsp ground cinnamon
3 lb boneless pork shoulder
¾ cup vegetable broth
¼ cup pineapple juice
1 lime, juiced

2 cloves garlic, crushed
2 bay leaves
4 corn tortillas, warmed
½ cup queso Cotija, crumbled

Directions

In a bowl, combine cumin, paprika, pepper, onion powder, oregano, salt, and cinnamon; toss in pork to coat. Place the pork in the pressure cooker and allow settling for 15 to 30 minutes. Add in broth, garlic, lime juice, bay leaves, and pineapple juice. Seal the lid and cook on High for 50 minutes. Release pressure naturally for 15 minutes.

Preheat oven to 450 F. Transfer the pork to a rimmed baking sheet and use two forks to shred the meat. Reserve juices in the Instant Pot. Bake in the oven for 10 minutes until crispy. Skim and get rid of fat from the liquid remaining in the pot. Dispose of the bay leaves. Over the pork, pour the liquid and serve alongside warm corn tortillas and queso fresco.

Mouthwatering Pork Tacos

Serves: 2-4 | Ready in about: 1 hour 25 minutes

Ingredients

2 lb pork shoulder, trimmed, cut into chunks

3 tbsp sugar
3 tsp taco seasoning
1 tsp black pepper
1 cup beer

1 cup vegetable broth
¼ cup plus
2 tbsp lemon juice
¼ cup mayonnaise

2 tbsp honey
2 tsp mustard
2 cups shredded cabbage
4 taco tortillas

Directions

In a bowl, combine sugar, taco seasoning, and black pepper. Rub onto pork pieces to coat well. Allow settling for 30 minutes. Into the pot, add ¼ cup lemon juice, broth, pork, and beer. Seal the lid and cook on High for 50 minutes. In a bowl, mix mayonnaise, mustard, 2 tablespoons lemon juice, cabbage, and honey until well coated.

Release pressure naturally for 15 minutes before doing a quick release. Transfer the pork to a cutting board and allow to cool before using two forks to shred. Skim and get rid of fat from liquid in the pressure cooker. Return pork to the pot and mix with the liquid. Top the pork with slaw on tacos before serving.

Onion Pork Ribs

Serves: 2-4 | Ready in about: 35 minutes

Ingredients

1 ½ cups tomato puree
1 tbsp garlic, minced
1 ½ cups water

Salt and black pepper to serve
½ tsp dried sage
1 ¼ cups sweet onions

½ cup carrots, thinly sliced
1 lb cut pork spare ribs
2 tbsp olive oil

Directions

Heat oil in your Instant Pot on Sauté and brown the ribs for 4-5 minutes on all sides. Pour in the remaining ingredients. Seal the lid and cook for 30 minutes on Pressure Cook on High. Once ready, do a quick pressure release. Serve warm.

Mushrooms & Celery Pork Butt

Serves: 2 | Ready in about: 354 minutes

Ingredients

¼ lb pork butt, sliced
½ cup mushrooms, sliced
½ cup celery stalk, chopped

1/6 cup white wine
¼ tsp garlic, minced
2 tbsp chicken broth

Salt and black pepper to taste
1 tbsp olive oil

Directions

Heat oil in your Instant Pot on Sauté. Brown the pork slices and for a few minutes. Stir in the remaining ingredients. Season with salt and pepper. Seal the lid and cook for 20 minutes on Meat/Stew on High. When done, do a quick release.

Red Wine Pork Chops

Serves: 2-4 | Ready in about: 30 minutes

Ingredients

4 pork chops
3 carrots, chopped
1 tomato, chopped
1 onion, chopped
2 garlic cloves, minced

¼ cup merlot red wine
½ cup beef broth
1 tsp dried oregano
2 tbsp olive oil
2 tbsp flour

2 tbsp water
2 tbsp tomato paste
1 beef bouillon cube
Salt and black pepper to taste

Directions

Heat the oil on Sauté in your Instant Pot. In a bowl, mix flour, pepper, and salt. Coat the pork chops. Place them in the cooker and cook for a few minutes, until browned on all sides. Add in the carrots, onion, garlic, and oregano. Cook for 2 minutes.

Stir in the remaining ingredients and seal the lid. Cook on Soup/Broth mode and cook for 25 minutes on High. When ready, do a natural pressure release for 10 minutes and serve immediately.

Mushroom & Pork with Pomodoro Sauce

Serves: 2-4 | Ready in about: 35 minutes

Ingredients

4 large bone-in pork chops
1 cup tomato sauce
1 cup white button mushrooms, sliced

1 small onion, chopped
1 garlic clove, minced
½ cup water

1 tbsp olive oil
Salt and black pepper to taste

Directions

Heat oil in your Instant Pot on Sauté. Add in garlic and onion and cook for 2 minutes, until soft and fragrant. Add pork and cook until browned on all sides. Stir in the remaining ingredients and seal the lid. Cook for 20 minutes on Meat/Stew on High. When ready, do a quick pressure release. Serve warm.

Plum Sauce Pork Chops

Serves: 2-4 | Ready in about: 20 minutes

Ingredients

4 pork chops
1 tsp cumin seeds

Salt and black pepper to taste
2 cups firm plums, pitted and chopped

1 tbsp vegetable oil
¾ cup vegetable stock

Directions

Sprinkle salt, cumin, and pepper on the pork chops. Set your Instant Pot on Sauté and warm oil. Add in the chops and cook for 3-5 minutes and set aside. Arrange plum slices at the bottom of the cooker. Place pork chops on top of the plumes.

Add any juice from the plate over the pork and apply stock around the edges. Seal lid and cook on High for 8 minutes. Do a quick pressure release. Transfer the pork chops to a serving plate and spoon over the plum sauce. Serve.

Squash Pork Chops with Mushroom Gravy

Serves: 2-4 | Ready in about: 45 minutes

Ingredients

2 tbsp olive oil
2 sprigs thyme, chopped
4 pork chops

1 cup mushrooms, chopped
2 cloves garlic, minced
1 cup chicken broth

1 tbsp soy sauce
1 lb butternut squash, cubed
1 tsp cornstarch

Directions

Set your Instant Pot to Sauté and heat the oil. Add in the pork chops and sear for 1 minute for each side until lightly browned; set aside. Add garlic and mushrooms in the pot and sauté pot for 5-6 minutes until tender. Pour in soy sauce and broth. Place pork chops on a wire trivet and place into the pot. Over the chops, place a cake pan. Add butternut squash in the pan.

Drizzle the squash with some olive oil. Seal the lid and cook on High for 10 minutes. Release the pressure quickly. Remove the pan and trivet. Stir cornstarch into the mushroom mixture for 3 minutes until the sauce thickens.

Transfer the mushroom sauce to food processor and pulse until you attain the desired consistency. Scoop sauce into a cup with a pour spout. Smash the squash into a purée. Set pork chops on a plate and ladle squash puree next to them. Top the pork chops with gravy. Sprinkle with thyme and serve warm.

Tasty Baby Back Ribs with BBQ Sauce

Serves: 2-4 | Ready in about: 45 minutes

Ingredients

2 lb baby back pork ribs
2 cups orange juice
2 tbsp honey

½ cup ketchup
1 tbsp Worcestershire sauce
1 tsp mustard

2 tsp paprika
½ tsp cayenne pepper
Salt to taste

Directions

Mix the honey, ketchup, mustard, paprika, cayenne pepper, Worcestershire sauce, and salt in a bowl until well incorporated. Set aside. Place ribs in your Instant Pot and add in orange juice and 1 cup of water. Seal the lid, press Meat/Stew, and cook on High for 20 minutes. Release pressure naturally for 15 minutes.

Preheat oven to 400°F. Line the sheet pan with aluminum foil. Transfer the ribs to the prepared sheet. Do away with the cooking liquid. Onto both sides of ribs, brush barbecue sauce. Bake ribs in the oven for 10 minutes until sauce is browned and caramelized; cut into individual bones to serve.

Apple Pork & Rutabaga

Serves: 2-4 | Ready in about: 40 minutes

Ingredients

1 tbsp olive oil
1 lb pork loin, cut into cubes
2 apples, peeled and chopped
2 rutabaga, peeled and chopped

1 onion, diced
1 celery stalk, diced
1 tbsp parsley, chopped
½ cup leeks, sliced

1 ½ cups beef broth
½ tsp cumin
½ tsp thyme

Directions

Heat half of the olive oil on Sauté. Add the beef and cook until it browned on all sides. Remove to a plate. Add leeks, onions, celery, and drizzle with the remaining oil. Stir to combine and cook for 3 minutes. Add the beef back to the cooker, pour the broth over, and stir in all herbs and spices. Seal the lid, and cook on High for 10 minutes.

After the beep, do a quick pressure release. Stir in the rutabaga and apples. Seal the lid again and cook for 5 minutes on High. Do a quick pressure release and serve right away.

Baby Carrot & Pork Cutlets

Serves: 2-4 | Ready in about: 30 minutes

Ingredients

1 lb pork cutlets
1 lb baby carrots
1 onion, sliced

1 tbsp butter
1 cup vegetable broth
1 tsp garlic powder

Salt and black pepper to taste

Directions

Season the pork with salt and pepper. Melt butter in your Instant Pot on Sauté and brown the pork on all sides. Stir in carrots and onions and cook for 2 more minutes, until soft. Pour in the broth, and add garlic powder. Season with salt and pepper. Seal the lid and cook for 20 minutes on Meat/Stew on High. When ready, release the pressure quickly. Serve warm.

Onion & Brussel Sprout Pork Chops

Serves: 2-4 | Ready in about: 40 minutes

Ingredients

1 lb pork chops
1 cup onions, sliced
1 cup carrots, sliced

1 tbsp butter
2 cups Brussel sprouts
1 tbsp arrowroot

1 tsp garlic, minced
1 cup chicken stock
½ tsp dried thyme

Directions

Melt butter on Sauté. Add the pork chops, and cook on all sides until golden in color. Transfer to a plate. Add the onions and garlic to the pot and cook for 3 minutes. Return the pork chops to the pot and pour the broth over. Seal the lid and cook on High for 15 minutes. When the timer goes off, do a quick pressure release. Stir in carrots and sprouts.

Seal the lid and cook for 3 minutes on High. Do a quick pressure release. Transfer the chops and veggies to a serving platter. Whisk the arrowroot into the pot and cook on Sauté until it thickens. Pour the sauce over the chops and veggies. Serve.

Chili & Sweet Pork

Serves: 2-4 | Ready in about: 40 minutes

Ingredients

1 lb pork loin, cut into chunks	¼ cup beef stock	2 tbsp soy sauce
2 tbsp white wine	2 tbsp sweet chili sauce	2 tbsp cornstarch
15 oz canned peaches with juice	2 tbsp honey	¼ cup water

Directions

Into the pot, mix soy sauce, beef stock, wine, the juice from the canned peaches, and sweet chili sauce. Stir in pork to coat. Seal the lid and cook on High for 5 minutes. Release pressure naturally for 10 minutes, then release the remaining pressure quickly. Remove the pork to a serving plate. Chop the peaches into small pieces.

In a bowl, mix water with cornstarch until well dissolved; stir the mixture into the pot. Press Sauté and cook for 5 minutes until you obtain the desired thick consistency. Add in the chopped peaches and stir well. Pour over the pork and serve.

Rutabaga & Apple Pork

Serves: 2-4 | Ready in about: 40 minutes

Ingredients

1 lb pork loin, cut into cubes	2 granny smith apples, peeled and diced	¼ tsp thyme
1 onion, diced	½ cup sliced leeks	½ tsp cumin
2 rutabagas, peeled and diced	1 tbsp vegetable oil	¼ tsp lemon zest
1 cup chicken broth	1 celery stalk, diced	Salt and black pepper to taste
½ cup white wine	2 tbsp dried parsley	

Directions

Season the pork with salt and pepper. Heat oil on Sauté. Add pork and cook for a few minutes, until browned. Add the onions and cook for 2 more minutes, until soft. Stir in the remaining ingredients, except for the apples.

Seal the lid and cook for 15 minutes on Pressure Cook mode on High. When ready, release the pressure quickly. Stir in apples, seal the lid again, and cook on High for another 5 minutes. Do a quick release.

Easy Pork Goulash

Serves: 2-4 | Ready in about: 40 minutes

Ingredients

12 oz pork neck, cut into bite-sized pieces

2 tbsp flour	1 carrot, chopped	4 cups beef broth
4 tbsp vegetable oil	1 celery stalk, chopped	1 chili pepper, chopped
2 onions, chopped	10 oz button mushrooms	1 tbsp cayenne pepper

Directions

Heat oil in your Instant Pot on Sauté. Add onions and cook for 2 minutes, until translucent. Add flour, chili pepper, carrot, celery, cayenne pepper, and continue to cook for 2 minutes, stirring constantly. Press Cancel and add meat, mushrooms, beef broth, and water. Seal the lid and cook on Manual mode for 30 minutes on High. Do a quick release and serve immediately.

Spicy Pork Meatloaf

Makes: 2-4 serves | Ready in about: 70 minutes

Ingredients

½ lb ground sausage	½ tsp cayenne powder	1 onion, diced
½ lb ground pork	½ tsp marjoram	2 tbsp brown sugar
1 cup cooked rice	2 eggs	1 cup ketchup
1 cup milk	2 garlic cloves, minced	

Directions

In a bowl, whisk the eggs with milk. Stir in the meat, cayenne, marjoram, rice, onion, and garlic. Mix well the ingredients to combine and form a meatloaf mixture. Grease a baking dish with cooking spray. Add and shape the meatloaf mixture inside.

Whisk together the ketchup and sugar and pour over the meatloaf. Place the trivet inside the pressure cooker and pour 1 cup of water. Lay the dish on top, seal the lid, and cook on Manual for 50 minutes on High. When ready, do a quick release.

Gourmet Bacon Casserole

Serves: 2-4 | Ready in about: 30 minutes

Ingredients

½ lb smoked bacon, chopped
½ cup carrots, sliced
2 cups water

1 cup chicken stock
¾ cup half and half
4 golden potatoes, peeled and chopped

4 endives, halved lengthwise
Salt and black pepper to taste

Directions

Set on Sauté and add the bacon. Cook for 2 minutes until slightly crispy. Add the potatoes, carrots, and chicken stock. Seal the lid and cook for 10 minutes on High. Release the pressure quickly. Add the endives and cook for 5 minutes on High.

Press Cancel again and quick-release the pressure. Strain the bacon and veggies and return them to the pressure cooker. Add the half and half and season with salt and pepper. Cook on Sauté for 3 more minutes. Serve.

Buttered Pork Tenderloin

Serves: 2-4 | Ready in about: 60 minutes

Ingredients

2 lb pork tenderloin
2 tbsp butter, unsalted
2 tbsp brown sugar

2 tbsp balsamic vinegar
2 garlic cloves, crushed
1 cup beef broth

Salt and black pepper to taste
1 tbsp cornstarch

Directions

Melt butter in your Instant Pot on Sauté and stir-fry garlic for 1 minute. Add in brown sugar and vinegar and cook for 1 more minute. Rub the meat with salt and pepper. Place it in the pot and pour in the broth. Seal the lid.

Cook on High for 35 minutes. Do a quick release and set the meat aside. Stir in cornstarch in the remaining liquid and cook for 1 minute on Sauté to thicken the sauce. Drizzle over meat and serve.

Bacon with Braised Red Cabbage

Serves: 2 | Ready in about: 20 minutes

Ingredients

¼ lb red cabbage, chopped
2 bacon slices, chopped

½ cup beef broth
½ tbsp butter

Salt and black pepper to taste

Directions

Add the bacon slices in IP, and cook for 5 minutes, until crispy, on Sauté. Stir in cabbage, salt, pepper, and butter. Seal the lid, select Manual, and cook for 10 minutes on High. When ready, release the pressure naturally for 10 minutes. Serve.

Herby Pork Butt with Yams

Serves: 2-4 | Ready in about: 20 minutes

Ingredients

1 lb pork butt, cut into 4 equal pieces
1 lb yams, diced
2 tsp butter

¼ tsp thyme
¼ tsp oregano
1 ½ tsp sage

1 ½ cups beef broth
Salt and black pepper to taste

Directions

Season the pork with thyme, sage, oregano, salt, and pepper. Melt the butter in your Instant Pot on Sauté. Add in the pork and cook until brown for 5-6 minutes. Stir in the yams and pour in the broth. Seal the lid and cook for 20 minutes on Meat/Stew on High. Do a quick release and serve hot.

Buckwheat & Pork Stew

Serves: 2-4 | Ready in about: 50 minutes

Ingredients

8 oz buckwheat porridge, cooked
1 lb pork tenderloin
1 carrot, chopped

1 onion, finely chopped
2 tbsp vegetable oil
1 tsp dry marjoram

Salt and black pepper to taste
½ cup white wine
2 cups chicken broth

Directions

Heat the olive oil in your Instant Pot on Sauté. Add in onion and stir-fry for 2 minutes, until fragrant and translucent. Add in carrot and meat. Cook for 5 minutes, until lightly browned. Add the remaining ingredients. Seal the lid and cook on High for 35 minutes. Do a quick release and stir in the porridge. Serve hot.

Apple & Prune Pork Chops

Serves: 2-4 | Ready in about: 30 minutes

Ingredients

4 pork chops	½ cup white wine	1 tbsp fruit jelly
¼ cup milk	2 apples, peeled and sliced	½ tsp ground ginger
8 prunes, pitted	¼ cup heavy cream	Salt and black pepper to taste

Directions

Place all ingredients, except the jelly, in your pressure cooker. Stir to combine well and season with salt and pepper. Seal the lid and cook on High for 15 minutes. Once done, wait 5 minutes and do a quick pressure release. Stir in the jelly and serve.

Spicy Pork with Onion & Garlic

Serves: 2-4 | Ready in about: 60 minutes

Ingredients

1 lb pork shoulder	2 Japones chilies	2 garlic cloves, crushed
2 tbsp olive oil	3 cups water	3 cups beef broth
3 Jalapeño peppers, seeded and chopped	1 large onion, chopped	

Directions

Heat the olive oil in your Instant Pot on Sauté and cook the jalapeno peppers for 3 minutes. Add in all the spices, garlic, and onion and stir-fry for another 2 minutes, until soft. Put in the pork shoulder, beef broth, and the pureed mixture. Seal the lid and cook on Meat/Stew for 30 minutes on High. Release the pressure quickly and serve hot.

Swedish Meatballs with Cauliflower

Serves: 2 | Ready in about: 1 hour

Ingredients

¼ lb ground beef	¼ tbsp water	¼ tsp red wine vinegar
¼ lb ground pork	Salt and ground black pepper to taste	¾ cup heavy cream
1 egg, beaten	1 tbsp butter	⅓ head cauliflower, cut into florets
¼ onion, minced	½ cup beef stock	2 tbsp sour cream
¼ cup breadcrumbs	1 tbsp flour	2 tbsp fresh chopped parsley

Directions

In a bowl, mix beef, onion, salt, breadcrumbs, pork, egg, water, and pepper; shape meatballs. Warm ½ tbsp of butter in your Instant Pot on Sauté. Add meatballs and cook until browned, about 5-6 minutes. Set aside to a plate. Pour beef stock in the pot to deglaze, scrape the pan to get rid of browned bits of food. Stir vinegar and flour with the liquid in the pot until smooth.

Bring to a boil. Stir half of the heavy cream into the liquid. Arrange meatballs into the gravy. Place trivet onto meatballs. Arrange cauliflower florets onto the trivet. Seal the lid and cook on High Pressure for 8 minutes. Release the Pressure quickly.

Set the cauliflower in a mixing bowl. Add in the remaining heavy cream, pepper, sour cream, salt, and the remaining butter and use a potato masher to mash the mixture until smooth. Spoon the mashed cauliflower onto serving bowls; place a topping of gravy and meatballs. Add parsley for garnishing.

Apple Pork Ribs

Serves: 2-4 | Ready in about: 40 minutes

Ingredients

½ cup apple cider vinegar	2 lb pork ribs	3 ½ cups apple juice

Directions

Pour apple juice and apple cider vinegar into the pressure cooker and lower a trivet. Place the pork ribs on top of the trivet and seal the lid. Cook on High for 30 minutes. Once it goes off, do a natural release for 10 minutes. Serve.

Chili Braised Pork Chops

Serves: 2-4 | Ready in about: 30 minutes

Ingredients

4 pork chops
1 onion, chopped
2 tbsp chili powder

14 oz canned tomatoes and green chilies
1 garlic clove, minced
½ cup beer

½ cup vegetable stock
1 tsp olive oil
Salt and black pepper to taste

Directions

Heat the olive oil in your Instant Pot on Sauté. Add onion, garlic, and chili powder and cook for 2 minutes. Add the pork chops and cook until browned on all sides. Stir in the tomatoes, broth, and beer. Season with salt and pepper. Seal the lid and cook for 20 minutes on Meat/Stew on High. When ready, quickly release the pressure. Serve hot.

Delicious Sauerkraut & Ground Pork

Serves: 2-4 | Ready in about: 25 minutes

Ingredients

1 lb ground pork
4 cups sauerkraut, shredded
1 cup tomato puree

1 cup chicken stock
1 red onion, chopped
2 garlic cloves, minced

2 bay leaves
Salt and black pepper to taste

Directions

Heat the olive oil in your Instant Pot on Sauté. Add in onion and garlic and cook until soft and fragrant, 3 minutes. Add the pork and cook it until lightly browned. Stir in the remaining ingredients. Seal the lid and cook for 20 minutes on Meat/Stew on High. When done, press Cancel and release the pressure quickly. Discard the bay leaves and serve

Mustard-Honey Pork Chops

Serves: 2-4 | Ready in about: 60 minutes

Ingredients

2 lb pork chops
1 cup beef broth
2 tbsp olive oil

¼ cup honey
1 tbsp Dijon mustard
½ tsp cinnamon

1 tsp ginger, grated
Salt and black pepper to taste

Directions

Season the chops with salt and pepper. Heat the olive oil in your Instant Pot on Sauté and brown the chops for 2-3 minutes on each side. In a bowl, mix honey, mustard, cinnamon, and ginger. Whisk together and drizzle over chops. Pour in broth and seal the lid. Cook on High for 30 minutes. Do a quick release and serve hot.

Saucy Pork Chops

Serves: 2-4 | Ready in about: 1 hour 15 minutes

Ingredients

4 pork loin chops, 1-inch thick
2 tbsp oil
1 tbsp butter

3 apples, peeled, cored, chopped
¼ cup soy sauce
1 cup beef broth

2 tbsp honey
¼ tsp cinnamon

Directions

Heat the olive oil in your Instant Pot on Sauté and briefly brown the chops for 3 minutes on each side. Remove and melt the butter. Add apples, soy sauce, broth, honey, and cinnamon. Cook until apples are half-done and slightly tender. Add the chops back, seal the lid and cook on Meat/Stew for 40 minutes on High. Do a quick release.

Thyme-Flavored Pork Stew

Serves: 2-4 | Ready in about: 45 minutes

Ingredients

1 lb pork tenderloin, cubed
1 onion, chopped
2 tbsp vegetable oil

4 tomatoes, peeled, diced
½ tbsp red wine
½ tbsp beef broth

A handful of fresh thyme
Salt and black pepper to taste

Directions

Heat the olive oil in your Instant Pot on Sauté and stir-fry the onion for 3 minutes. Add the meat, salt, pepper, wine, and thyme. Cook for 10 minutes. Pour in broth, seal the lid and cook on High for 25 minutes. Do a quick release. Serve.

Root Veggies & BBQ Rib Chops

Serves: 2-4 | Ready in about: 25 minutes

Ingredients

4 pork rib chops	1 cup turnips, thinly sliced	1 ½ cups BBQ sauce
1 cup carrots, thinly sliced	1 cup onions, slice into rings	2 cups water

Directions

Add the pork cutlets in your cooker. Pour in a half cup of BBQ sauce and 2 cups of water. Select Meat/Stew. Stir in the onions, turnip, and carrots. Lock the lid and cook for 20 minutes on High. Once ready, release the pressure quickly. Open the lid, drizzle with the remaining BBQ sauce and serve.

Green Onion Pork Frittata

Serves: 2-4 | Ready in about: 30 minutes

Ingredients

1 tbsp butter, melted	1 lb ground pork	Salt and black pepper to taste
1 cup green onions, chopped	6 eggs	1 cup water

Directions

In a bowl, whisk the eggs until frothy. Mix in the onions and ground meat and season with the salt and pepper. Grease a casserole dish with melted butter. Pour the egg mixture into the dish. Place a trivet in the pressure cooker and add 1 cup of water. Select Rice mode and cook for 25 minutes on High. Do a quick pressure release and serve immediately.

Brussel Sprouts with Pork Chops

Serves: 2-4 | Ready in about: 30 minutes

Ingredients

4 pork chops	1 ½ cups beef stock	1 cup celery stalk, chopped
½ lb Brussel sprouts	2 shallots, chopped	1 tbsp coriander
¼ cup sparkling wine	1 tbsp olive oil	Salt and black pepper to taste

Directions

Heat the olive oil in your Instant Pot on Sauté. Add the pork chops and cook until browned on all sides. Stir in the remaining ingredients. Seal the lid and cook for 20 minutes on Meat/Stew on High. Release the pressure quickly. Serve.

Jalapeno Beef Taco Quinoa

Serves: 2-4 | Ready in about: 20 minutes

Ingredients

1 tbsp olive oil	1 jalapeño pepper, minced	1 (14 oz) can diced tomatoes
1 lb ground beef	1 cup corn, fresh or frozen	2 ½ cups chicken broth
Salt and black pepper to taste	1 tsp ground cumin	1 cup grated cheddar cheese, grated
1 onion, finely diced	1 tbsp chili seasoning	2 tbsp chopped cilantro
2 garlic cloves, minced	1 (8 oz) can black beans, rinsed	2 limes, cut into wedges for garnishing
1 red bell pepper, deseeded and chopped	1 cup quick-cooking quinoa	

Directions

Set your Instant Pot to Sauté. Heat olive oil and cook beef until no longer pink, 5 minutes. Season with salt and pepper. Add in onion, garlic, red bell pepper, jalapeño pepper, and corn. Cook until bell pepper softens, 5 minutes.

Season with cumin and chili and add black beans, quinoa, tomatoes, and broth; stir. Seal the lid, select Manual on High, and cook for 1 minute. After cooking, do a quick pressure to release steam, and unlock the lid.

Select Sauté and sprinkle the food with cheddar cheese and half of the cilantro. Cook until cheese melts, 3-4 minutes. Spoon quinoa into serving bowls and garnish with remaining cilantro and lime wedges. Serve warm.

Homemade Chili con Carne

Serves: 2 | Ready in about: 1 hour 25 minutes

Ingredients

⅓ tbsp ground black pepper
Garlic salt to taste
⅓ tsp sweet paprika
⅓ tsp cayenne pepper

⅓ tsp chili powder
1/8 tsp onion powder
1 lb beef brisket
⅓ cup beef broth

1 bay leaf
1 tbsp Worcestershire sauce
5 oz canned black beans, drained

Directions

In a bowl, combine black pepper, paprika, chili powder, cayenne pepper, salt, onion powder, and garlic salt; rub onto brisket pieces to coat. Add the brisket to your Instant Pot. Cover with Worcestershire sauce and water. Seal the lid and cook on High Pressure for 50 minutes. Release the pressure naturally for 10 minutes. Transfer the brisket to a cutting board.

Drain any liquid present in the pot using a fine-mesh strainer; get rid of any solids and fat. Slice brisket and arrange the slices onto a platter. Add the black beans on the side. Spoon the cooking liquid over the slices and beans and serve.

Smoked Bacon & Beef Chili

Serves: 2 | Ready in about: 50 minutes

Ingredients

½ lb stewing beef, trimmed
Salt and black pepper to taste
3 slices smoked bacon, cut into strips
1 tsp olive oil
⅓ onion, diced

½ bell pepper, diced
1 garlic clove, minced
⅓ tbsp ground cumin
⅓ tsp chili powder
1/8 tsp cayenne pepper

⅓ chipotle in adobo sauce, chopped
½ cup beef broth
10 oz canned whole tomatoes
5 oz canned kidney beans, drained

Directions

Set your Instant Pot to Sauté in and fry the bacon until crispy, about 5 minutes. Set aside. Rub the beef with pepper and salt to taste. In the bacon fat, brown beef for 5-6 minutes; transfer to a plate. Warm the oil in the pot. Add in garlic, bell pepper, and onion and sauté for 3 minutes until soft. Stir in cumin, cayenne pepper, salt, pepper, chipotle sauce, and chili powder.

Cook for 30 seconds until soft. Return beef and bacon and add in tomatoes and broth. Seal the lid and cook on High Pressure for 30 minutes. Release the pressure quickly. Stir in beans. Simmer on Sauté for 10 minutes until flavors combine. Serve.

Beef Steaks with Mushroom Sauce

Serves: 2 | Ready in about: 40 minutes

Ingredients

2 beef steaks, boneless
Salt and black pepper to taste
2 tbsp olive oil

4 oz mushrooms, sliced
½ onion, chopped
1 cup vegetable stock

1 tsp parsley, chopped
1 ½ tbsp cornstarch
1 tbsp half and half

Directions

Rub the beef with salt and pepper. Set your Instant Pot to Sauté and warm the oil. Place in the beef and sear it for 2 minutes per side. Remove to a plate. Put in the mushrooms and cook for 5 minutes. Add in onion and cook for 2 minutes until fragrant. Return the steaks to the pot and pour in the stock. Seal the lid, select Manual, and cook for 15 minutes on High.

When done, perform a quick pressure release to let out the steam. Unlock the lid and transfer the chops to a plate. Select Sauté. In a bowl, combine cornstarch and half and half and mix well. Pour the slurry into the pot and cook until the sauce reaches the desired consistency. Serve topped with parsley.

Garbanzo & Beef Chili

Serves: 2 | Ready in about: 45 minutes

Ingredients

½ cup garbanzo beans, soaked overnight
½ tbsp olive oil
½ onion, finely chopped
½ lb ground beef
⅓ jalapeño pepper with seeds, minced

1 garlic clove, minced
½ tbsp chili powder
½ tbsp ground cumin
Salt to taste
1/5 tsp smoked paprika

1/5 tsp dried oregano
1/5 tsp garlic powder
1/8 tsp cayenne pepper
½ cup beef broth
2 oz canned tomato puree

Directions

Add the garbanzo beans in your Instant Pot and pour in water to cover it by 1 inch. Seal the lid and cook for 20 minutes on High. Release the pressure quickly. Drain beans. Wipe clean the pot and set to Sauté. Warm olive oil, add in onion, and sauté for 3 minutes until soft. Add jalapeño pepper, beef, and garlic, and stir-fry for 5 minutes until everything is cooked through.

Stir in chili powder, salt, garlic powder, paprika, cumin, oregano, and cayenne pepper, and cook until soft, about 30 seconds. Pour in broth, beans, and tomato puree. Seal the lid and cook for 20 minutes on High. Release the pressure naturally for 10 minutes. Press Sauté, and cook as you stir until desired consistency is attained. Spoon chili into bowls and serve.

Southern Pot Roast with Potatoes

Serves: 2 | Ready in about: 1 hour 40 minutes

Ingredients

½ tbsp canola oil
½ lb chuck roast
Salt and black pepper to taste
2 tbsp butter
⅓ onion, finely chopped

⅓ tsp onion powder
⅓ tsp garlic powder
¼ tsp dried thyme
¼ tsp dried parsley
2 cups beef broth

1/6 cup pepperoncini juice
3 pepperoncini
2 potatoes, chopped
1 bay leaf

Directions

Warm canola oil in your Instant Pot on Sauté. Season chuck roast with pepper and salt, then sear for 2-4 minutes per side until browned. Set aside. Melt butter and cook onion for 3 minutes until fragrant. Sprinkle with dried parsley, onion powder, dried thyme, and garlic powder and stir for 30 seconds. Stir in bay leaf, broth, pepperoncini juice, potatoes, and pepperoncini.

Nestle chuck roast down into the liquid. Seal the lid and cook on High for 60 minutes. Release pressure naturally for about 10 minutes. Set the chuck roast to a cutting board and use two forks to shred. Serve immediately.

Beef Empanadas

Serves: 2 | Ready in about: 35 minutes

Ingredients

1 cup olive oil
1 garlic clove, minced
½ white onion, chopped
¼ lb ground beef

6 green olives, pitted and chopped
¼ tsp cumin powder
¼ tsp paprika
¼ tsp cinnamon powder

2 small tomatoes, chopped
8 square wonton wrappers
1 egg, beaten

Directions

Select Sauté on your Instant Pot and heat 1 tbsp of the olive oil. Cook garlic, onion, and ground beef for 5 minutes until it is fragrant, and the meat is no longer pink. Stir in olives, cumin, paprika, and cinnamon and cook for 3 minutes. Add the tomatoes and 1 cup water, and cook for 1 more minute. Seal the lid, select Manual on High, and set time to 8 minutes.

After cooking, perform a natural pressure release for 10 minutes. Spoon the beef mixture into a plate and allow cooling for a few minutes. Lay the wonton wrappers on a flat surface. Place 2 tbsp of the beef mixture in the middle of each wrapper.

Brush the edges of the wrapper with egg and fold in half to form a triangle. Pinch the edges together to seal. Wipe out the inner pot. Heat the remaining oil and fry the empanadas in a single layer, about 20 seconds per side. Remove to paper towels to soak up excess fat before serving.

Beef Meatballs with Marinara Sauce

Serves: 2 | Ready in about: 35 minutes

Ingredients

½ lb ground beef
2 tbsp warm water
2 tbsp grated Parmigiano-Reggiano
¼ cup breadcrumbs

1 egg
1 tbsp fresh parsley
1/8 tsp garlic powder
1/8 tsp dried oregano

Salt and black pepper to taste
¼ cup capers
½ tsp olive oil
1 cup marinara sauce

Directions

In a bowl, mix ground beef, garlic powder, pepper, oregano, crumbs, egg, and salt; shape into meatballs. Warm the olive oil in your Instant Pot on Sauté. Add in the meatballs and brown them for 2-3 minutes on all sides.

Pour warm water and marinara sauce over the meatballs. Seal the lid and cook on High Pressure for 10 minutes. Release the pressure quickly. Serve in large bowls topped with capers and Parmigiano-Reggiano cheese.

Eggplant & Beef Casserole

Serves: 2 | Ready in about: 35 minutes

Ingredients

2 eggplants, peeled and sliced lengthwise
1 cup lean ground beef
1 onion, chopped
1 tsp olive oil
¼ tsp freshly ground black pepper
2 tomatoes, chopped

Directions

Heat oil in your Instant Pot on Sauté. Stir-fry onion for 2 minutes until soft. Add in ground beef and tomatoes and cook for 5 minutes; season with salt. Remove from the pot and transfer to a deep bowl. Make a layer with eggplant slices in the pot.

Spread the ground beef mixture over and sprinkle with parsley. Make another layer with eggplants and repeat until you've used up all ingredients. Seal the lid and cook on High Pressure for 12 minutes. Do a quick release. Serve.

Pumpkin & Beef Stew

Serves: 2 | Ready in about: 35 minutes

Ingredients

1 tbsp canola oil
½ lb stew beef, cut into 1-inch chunks
⅓ cup red wine
⅓ onion, chopped
⅓ tsp garlic powder
Salt to taste
1 whole clove
½ bay leaf
1 carrot, chopped
1 cup butternut pumpkin, chopped
½ tbsp cornstarch
1 tbsp water

Directions

Warm canola oil in your Instant Pot on Sauté. Brown the beef for 5 minutes per side. Deglaze the pot with wine by scraping the bottom to get rid of any browned beef bits. Add in onion, salt, bay leaf, clove, and garlic powder. Seal the lid, press Meat/Stew, and cook on High for 15 minutes. Release the pressure quickly. Add in pumpkin and carrots without stirring.

Seal the lid and cook on High Pressure for 5 minutes. Release the pressure quickly. In a bowl, mix water and cornstarch until cornstarch dissolves completely; mix into the stew. Allow the stew to simmer on Sauté for 5 minutes until thickened. Serve.

Sticky BBQ Baby Back Ribs

Serves: 2 | Ready in about: 40 minutes

Ingredients

½ tbsp olive oil
⅓ rack baby back ribs, cut into bones
Salt and black pepper to taste
⅓ tbsp mustard powder
⅓ tbsp smoked paprika
⅓ tbsp dried oregano
2 tbsp ketchup
⅓ cup barbecue sauce
2 tbsp apple cider

Directions

In a bowl, combine salt, mustard, paprika, oregano, and pepper. Rub the mixture over the ribs. Warm the olive oil in your Instant Pot on Sauté. Add in the ribs and sear for 2 minutes for each side. Pour apple cider and barbecue sauce into the pot. Turn the ribs to coat. Seal the lid, press Manual, and cook on High Pressure for 30 minutes. Release the pressure quickly.

Preheat the broiler. Cook the ribs with the sauce under the broiler for about 7 until the ribs become sticky and have a dark brown color. Transfer the ribs to a serving plate. Baste with the sauce to serve.

Turnip & Beef Chili

Serves: 2 | Ready in about: 30 minutes

Ingredients

½ tbsp olive oil
⅓ yellow onion, chopped
Salt to taste
1 garlic clove, minced
1 tbsp tomato puree
⅓ tbsp chili powder
½ tsp ground cumin
⅓ tsp dried oregano
1/8 tsp ground turmeric
½ tsp cayenne pepper
⅓ lb ground beef meat
1 cup canned whole tomatoes
½ cup beef stock
1 lb turnips, peeled and cubed
½ bell pepper, chopped

Directions

Heat oil in your Instant Pot on Sauté. Add in onion and cook for 3 minutes until softened. Stir in garlic, chili powder, turmeric, cumin, tomato paste, oregano, and cayenne pepper; cook for 2-3 minutes as you stir until very soft and sticks to the pot's bottom. Add beef and cook for 5 minutes until completely browned. Stir in tomatoes, turnips, bell pepper, and stock. Seal the lid and cook on High Pressure for 15 minutes. Release the pressure quickly. Adjust the taste and serve.

Veggies & Beef Stew

Serves: 2 | Ready in about: 1 hour 15 minutes

Ingredients

1 ¼ tbsp flour
Salt and black pepper to taste
⅓ tsp paprika
½ lb beef chuck, cubed
½ tbsp olive oil
½ tbsp butter

⅓ onion, diced
1 garlic clove, minced
⅓ cup dry red wine
½ cups beef stock
⅓ tbsp dried Italian seasoning
½ tsp Worcestershire sauce

1 potato, diced
½ celery stalk, chopped
1 cup carrots, chopped
1 tomato, chopped
1 bell pepper, chopped
1 tbs fresh parsley, chopped

Directions

In a bowl, mix beef, flour, paprika, pepper, and salt. Toss the ingredients and ensure the meat is well-coated. Warm butter and oil in your Instant Pot on Sauté. Add in beef and cook for 8- 10 minutes until browned. Set aside. To the same fat, add garlic, onion, celery, and bell pepper and cook for 4-5 minutes. Add in wine, scrape the bottom to get rid of any browned beef bits.

Pour in beef stock, Worcestershire sauce, and Italian seasoning. Return the beef to the pot; add carrots, tomatoes, and potatoes. Seal the lid, press Meat/Stew, and cook on High Pressure for 35 minutes. Release pressure naturally for 10 minutes. Taste and adjust the seasonings as necessary. Serve on plates and scatter over the parsley.

Cajun Marinated Flank Steak

Serves: 2-4 | Ready in about: 30 minutes + marinating time

Ingredients

1 tbsp olive oil
½ lb beef flank steak
1 cup beef broth

1 onion, diced
1 carrot, chopped
½ tsp Cajun seasoning

1 tsp garlic, minced
¼ cup soy sauce
1 tbsp sesame oil

Directions

Combine soy sauce, Cajun seasoning, garlic, and sesame oil in a bowl and mix well. Add in the beef and let marinate for 30 minutes. Heat olive oil in your Instant Pot on Sauté. Add in onion and carrot and cook for 3 minutes until soft. Add the beef along with the marinade and broth. Seal the lid and cook for 20 minutes on Manual on High. Do a quick release and serve.

Onion-Flavored Steaks with Gravy

Serves: 2-4 | Ready in about: 30 minutes

Ingredients

4 round steaks
2 onions, sliced
1 ½ cups beef broth
1 tsp garlic, minced

1 tbsp dried parsley
½ tsp rosemary
1 tbsp oil
½ tsp red pepper flakes

¼ cup half and half
2 tbsp flour
¼ tsp salt
¼ tsp black pepper

Directions

Heat the olive oil in your Instant Pot on Sauté. Add the beef and brown the steaks on all sides. Remove to a plate. Sauté the onions and garlic for 2 minutes, until translucent and fragrant. Return the steaks to the pressure cooker.

Stir in broth, pepper flakes, rosemary, parsley, salt, and pepper. Seal the lid and cook for 20 minutes on Meat/Stew on High. When ready, do a quick pressure release. Stir in flour and half and half. Cook for 3 minutes until thickened on Sauté. Serve.

Asian-Style Rice Porridge

Serves: 2 | Ready in about: 1 hour

Ingredients

⅓ cup jasmine rice
1 clove garlic, minced
1 (½ inch) piece fresh ginger, minced

2 cups beef stock
⅓ cup kale, roughly chopped
⅓ cup water

½ lb ground beef
Salt and ground black pepper to taste
1 tbsp fresh cilantro, chopped

Directions

Run cold water and rinse rice. Add garlic, rice, and ginger into the pot. Pour water and stock into the pot and Spread the beef on top of rice. Seal the lid and cook on High Pressure for 30 minutes. Release pressure naturally for 10 minutes. Stir in kale to obtain the desired consistency. Season with pepper and salt. Divide into serving plates and top with cilantro.

Vietnamese Beef with Swiss Chard

Serves: 2 | Ready in about: 1 hour 10 minutes

Ingredients

⅓ tbsp coconut oil
⅓ onion, chopped
⅓ tbsp minced fresh ginger
⅓ tsp coriander seeds
⅓tsp ground cinnamon

⅓ tsp ground cloves
1 lb beef neck bones
Salt and black pepper to taste
2 ½ oz rice noodles
½ tbsp fish sauce

½ lb beef sirloin steak
½ tbsp fresh cilantro, chopped
1 scallion, chopped
½ jalapeño pepper, chopped
1 cup swiss chard, chopped

Directions

Heat coconut oil in your Instant Pot on Sauté. Add ginger and onion and cook for 4 minutes until softened. Stir in ground cloves, cinnamon, and coriander seeds and cook for 1 minute. Add in beef neck bones, sirloin steak, and 2 cups water. Seal the lid and cook on High Pressure for 30 minutes. Release the pressure naturally for 10 minutes.

Transfer the meat to a large bowl; cover with it enough water and soak for 10 minutes. Drain the water and slice the beef. In hot water, soak rice noodles for 8 minutes until softened and pliable; drain and rinse with cold water. Drain the liquid from the cooker into a separate pot through a fine-mesh strainer; get rid of any solids.

Add fish sauce and sugar to the broth. Transfer into the cooker and simmer on Sauté. Spoon the noodles in bowls. Top with steak slices, scallions, swiss chard, jalapeño pepper, cilantro, red onion, and pepper. Spoon the broth over each bowl to serve.

Chili Beef Brisket

Serves: 2-4 | Ready in about: 1 hour 10 minutes

Ingredients

2 tsp smoked paprika
Salt and black pepper to taste
1 tbsp Worcestershire sauce
½ tsp ground cumin

½ tsp garlic powder
1 tsp chipotle powder
¼ tsp cayenne pepper
1 lb beef brisket

2 tbsp olive oil
1 cup beef broth
¼ cup red wine
2 tbsp fresh parsley, chopped

Directions

In a bowl, combine cumin, cayenne, garlic, salt, paprika, pepper, Worcestershire sauce, and chipotle powder. Rub the seasoning mixture on the beef to coat. Warm olive oil in your Instant Pot on Sauté. Add in beef and cook for 3 to 4 minutes each side until browned completely. Pour in beef broth and red wine. Seal the lid and cook on High Pressure for 50 minutes.

Release the pressure naturally for about 10 minutes. Place the beef on a cutting board and allow to cool for 10 minutes before slicing. Arrange the beef slices on a serving platter, Pour the cooking sauce over and scatter with parsley to serve.

Classic Beef Stroganoff

Serves: 2 | Ready in about: 1 hour 15 minutes

Ingredients

1 ¼ tbsp flour
Salt and black pepper to taste
¼ lb beef stew meat
1 tbsp olive oil

⅓ onion, chopped
1 garlic clove, minced
⅓ cup beef broth
1 cup fresh mushrooms, chopped

½ cup sour cream
⅓ tbsp chopped fresh parsley
½ cup long-grain rice, cooked

Directions

In a large bowl, combine salt, pepper, and flour and mix well. Add in beef and massage to coat beef in flour mixture. Warm the olive oil in your Instant Pot on Sauté. Brown the beef for 4 to 5 minutes. Add garlic and onion and cook for 3 minutes until fragrant. Add beef broth to the pot. Seal the lid and cook on High Pressure for 35 minutes. Release the pressure quickly.

Open the lid and stir mushrooms and sour cream into the beef mixture. Seal the lid again and cook on High Pressure for 2 minutes. Release the pressure quickly. Season the stroganoff with pepper and salt; scoop over cooked rice before serving.

Lemon-Mustardy Beef Steak

Serves: 2 | Ready in about: 55 minutes

Ingredients

2 rib-eye steaks, boneless
1 tbsp lemon juice

2 tbsp olive oil
2 tbsp Dijon mustard

Salt and black pepper to taste
2 cups beef broth

Directions

In a bowl, mix lemon juice, oil, mustard, salt, and pepper. Brush the steaks with this mixture and set aside. Pour the beef broth in the Instant Pot. Place the steamer tray and arrange the steaks on top. Seal the lid and cook on High Pressure for 35 minutes. Do a quick release and remove the broth. Press Sauté and brown steaks on both sides for 3-4 minutes.

Fall Goulash Stew

Serves: 2 | Ready in about: 55 minutes

Ingredients

½ lb beef stew meat
1 potato, cut into chunks
½ large onion, roughly chopped
½ carrot, chopped

⅓ cabbage head, shredded
⅓ cup sun-dried tomatoes, diced
1 ½ cups beef broth
1 tbsp tomato paste

⅓ tsp tabasco
Salt and white pepper to taste
1 tbsp butter

Directions

Melt the butter in your Instant Pot on Sauté and cook the onion until translucent, about 2 minutes. Add the tomato paste and stir. Add the remaining ingredients and seal the lid. Cook on High Pressure for 35 minutes. Do a quick release. Serve.

Beef Stew with Cauliflower

Serves: 2 | Ready in about: 20 minutes

Ingredients

½ lb beef stew meat, cubed
⅓ tbsp cauliflower, chopped
⅓ onion, chopped

½ cups beef broth
½ cups heavy cream
⅓ cup water

⅓ tsp Italian seasoning mix
Salt and chili pepper to taste

Directions

Add all ingredients in your Instant Pot. Seal the lid and cook on High Pressure for 15 minutes. When ready, do a quick release and serve immediately.

Parsley Buttered Beef

Serves: 2 | Ready in about: 50 minutes

Ingredients

½ lb beef fillets, cut into bite-sized pieces
1 onion, chopped

1 tbsp tomato paste
1 tbsp oil

½ tbsp fresh parsley, chopped
Salt and black pepper to taste

Directions

Grease your Instant Pot with olive oil. Make the first layer of meat. Add onion, tomato paste, parsley, salt, and pepper and stir. Pour in ½ cup of water. Seal the lid and cook on Meat/Stew for 30 minutes on High. Release the steam naturally for about 10 minutes. Serve warm.

Cuban Ropa Vieja

Serves: 2 | Ready in about: 1 hour 10 minutes

Ingredients

Salt and ground black pepper to taste
½ lb beef skirt steak
1 cup beef stock
1 small bay leaf
1 tbsp olive oil

⅓ red onion, halved and chopped
⅓ green bell pepper, chopped
⅓ red bell pepper, chopped
1 tbsp minced garlic
⅓ tsp dried oregano

⅓ tsp ground cumin
⅓ cup tomato sauce
⅓ cup dry red wine
⅓ tbsp vinegar
2 tbsp cheddar cheese, shredded

Directions

Season the steak with pepper and salt. Add water to the cooker and mix in bay leaves and flank steak. Seal the lid and cook on High Pressure for 35 minutes. Release the pressure quickly. Remove skirt steak to a cutting board and allow to sit for about 5 minutes. When cooled, shred the beef using two forks. Drain the pressure cooker and reserve the bay leaves and 1 cup liquid.

Warm the olive oil in your Instant Pot on Sauté. Add onion, bell pepper, cumin, garlic, and oregano and cook for 5 minutes until vegetables are softened. Stir in reserved liquid, tomato sauce, bay leaf, and wine. Return beef to the pot with vinegar. Seal the lid and cook on High Pressure for 15 minutes. Release pressure naturally for 10 minutes. Serve with shredded cheese.

Short Ribs with Asparagus Sauce

Serves: 2 | Ready in about: 1 hour 15 minutes

Ingredients

1 lb boneless beef short ribs, cut into pieces
Salt and black pepper to taste
1 tbsp olive oil
⅓ onion, diced
⅓ cup dry red wine

⅓ tbsp tomato puree
½ carrot, peeled and chopped
1 garlic clove, minced
1 sprig parsley, chopped
1 sprig rosemary, chopped

1 sprig oregano, chopped
1 ⅓ cup beef stock
3 oz mushrooms, quartered
⅓ cup asparagus, trimmed chopped
⅓ tbsp cornstarch

Directions

Season the ribs with black pepper and salt. Warm the olive oil in your Instant Pot on Sauté. Add the short ribs to the oil and cook for 3-5 minutes each side until browned. Set aside. Add onions to the pot and sauté for 4 minutes. Add in tomato puree and red wine to deglaze, scrape the bottom to get rid of any browned beef bits. Cook for 2 minutes until wine reduces slightly.

Return the ribs to the pot and top with carrot, oregano, rosemary, and garlic. Add in broth. Seal the lid, press Manual, and cook on High for 35 minutes. Release pressure quickly. Transfer ribs to a plate. Strain and get rid of herbs and vegetables and return cooking broth to the inner pot. Add mushrooms and asparagus to the broth. Press Sauté and cook for 2 minutes.

In a bowl, mix 1 tbsp water and cornstarch until cornstarch dissolves. Add the mixture to the broth as you stir for 1-3 minutes until the broth thickens slightly. Season with pepper and salt. Pour the sauce over ribs add chopped parsley before serving.

Eggplant & Parmesan Beef Stew

Serves: 2 | Ready in about: 50 minutes

Ingredients

3 oz beef neck, cut into bite-sized pieces
⅓ eggplant, chopped
½ cups fire-roasted tomatoes
½ tbsp fresh green peas

⅓ tbsp beef broth
1 tbsp olive oil
½ tbsp tomato paste
⅓ tbsp ground chili pepper

Salt to taste
1 tbsp Parmesan cheese, grated
1 tbsp fresh parsley, chopped

Directions

Rub the meat with salt, cayenne, and chili pepper. Grease the Instant Pot with oil and brown the meat for 5-7 minutes, or until golden, on Sauté. Add all the remaining ingredients and seal the lid. Cook on Meat/Stew mode for 40 minutes on High. Do a natural release for 10 minutes. Serve warm sprinkled with freshly grated Parmesan cheese and parsley.

Mushroom & Beef Northern Stew

Serves: 2 | Ready in about: 35 minutes

Ingredients

½ lb beef steak, cut into bite-sized pieces
⅓ cup button mushrooms, chopped
⅓ cup sour cream

½ cups beef broth
1 tbsp Worcestershire sauce
1 tbsp olive oil

⅓ tbsp flour
⅓ onion, chopped
Salt and black pepper to taste

Directions

In a bowl, mix flour, salt, and pepper. Coat steaks with the mixture. Place the meat and broth in your Instant Pot. Seal the lid and cook for 10 minutes on High. Do a quick release. Add mushrooms, onion, and Worcestershire sauce. Seal the lid and cook on High Pressure for 5 minutes. Do a quick release. Stir in sour cream. Let simmer for 10 minutes. Serve.

Jalapeno Beef

Serves: 2 | Ready in about: 45 minutes

Ingredients

½ lb lean beef, cut into bite-sized pieces
1 onion, chopped
1 garlic clove, crushed

⅓ jalapeno pepper, chopped
⅓ bell pepper, chopped
Salt and black pepper to taste

⅓ tsp cayenne pepper
½ tbsp tomato sauce
½ tbsp vegetable oil

Directions

Heat vegetable oil in your Instant Pot on Sauté. Stir-fry the onion and garlic for 3 minutes. Add in the meat, salt, pepper, cayenne pepper, and tomato sauce. Mix well and pour enough water to cover. Seal the lid and cook for 20 minutes on High Pressure. Do a quick pressure release. Serve warm.

Creamy Braised Short Ribs

Serves: 2 | Ready in about: 1 hour 55 minutes

Ingredients

1 lb beef short ribs	⅓ celery stalk, chopped	1 tbsp red wine vinegar
Salt and black pepper to taste	1 garlic clove, chopped	1 bay leaf
½ tbsp olive oil	½ cup beef broth	1/8 tsp red pepper flakes
⅓ onion, chopped	5 oz canned diced tomatoes	½ tbsp chopped parsley
⅓ large carrot, chopped	2 tbsp dry red wine	¼ cup cheese cream

Directions

Season short ribs with black pepper and salt. Warm olive oil in your Instant Pot on Sauté. Add in short ribs and sear for 3 minutes each side until browned. Set aside on a bowl. Drain everything only to be left with 1 tablespoon of the remaining fat from the pot. Stir-fry the garlic, carrot, onion, and celery in the hot fat for 4 to 6 minutes until fragrant.

Stir in broth, wine, red pepper flakes, vinegar, tomatoes, and bay leaf. Set to Sauté and bring the mixture to a boil. With the bone-side up, lay short ribs into the braising liquid. Seal the lid and cook on High Pressure for 40 minutes.

Once ready, release the pressure quickly. Set the short ribs on a plate. Get rid of bay leaf. Skim and get rid of the fat from the surface of the braising liquid. Using an immersion blender, blend the juice for 1 minute. Add in cream cheese, pepper, and salt and blitz until smooth. Arrange the ribs onto a serving plate, pour the sauce over, and top with parsley to serve.

Roast Beef with Bearnaise Sauce

Serves: 2 | Ready in about: 40 minutes

Ingredients

½ lb beef scotch fillet	⅓ cup white wine	1 egg yolk
1 tbsp oil	⅓ onion, chopped	½ tbsp lemon juice
2 tbsp butter	⅓ tsp fresh basil, chopped	2 peppercorns

Directions

Melt butter in your Instant pot on Sauté and stir-fry the onion until translucent, about 3 minutes. Pour in the wine, basil, peppercorns, and lemon juice. Stir egg yolks. Add in beef fillets and 1 cup of water and seal the lid. Cook on Meat/Stew for 25 minutes on High Pressure. Do a quick release. Serve warm.

Vegetable Beef Stew

Serves: 2 | Ready in about: 35 minutes

Ingredients

½ lb beef meat for stew	2 oz baby carrots, chopped	1 ½ cups beef broth
2 tbsp red wine	1 sweet potato, cut into chunks	¼ cup green peas
⅓ tbsp ghee	⅓ onion, finely chopped	⅓ tsp dried thyme
2 oz tomato paste	Salt to taste	1 garlic clove, crushed

Directions

Heat the ghee in your Instant Pot on Sauté. Add beef and brown for 5-6 minutes. Add onion and garlic and keep stirring for 3 more minutes. Add the remaining ingredients and seal the lid. Cook on Manual for 20 minutes. Do a quick release and serve.

Carrots & Potato Spicy Beef

Serves: 2-4 | Ready in about: 35 minutes

Ingredients

1 lb beef shoulder	4 tbsp olive oil	1 tbsp fresh celery, chopped
1 lb potatoes, cut into chunks	2 tbsp tomato paste	1 tbsp fresh parsley, chopped
2 carrots, chopped	1 tbsp flour	1 cayenne pepper, chopped
1 onion, finely chopped	4 cups beef broth	Salt and black pepper to taste

Directions

Warm oil in your Instant Pot on Sauté. Stir-fry onions, carrots, and potatoes for 7-8 minutes. Stir in flour and press Cancel. Add the remaining ingredients. Seal the lid and cook on High Pressure for 40 minutes. Do a quick release.

Mushrooms Beer-Braised Short Ribs

Serves: 2-4 | Ready in about: 1 hour

Ingredients

1 lb beef short ribs	1 tbsp olive oil	⅓ cup beef broth
1 tsp smoked paprika	1 small onion, chopped	1 cup crimini mushrooms, chopped
½ tsp cayenne pepper	2 garlic cloves, smashed	1 tbsp soy sauce
Salt and black pepper to taste	1 cup beer	1 bell pepper, diced

Directions

In a bowl, combine pepper, paprika, cayenne, and salt. Rub the seasoning mixture on all sides of the short ribs. Warm oil in your Instant Pot on Sauté. Add mushrooms and cook until browned, about 6-8 minutes. Set aside. Add short ribs to the pot and cook for 3 minutes for each side until browned; set aside. Throw garlic and onion to the oil and stir-fry for 2 minutes.

Add in beer to deglaze by scraping the pot's bottom to eliminate any browned bits of food. Bring to a simmer and cook for 2 minutes until reduced slightly. Stir in soy sauce, bell pepper, and beef broth. Dip short ribs into the liquid in a single layer.

Seal the lid, press Meat/Stew, and cook on High for 40 minutes. Release pressure naturally for about 10 minutes. Divide the ribs with the sauce into bowls and top with fried mushrooms.

Homemade Beef Gyros

Serves: 2-4 | Ready in about: 55 minutes

Ingredients

1 lb beef sirloin, cut into thin strips	2 tbsp olive oil	4 slices pita bread
1 onion, chopped	2 tsp dry oregano	1 cup Greek yogurt
⅓ cup beef broth	1 clove garlic, minced	2 tbsp fresh dill, chopped
2 tbsp fresh lemon juice	Salt and black pepper to taste	

Directions

In the pot, mix beef, beef broth, oregano, garlic, lemon juice, pepper, onion, olive oil, and salt. Seal the lid and cook on High Pressure for 30 minutes. Release pressure naturally for 15 minutes, then turn the steam vent valve to Venting to release the remaining pressure quickly. Divide the beef mixture between the pita bread, Top with yogurt and dill, and roll up to serve.

Beef Sandwiches with Pesto

Serves: 2-4 | Ready in about: 50 mi

Ingredients

1 lb beef steak, cut into strips	1 cup beef broth	4 hoagie rolls, halved
Salt and black pepper to taste	1 tbsp oregano	8 slices mozzarella cheese
1 tbsp olive oil	1 tsp onion powder	4 tbsp pesto
¼ cup dry red wine	1 tsp garlic powder	

Directions

Season the beef cubes with salt and pepper. Warm oil on Sauté and sear the beef for 2 to 3 minutes for each side until browned. Add wine into the pot to deglaze and scrape the bottom to eliminate any browned beef bits. Stir garlic powder, beef broth, onion powder, and oregano into the pot.

Seal the lid, press Meat/Stew, and cook for 25 minutes on High. Release pressure naturally for 10 minutes. Spread each bread half with pesto, put beef and mozzarella cheese on top, and cover with the second half of bread to serve.

Spicy Beef Beans

Serves: 2-4 | Ready in about: 30 minutes

Ingredients

14.5 oz canned beans	1 garlic clove, minced	Salt and black pepper to taste
12 oz beef bones	1 carrot, chopped	1 tsp cayenne pepper
1 onion, chopped	1 bay leaf	2 tbsp vegetable oil

Directions

Place all other ingredients in the Instant Pot and cover them with water. Seal the lid and cook on High Pressure for 15 minutes. When ready, release the steam naturally for 10 minutes. Let it chill for a while before serving.

Beef Pot Roast with Pancetta

Serves: 2-4 | Ready in about: 1 hour 30 minutes

Ingredients

2 lb beef brisket, trimmed
Salt and black pepper to taste
2 tbsp olive oil
1 onion, chopped

3 garlic cloves, minced
1 cup beef broth
¾ cup dry red wine
2 fresh thyme sprigs

2 fresh rosemary sprigs
4 oz pancetta, chopped
6 carrots, chopped
1 bay leaf

Directions

Warm oil in your Instant Pot and pour on Sauté. Fry the pancetta for 4-5 minutes until crispy. Set aside. Season the beef with pepper and salt and brown in the pot for 5-7 minutes. Remove to a plate. In the same oil, fry garlic and onion for 3 minutes. Pour in red wine and beef broth to deglaze the bottom, scrape the bottom of the pot to get rid of any browned bits of food.

Return the beef and pancetta to the pot and add rosemary and thyme. Seal the lid and cook for 50 minutes on High Pressure. Release the pressure quickly. Add carrots and bay leaf to the pot. Seal the lid and cook for an additional 4 minutes on High Pressure. Release the pressure quickly. Get rid of the thyme, bay leaf, and rosemary sprigs. Serve.

Vegetable Beef Steaks

Serves: 2-4 | Ready in about: 45 minutes

Ingredients

2 large beef cutlets
3 potatoes, chopped
1 onion, chopped
1 carrot, chopped

6 oz cauliflower, into florets
2 tbsp olive oil
1 tbsp butter
1 tsp salt

¼ tsp black pepper
½ tbsp chili pepper, ground
3 cups beef broth

Directions

Warm the olive oil in your Instant Pot. Add in onion, carrot, and cauliflower and sauté for 3 minutes. Sprinkle the beef with salt and pepper and place it in the pot. Pour in broth, seal the lid, and cook on High Pressure for 25 minutes.

Release the pressure naturally for about 10 minutes. Remove the meat and vegetables to a serving bowl. Melt the butter on Sauté and add chili pepper. Stir for 1 minute and pour over the stew. Serve warm.

Macaroni with Beef & Tomato Sauce

Serves: 2-4 | Ready in about: 45 minutes

Ingredients

16 oz macaroni
6 oz beef, braising steak cut into chunks
1 onion, chopped

1 tomato, peeled, diced
1 tbsp tomato paste
3 tbsp butter, unsalted

¼ tsp ground black pepper
1 tsp cayenne pepper
1 tbsp vegetable oil

Directions

Heat oil in your Instant Pot on Sauté and stir-fry the onion until translucent. Add tomato, paste, butter, a pinch of salt, black and cayenne pepper. Cook until tomato softens, stirring occasionally. Add beef chunks and 1 cup of water. Give it a good stir.

Seal the lid and cook for 14 minutes on High. Do a quick release. Set the meat aside. Add macaroni and 2 cups of water to the pot. Seal the lid and cook on High for 4 minutes. Do a quick release. Stir in the beef and serve.

Wax Beans with Beef

Serves: 2-4 | Ready in about: 20 minutes

Ingredients

1 lb ground beef
1 lb wax beans
1 small onion, chopped
1 tbsp tomato paste

2 cups beef broth
2 garlic cloves, crushed
2 tbsp olive oil
2 tbsp fresh parsley, finely chopped

1 tsp salt
½ tsp paprika
1 tbsp Parmesan cheese, grated

Directions

Grease the pot with olive oil. Stir-fry the onion and garlic for 3 minutes until translucent on Sauté. Add beef, tomato paste, parsley, salt, and paprika. Cook for 5 more minutes, stirring constantly. Add wax beans and beef broth. Press Cancel and seal the lid. Cook on High Pressure for 4 minutes. Do a natural release for 10 minutes. Top with Parmesan and serve.

Rice & Beef Stuffed Onions

Serves: 2-4 | Ready in about: 30 minutes

Ingredients

10 sweet onions, peeled
1 lb lean ground beef
½ cup rice
1 tbsp olive oil

1 tbsp dry mint, ground
1 tsp cayenne pepper, ground
½ tsp cumin, ground
1 tsp salt

½ tbsp tomato paste
½ cup bread crumbs
1 tbsp fresh parsley, finely chopped

Directions

Cut a ¼-inch slice from top of each onion and trim a small amount from the bottom end; this will make the onions stand upright. Place onions in a microwave-safe dish and pour 1 cup water. Cover with a tight lid and microwave for 8 minutes until softened. Remove and cool slightly. Remove inner layers of onions with a paring knife, leaving about ¼-inch onion shell.

In a bowl, combine beef, rice, oil, mint, cayenne pepper, cumin, salt, and bread crumbs. Use one tablespoon of the mixture to fill the onions. Grease the inner pot with oil. Add onions and pour 2.5 cups of water. Seal the lid and cook on Manual for 10 minutes on High. Do a quick release. Top with parsley and serve with sour cream and pide bread.

Traditional Beef Bourguignon

Serves: 2-4 | Ready in about: 40 minutes

Ingredients

1 lb boneless chuck steak, cut into chunks
¼ cup flour
Salt and black pepper to taste
1 cup pancetta, chopped

½ cup red burgundy wine
1¼ cup beef broth
1 carrot, diced
1 cup portobello mushrooms, quartered

4 shallots, chopped
3 garlic cloves, crushed
1 tbsp fresh parsley, chopped

Directions

Toss beef with black pepper, salt, and flour in a large bowl to coat. Set in your Instant Pot and pour on Sauté. Cook pancetta for 5 minutes until brown and crispy. Pour in approximately half the beef and cook for 5 minutes each side until browned all over. Transfer the pancetta and beef to a plate. Sear remaining beef and transfer to the plate.

Add beef broth and wine to the cooker to deglaze the pan, scrape the pan's bottom to get rid of any browned bits of food. Return the beef and pancetta to cooker and stir in garlic, carrot, shallots, and mushrooms. Seal the lid and cook on High Pressure for 32 minutes. Release the pressure quickly. Garnish with fresh chopped parsley and serve.

Beef Steaks with Mushrooms

Serves: 2-4 | Ready in about: 35 minutes

Ingredients

1 lb beef steaks
1 lb button mushrooms, chopped
2 tbsp vegetable oil

1 tsp salt
½ tsp ground black pepper
1 bay leaf

1 tbsp dried thyme
6 oz cherry tomatoes

Directions

Rub steaks with salt, pepper, and thyme. Place in the Instant Pot. Pour in 3 cups of water, add bay leaf, and seal the lid. Cook on High Pressure for 13 minutes. Do a quick release. Set the steaks aside. Heat the vegetable oil in the pot on Sauté and stir-fry mushrooms and tomatoes for 5 minutes. Add steaks and cook for 2-3 minutes. Serve.

Crispy Beef with Rice

Serves: 2-4 | Ready in about: 55 minutes

Ingredients

2 lb beef shoulder
1 cup rice

2 cups beef broth
3 tbsp butter

1 tsp salt
½ tsp pepper

Directions

Season the beef with salt. Place it in the pot and pour in broth. Seal the lid and cook on Meat/Stew for 25 minutes on High Pressure. Do a quick release, remove the meat but keep the broth. Add rice and stir in 1 tbsp of butter.

Seal the lid, and cook on Rice mode for 8 minutes on High. Do a quick release. Remove the rice and wipe the pot clean. Melt 2 tbsp of butter on Sauté. Add meat and lightly brown for 10 minutes. Serve with rice and Season with pepper and salt.

Cherry & Beef Tagine

Serves: 2-4 | Ready in about: 1 hour 20 minutes

Ingredients

2 tbsp olive oil
1 onion, chopped
1 ½ lb stewing beef, trimmed
1 tsp ground cinnamon
½ tsp paprika

½ tsp turmeric
½ tsp salt
¼ tsp ground ginger
¼ tsp ground allspice
1-star anise

1 cup water
1 tbsp honey
1 cup dried cherries, halved
¼ cup toasted almonds, slivered

Directions

Set your Instant Pot to Sauté and warm the olive oil. Add in onion and cook for 3 minutes until fragrant. Mix in beef and cook for 2 minutes each side until browned. Stir in anise, cinnamon, turmeric, allspice, salt, paprika, and ginger; cook for 2 minutes until aromatic. Add in honey and water. Seal the lid, press Meat/Stew, and cook on High Pressure for 50 minutes.

In a bowl, soak dried cherries in hot water until softened. Once ready, release pressure naturally for 15 minutes. Drain cherries and stir into the tagine. Top with toasted almonds before serving.

Mustard T-Bone Steak

Serves: 2-4 | Ready in about: 1 hour 35 minutes

Ingredients

1 lb T-bone steak (2 pieces)
1 tsp pink salt

¼ tsp freshly ground black pepper
2 tbsp Dijon mustard

¼ cup oil
½ tsp dried basil, crushed

Directions

Whisk together oil, mustard, salt, pepper, and basil. Brush each steak and Refrigerate for 1 hour. Meanwhile, insert the steamer tray in the Instant Pot. Pour 3 cups of water and arrange the steaks on the tray.

Seal the lid, press Manual, and cook for 25 minutes on High. Do a quick release and open the pot. Discard the liquid, remove the tray, and hit Sauté. Brown the steaks, one at the time for 5 minutes, turning once. Serve.

Celery Beef Sirloin

Serves: 2-4 | Ready in about: 25 minutes

Ingredients

2 lb beef sirloin
1 cup red wine
2 cups beef consomme
2 bay leaves

2 tbsp olive oil
Salt and black pepper to taste
1 large onion, chopped
1 stalk celery, diced

1 tbsp tomato puree
2 cloves garlic, minced
2 sprigs fresh parsley

Directions

Rub the meat with salt and pepper. Heat oil in your Instant Pot and pour on Sauté and sear the beef for 4-5 minutes. Set aside. In the same oil, add onion, celery, garlic, and tomato puree. Cook for 4-5 minutes, until soft. Pour in wine to deglaze the bottom of the pot, scrape to remove browned bits.

Bring the meat back to the pot and add parsley and bay leaf. Seal the lid and cook on High Pressure for 50 minutes. Do a natural pressure release for 10 minutes and serve immediately.

Potato Beef Moussaka

Serves: 2-4 | Ready in about: 30 minutes

Ingredients

2 lb potatoes, peeled, chopped
1 lb lean ground beef
1 onion, peeled, chopped

Salt and black pepper to taste
½ cup milk
2 eggs, beaten

1 tbsp vegetable oil
Sour cream for serving

Directions

Grease the bottom of the pot with oil. Make one layer of potatoes and brush with milk. Spread the ground beef on top and make another layer of potatoes. Brush with the remaining milk. Seal the lid, and cook for 15 minutes on High Pressure.

When ready, do a quick release. Open the lid, and make the final layer with the beaten eggs. Seal the lid and let it stand for about 10 minutes. Top with sour cream to serve.

Ricotta & Beef Meatloaf with Potato Mash

Makes: 2-4 serves | Ready in about: 45 minutes

Ingredients

1 lb ground beef
1 onion, diced
1 egg
½ breadcrumbs

¼ cup tomato puree
1 tsp garlic powder
4 potatoes, chopped
½ cup milk

2 tbsp butter
Salt and black pepper to taste
1 cup ricotta cheese

Directions

In a bowl, combine ground beef, eggs, pepper, garlic powder, breadcrumbs, onion, and tomato puree and mix to obtain a consistent texture. Shape the mixture into a meatloaf and place it onto an aluminum foil.

Put potatoes in the pot and cover with water. Place a trivet onto potatoes and set the foil sheet with meatloaf onto the trivet. Seal the lid and cook on High Pressure for 22 minutes. Release the pressure quickly. Leave to cool the meatloaf before slicing.

Drain the liquid out of the pot. Mash the potatoes in the pot. Mix in milk, ricotta cheese, butter, pepper, and salt until smooth and all the liquid is absorbed. Divide mash into plates and lean a meatloaf slice to one side of the potato pile. Serve.

Layered Moussaka with Almonds & Capers

Serves: 2-4 | Ready in about: 30 minutes

Ingredients

3 eggplants, halved
2 tomatoes, chopped
2 red bell peppers, chopped

¼ tbsp tomato paste
1 bunch of fresh parsley, chopped
3 oz toasted almonds, chopped

2 tbsp capers, rinsed, drained
¼ cup extra virgin olive oil
1 tsp sea salt

Directions

Grease the Instant Pot with some olive oil. Make the first layer with halved eggplants tucking the ends gently to fit in. Make the second layer with tomatoes and red bell peppers.

Spread the tomato paste evenly over the vegetables, sprinkle with almonds and salted capers. Add the remaining olive oil, salt, and pepper. Pour 1 ½ cups of water and seal the lid. Cook on High Pressure for 13 minutes. Do a quick release.

Beef Meatballs with Potatoes

Serves: 2-4 | Ready in about: 40 minutes

Ingredients

1 lb ground beef
6 oz rice
1 onion, chopped

2 garlic cloves, crushed
1 egg, beaten
1 large potato, peeled, chopped

3 tbsp olive oil
1 tsp salt

Directions

In a bowl, combine beef, rice, onions, garlic, egg, and salt. Shape the mixture into 15-16 meatballs. Grease your Instant Pot with 1 tbsp of olive oil. Press Sauté and cook the meatballs for 3-4 minutes, or until slightly brown.

Remove the meatballs. Add the remaining oil and make a layer of potatoes. Top with meatballs, cover with water, and seal the lid. Adjust the release steam handle. Cook on Meat/Stew mode for 15 minutes on High. Do a quick release.

Red Peppers with Beef Stuffing

Serves: 2-4 | Ready in about: 35 minutes

Ingredients

4 red peppers, stems and seeds removed
1 onion, finely chopped
1 lb ground beef

¼ cup rice
½ cup tomatoes
1 tomato, chopped

½ tsp salt
1 tsp cayenne pepper
3 tbsp olive oil

Directions

In a bowl, combine meat, onion, rice, tomatoes, salt, and cayenne. Stir well to combine. Use 2 tbsp of this mixture and fill each pepper. Make sure to leave at least ½ inch of headspace. Grease the bottom of your Instant Pot with cooking spray.

Make the first layer with tomato slices. Arrange the peppers and add two cups of water. Seal the lid, and cook on High Pressure for 15 minutes. Do a natural pressure release for 10 minutes.

Spring Beef Stew

Serves: 2-4 | Ready in about: 50 minutes

Ingredients

1 lb beef stew meat, chopped
2 spring onions, chopped
4 new potatoes, chopped

1 cup green peas
1 tsp salt
1 tsp cayenne pepper

1 tbsp apple cider vinegar
2 tbsp olive oil
3 cups beef broth

Directions

Heat oil in your Instant Pot on Sauté. Stir-fry the onions for 3 minutes. Add the meat and potatoes, and brown for about 10 minutes. Add peas and season with salt and cayenne pepper. Pour in broth and apple cider. Seal the lid and set on Meat/Stew for 25 minutes on High. Do a quick release. Serve warm.

Beef Calf's Liver

Serves: 2 | Ready in about: 10 minutes

Ingredients

1 lb calf's liver, rinsed
3 tbsp olive oil

2 garlic cloves, crushed
1 tbsp fresh mint, finely chopped

½ tsp cayenne pepper
½ tsp Italian seasoning

Directions

In a bowl, mix oil, garlic, mint, cayenne, and Italian seasoning. Brush the liver and chill for 30 minutes. Remove from the fridge and pat dry with paper. Place the liver into the inner pot. Seal the lid and cook on High Pressure for 5 minutes. When ready, release the steam naturally for about 10 minutes. Serve.

Thyme Meatloaf

Makes: 2-4 serves | Ready in about: 60 minutes

Ingredients

1 lb ground beef
1 large egg

1 garlic clove, minced
½ cup all-purpose flour

2 tbsp olive oil
½ tsp salt

Directions

In a bowl, combine the meat, flour, egg, and salt. Mix with hands until well incorporated and set aside. Grease a baking dish with oil. Form the meatloaf at the bottom. Add 1 cup of water and place a trivet in the cooker. Lay the baking dish on the trivet. Seal the lid, press Meat/Stew, and cook for 40 minutes on High. Do a quick release. Slice the meatloaf and serve warm.

Paprika Beef Pastrami

Serves: 2 | Ready in about: 60 minutes

Ingredients:

¼ tbsp onion powder
¼ tbsp brown sugar
¼ tbsp garlic powder

½ tsp paprika
⅛ tsp ground cloves
1 lb corned beef

1 cup water
1 tbsp vegetable oil

Directions

Pour the water into your Instant Pot. Lower the trivet, and add the beef. Select Manual, and cook on High for 45 minutes. Once ready, release the pressure naturally for 10 minutes. Coat the meat with oil, and rub the spices onto it. Set the Instant Pot to Sauté, and cook the meat for about a minute per side. Serve immediately.

Effortless Beef Casserole

Serves: 2 | Ready in about: 20 minutes

Ingredients

½ lb lean beef, with bones
1 carrot

1 potato, peeled and sliced
2 tbsp olive oil

½ tsp salt

Directions

Mix all ingredients in your Instant Pot. Pour water enough to cover and seal the lid. Cook on High Pressure for 15 minutes. Do a quick release and serve hot.

Green Pea Beef Stew

Serves: 2-4 | Ready in about: 15 minutes

Ingredients

2 lb beef, tender cuts, boneless and cubed
2 cups green peas
1 onion, diced
1 tomato, diced

3 cups beef broth
½ cup tomato paste
1 tsp cayenne pepper, ground
1 tbsp flour

1 tsp salt
½ tsp dried thyme, ground
½ tsp red pepper flakes

Directions

Add all ingredients in the Instant Pot. Seal the lid, press Manual, and cook for 10 minutes on High Pressure. When done, release the steam naturally for 10 minutes and serve.

Beef Sweet Short Ribs

Serves: 2 | Ready in about: 40 minutes + marinating time

Ingredients:

½ cup water
Juice of ½ orange
1 garlic clove, crushed

¼ tbsp sesame oil
2 beef short ribs
¼ cup brown sugar

⅓ cup soy sauce
½ tsp grated ginger

Directions

Whisk together all of the ingredients, except the ribs, in a bowl. Add the ribs, cover the bowl, and store the marinade in the fridge for 4 hours. Then, transfer the beef to the Instant Pot along with the marinade. Seal the lid, and select High Pressure. Cook for 30 minutes. Once ready, release the pressure naturally for 10 minutes and serve hot.

Veal Chops with Greek Yogurt Topping

Serves: 2-4 | Ready in about: 60 minutes

Ingredients

2 lb boneless veal shoulder, cubed
3 large tomatoes, roughly chopped
2 tbsp flour

3 tbsp butter
1 tbsp cayenne pepper
1 tsp salt

1 tbsp parsley, finely chopped
1 cup Greek yogurt for serving
1 pide bread

Directions

Grease the bottom of the inner pot with 1 tbsp of butter. Make a layer with veal pieces and Pour water to cover. Season with salt and seal the lid. Cook on High Pressure for 45 minutes. Do a quick release.

Melt the remaining butter in a skillet. Add the cayenne pepper and flour and briefly stir-fry for 2 minutes. Slice pide bread and arrange on a serving plate. Place the meat and tomato on top. Drizzle with cayenne pepper. Top with yogurt and parsley.

Veal with Chicken & Mushrooms

Serves: 2-4 | Ready in about: 35 minutes

Ingredients

1 lb veal cuts, cut into bite-sized pieces
1 lb chicken breasts, cubed
12 oz button mushrooms, sliced

1 carrot, chopped
2 tbsp butter, softened
1 tbsp cayenne pepper

Salt and black pepper to serve
A bunch fresh of celery leaves, chopped
3 oz celery root, finely chopped

Directions

Melt the butter in your Instant Pot on Sauté. Add in veal, chicken breasts, carrot, salt, pepper, cayenne pepper, and celery and cook for 5 minutes. Pour in 2 cups water. Seal the lid and cook on High Pressure for 20 minutes. Do a quick release. Press Sauté and add mushrooms and celery. Cook for 10 minutes. Serve.

Roast Lamb with Rosemary

Serves: 2-4 | Ready in about: 40 minutes

Ingredients

2 lb lamb leg
1 tbsp garlic powder

3 tbsp extra virgin olive oil
Salt and black pepper to taste

4 rosemary sprigs, chopped

Directions

Grease the inner pot with oil. Rub the meat with salt, pepper, and garlic powder, and place it in the Instant Pot. Pour enough water to cover and seal the lid. Cook on Meat/Stew for 30 minutes on High. Do a quick release. Make sure the meat is tender and falls off the bones. Top with cooking juices and rosemary.

Sage Lamb Stew

Serves: 2-4 | Ready in about: 40 minutes

Ingredients

2 lb lamb, cubed
2 garlic cloves, minced
1 cup onions, chopped
1 cup red wine

2 cups beef stock
2 tbsp butter, softened
2 celery stalks, chopped
1 tbsp fresh sage

1 bay leaf
2 tbsp flour
Salt and black pepper to taste

Directions

Rub the lamb with salt and pepper. Melt butter in your Instant Pot and pour on Sauté and cook onion, celery, and garlic for 5 minutes until tender. Add lamb and stir-fry until browned for about 5-6 minutes. Dust the flour and stir.

Pour in the stock, red wine, and bay leaf, seal the lid, and cook on High Pressure for 30 minutes. Do a natural release for 10 minutes. Remove and discard the bay leaf and serve garnished with sage.

Thyme Roast Leg of Lamb with Potatoes

Makes: 4-6 | Ready in about: 35 minutes

Ingredients

2 lb lamb leg
2 garlic cloves
1 tbsp fresh thyme, chopped

1 lb potatoes
1 lemon, chopped
3 tbsp oil

¼ cup red wine vinegar
1 tsp brown sugar
1 tsp salt

Directions

Place the potatoes in the pot, and pour enough water to cover. Season with salt, add garlic, and seal the lid. Set your Instant Pot to Meat/Stew. Cook for 20 minutes on High Pressure. Do a quick release and remove potatoes; reserve the liquid.

Rub the meat with oil and thyme. Place it in the pot. Pour in red wine vinegar, sugar, and add lemon. Add 1 cup of the reserved liquid and seal the lid. Cook on High Pressure for 7 minutes. Do a quick release.

Potato & Carrot Lamb Stew

Serves: 2-4 | Ready in about: 60 minutes

Ingredients

1 lb lamb neck, boneless
2 potatoes, cut into bite-sized pieces
2 large carrots, chopped

1 tomato, diced
1 small red bell pepper, chopped
1 garlic head, whole

2 tbsp fresh parsley, chopped
¼ cup lemon juice
Salt and black pepper to serve

Directions

Season the meat with salt and place it in your Instant Pot. Add in the remaining ingredients, tuck in one garlic head in the middle of the pot, and add 2 cups of water. Seal the lid, press Manual, and cook for 25 minutes. Do a quick release. Serve.

Lamb Leg with Garlic & Pancetta

Makes: 4-6 | Ready in about: 60 minutes

Ingredients

2 lb lamb leg
6 garlic cloves
1 large onion, chopped

6 pancetta slices
1 tsp rosemary
½ tsp salt

¼ tsp ground black pepper
2 tbsp oil
3 cups beef broth

Directions

Heat oil in your Instant Pot on Sauté. Add in pancetta and onion, making two layers. Season with salt and cook for 3 minutes, until lightly browned. With a sharp knife, make 6 incisions into the lamb leg and place a garlic clove in each.

Rub the meat with spices and transfer to the pot. Press Cancel and pour in beef broth. Seal the lid and cook on High Pressure for 25 minutes. When done, do a natural pressure release for about 10 minutes.

Sesame Lamb with Green Peas

Serves: 2-4 | Ready in about: 40 minutes

Ingredients

1 cup rice	3 tbsp sesame seeds	1 bay leaf
1 cup green peas	4 cups beef broth	½ tsp dried thyme
12 oz lamb, tender cuts, ½-inch thick	1 tsp sea salt	1 tbsp butter

Directions

Place the lamb and broth in your Instant Pot. Seal the lid and cook on High Pressure for 18 minutes. Do a quick release. Remove the meat but keep the liquid. In the pot, add rice, green peas, salt, bay leaf, and thyme. Stir well and top with the meat. Seal the lid and cook on Rice mode for 8 minutes. Do a quick release and stir in butter and sesame seeds. Serve.

Traditional Lamb Ragout

Serves: 2 | Ready in about: 25 minutes

Ingredients

⅓ lb lamb chops, 1-inch thick	1 onion, chopped	1 tbsp olive oil
⅓ cup green peas, rinsed	1 potato, chopped	⅓ tbsp paprika
1 carrot, chopped	1 tomato, roughly chopped	Salt and ground black pepper to taste

Directions

Grease the Instant Pot with olive oil. Rub salt onto the meat and make a bottom layer. Add peas, carrots, onions, potatoes, and tomato. Season with paprika. Add olive oil, ⅓ cup water, salt, and pepper. Give it a good stir and seal the lid. Cook on Meat/Stew mode for 20 minutes on High Pressure. When ready, do a natural pressure release for about 10 minutes. Serve.

Rosemary Lamb Chops with Mashed Potatoes

Serves: 2 | Ready in about: 40 minutes

Ingredients

2 lamb cutlets	⅓ tbsp olive oil	1 potato, peeled and chopped
Salt to taste	⅓ tbsp tomato puree	2 tbsp milk
1 sprig rosemary leaves, chopped	⅓ green onion, chopped	2 cilantro leaves, for garnish
1 tbsp butter, softened	⅓ cup beef stock	

Directions

Rub rosemary leaves and salt to the lamb chops. Warm oil and ½ tbsp of butter in your Instant Pot on Sauté. Brown lamb chops for 1 minute per each side; set aside on a plate. In the pot, mix tomato puree and green onion; cook for 2-3 minutes. Add the beef stock into the pot to deglaze, scrape the bottom to get rid of any browned bits of food.

Return lamb cutlets alongside any accumulated juices to the pot. Set a steamer rack on lamb cutlets. Place a steamer basket on the rack. Put in the potatoes. Seal the lid and cook on High Pressure for 4 minutes. Release the pressure quickly. Remove trivet and steamer basket from the pot.

In a blender, add potato, milk, salt, and remaining butter. Blend until you obtain a smooth consistency. Divide the potato mash onto serving dishes. Lay lamb chops on the mash. Drizzle with cooking liquid and sprinkle with cilantro to serve.

Pearl Barley & Lamb Soup

Serves: 2 | Ready in about: 40 minutes

Ingredients

½ tbsp olive oil	½ small onion, chopped	½ tsp ground cumin
½ lamb meat, chopped	½ celery stalk, cut into squares	1 bay leaf
1 tbsp white wine	1 carrot, chopped	2 cups vegetable broth
½ cup pearl barley	½ tsp garlic powder	1 tsp fresh parsley, chopped

Directions

Warm oil in your Instant Pot on Sauté. Brown the lamb on all sides for about 6 minutes, stirring often. Transfer the lamb to a bowl. Into the pot, add wine to deglaze, scraping any brown bits present at the cooker's bottom

Mix the wine with pearl barley, cumin, stock, onion, carrots, celery, garlic powder, and bay leaf. Seal the lid, press Manual, and cook on High for 20 minutes. Release pressure naturally for 10 minutes. Divide into plates and add parsley for garnish.

SOUPS & SAUCES

Beef Barley Soup

Serves: 2-4 | Ready in about: 45 minutes

Ingredients

1 tbsp olive oil
½ lb stewing beef, cut into ½-inch cubes
Salt and black pepper to taste
1 celery stalk, chopped

1 carrot, chopped
1 onion, diced
1 cup quartered cremini mushrooms
1 tsp Italian seasoning

1 cup pearl barley
½ cup diced tomatoes
2 cups beef broth
2 tbsp chopped parsley

Directions

Set your Instant Pot to Sauté and heat olive oil. Season beef with salt and pepper, and sear in oil until lightly brown, 4 minutes. Add celery, carrots, onion, garlic, mushrooms, and Italian seasoning; sauté until slightly softened, 4 minutes. Stir in barley, tomatoes, and beef broth. Seal the lid, select Manual/Pressure Cook on High, and cook for 20 minutes.

After cooking, do a natural pressure release for 10 minutes, then a quick pressure release to let out remaining steam. Unlock the lid, stir in parsley, and adjust taste with salt and black pepper. Spoon soup into serving bowls and serve.

Over medium heat, heat a skillet. With butter sides down, place the sandwiches on the skillet. Spread 1 tbsp butter on top of each sandwich. Cook each side for 3 to 5 minutes until browned and all cheese melt. Transfer sandwiches to a cutting board and chop into bite-sized pieces. Divide the soup into serving plates and top with parsley cheese croutons before serving.

Vegetarian Minestrone with Navy Beans

Serves: 2-4 | Ready in about: 25 minutes

Ingredients

2 tbsp olive oil
1 onion, diced
1 cup celery, chopped
1 carrot, peeled and diced
1 green bell pepper, chopped
2 cloves garlic, minced

3 cups chicken broth
½ tsp dried parsley
½ tsp dried oregano
½ tsp salt
¼ tsp black pepper
2 bay leaves

28 oz canned diced tomatoes
6 oz canned tomato paste
2 cups kale
14 oz canned Navy beans, rinsed
½ cup white rice
¼ cup Parmesan cheese, shredded

Directions

Warm the oil in your Instant Pot on Sauté. Stir in carrot, garlic, celery, and onion and cook for 5 minutes until soft. Add in bell pepper and cook for 2 minutes as you stir until aromatic. Stir in pepper, stock, salt, parsley, oregano, tomatoes, bay leaves, and tomato paste to dissolve. Mix in rice. Seal the lid and cook on High Pressure for 15 minutes. Do a quick release.

Add kale to the liquid and stir. Use residual heat in slightly wilting the greens. Discard bay leaves. Stir in navy beans and serve topped with Parmesan cheese.

Bengali Parsnip Soup

Serves: 2-4 | Ready in about: 15 minutes

Ingredients

2 tbsp vegetable oil
1 red onion, finely chopped
3 parsnips, chopped
2 garlic cloves, crushed

2 tsp garam masala
½ tsp chili powder
1 tbsp plain flour
4 cups vegetable stock

1 whole lemon, juiced
1 tsp salt
½ tsp black pepper, ground
Strips of lemon rind, to garnish

Directions

Heat the vegetable oil in your Instant Pot on Sauté and stir-fry onion, parsnips, and garlic for 5 minutes or until soft but not change color. Stir in garam masala and chili powder and cook for 30 seconds. Stir in the flour for another 30 seconds.

Pour in the stock, lemon rind, and lemon juice, and seal the lid. Cook on Manual/Pressure Cook for 5 minutes on High. Do a quick release, remove a third of the vegetable pieces with a slotted spoon and reserve.

Process the remaining soup and vegetables in a food processor for about 1 minute, to a smooth puree. Return to the pot, and stir in the reserved vegetables. Press Keep Warm and heat the soup for 2 minutes until piping hot. Season with salt and pepper, then ladle into bowls. Garnish with strips of lemon to serve.

Spinach & Mushroom Cream Soup

Serves: 2-4 | Ready in about: 25 minutes

Ingredients

1 tbsp olive oil
8 button mushrooms, sliced
1 cup spinach, chopped
1 red onion, chopped

4 cups vegetable stock
2 sweet potatoes, peeled and chopped
2 tbsp white wine
1 tbsp dry porcini mushrooms, soaked

Sea salt and black pepper to taste
1 cup creme fraiche
2 tbsp fresh parsley, chopped

Directions

Set on Sauté and add in olive oil and mushrooms. Sauté for 3 to 5 minutes until browning on both sides; set aside. Add onion and spinach and cook for 3 minutes until translucent. Stir in chopped mushrooms and parsley and cook for 5 minutes, stirring occasionally until golden brown. Pour in wine to deglaze the bottom of the pot, scrape to remove browned bits.

Cook for 5 minutes until wine evaporates. Mix in the remaining mushrooms, potatoes, soaked mushrooms, wine, stock, and salt. Seal the lid and cook on High Pressure for 5 minutes. Quick-release the pressure. Mix in pepper and creme fraiche. With an immersion blender, whizz the mixture until smooth. Stir in the sautéed mushrooms. Top with reserved mushrooms.

Traditional Tomato Soup with Cheese Croutons

Serves: 2 | Ready in about: 1 hour

Ingredients

1 tbsp olive oil
½ onion, chopped
½ carrot, peeled and chopped
Salt and black pepper to taste

1 cup vegetable stock
10 oz canned tomatoes
1 cup heavy cream
2 slices Monterey Jack cheese

2 slices bread
1 slice Gouda cheese
2 tbsp butter, at room temperature
1 tbsp parsley, finely chopped

Directions

Warm oil in your Instant Pot on Sauté. Stir-fry onion, carrot, pepper, and salt for 6 minutes. In the pot, add stock to deglaze. Scrape any brown bits from it. Mix the stock with tomatoes. Seal the lid and cook on High Pressure for 30 minutes.

Allow for a quick release. Transfer soup to a blender and process until smooth. Add in heavy cream, salt, and pepper and stir. Place 2 slices Monterey Jack cheese onto 1 bread slice and cover with 1 Gouda cheese slice and the second slice of bread. Spread 1 tbsp of butter and parsley over the top. Do the same with the rest of the cheese, bread, parsley, and butter.

Fall Spicy Squash Soup

Serves: 2-4 | Ready in about: 25 minutes

Ingredients

4 cups vegetable broth
2 tbsp butter
1 onion, diced

1 acorn squash, chopped
2 carrots, peeled and diced
½ tsp ground cinnamon

¼ tsp chili pepper
½ cup coconut milk
⅓ cup sour cream

Directions

Melt butter in your Instant Pot on Sauté. Add onion, carrots, cinnamon, squash, salt, and chili pepper and cook for 5 minutes until tender. Pour in the vegetable stock. Seal the lid and cook for 12 minutes on High. Quick-release the pressure.

Add soup to a food processor and puree to obtain a smooth consistency. Take the soup back to the cooker, stir in coconut milk until you get a consistent color. Serve hot with a dollop of sour cream.

Pumpkin Chipotle Cream Soup

Serves: 2-4 | Ready in about: 25 minutes

Ingredients

1 tbsp olive oil
1 onion, chopped
2 chipotle peppers, seeded and minced

¼ tsp ground cloves
¼ ground cinnamon
1 butternut pumpkin, cubed

4 cups vegetable broth
Salt and black pepper to taste
1 cup half-and-half

Directions

Warm oil in your Instant Pot on Sauté. Cook onion, nutmeg, pepper, salt, ground cloves, and cinnamon for 3 minutes. Add pumpkin and cook for 5 minutes, stirring infrequently. Pour in broth and add chipotle peppers. Seal the lid and cook on High for 10 minutes. Release pressure quickly. Stir in half-and-half and transfer to a blender to purée until smooth. Serve.

Asian Pork Soup

Serves: 2-4 | Ready in about: 40 minutes

Ingredients

2 tbsp olive oil
1 onion, halved
1 piece fresh ginger, grated
1 tsp red pepper flakes

½ tsp coriander seeds
10 black peppercorns
2-star anise
½ lb pork tenderloin, cut into strips

1 tsp salt
8 oz rice noodles
1 lime, cut into wedges
2 tbsp fresh cilantro, chopped

Directions

Warm the olive oil in your Instant Pot on Sauté. Add ginger and onion and cook for 4 minutes. Add in flakes, anise, peppercorns, and coriander seeds and cook for 1 minute as you stir. Add in 2-3 cups of water, salt, and pork. Seal the lid and cook on High Pressure for 60 minutes. Release the pressure naturally for 10 minutes.

As the pho continues to cook, soak rice noodles in hot water for 8 minutes until softened and pliable; stop the cooking process by draining and rinsing with cold water. Separate the noodles into soup bowls.

Remove the pork from the cooker and ladle among bowls. Strain the broth to get rid of solids. Pour it over the pork and noodles; Season with red pepper flakes. Garnish with lime wedges and cilantro and serve.

Chicken Soup with Vermicelli

Serves: 2-4 | Ready in about: 45 minutes

Ingredients

2 tbsp olive oil
1 yellow onion, chopped
2 celery stalks, chopped
2 large carrots, chopped
5 garlic cloves, minced

2 chicken breasts, cut into ½-inch cubes
4 cups chicken stock
2 tsp Italian seasoning
2 bay leaves
Salt and black pepper to taste

½ tsp chili powder
½ lemon, juiced
3 cups chopped artichoke hearts
¼ cup vermicelli

Directions

Set your Instant Pot to Sauté. Heat olive oil in the inner pot, sauté onion, celery, carrots, and cook until softened, 3 minutes. Stir in garlic until softened, 3 minutes. Mix in chicken breasts, stock, Italian seasoning, bay leaves, salt, pepper, and chili powder. Seal the lid, select Manual/Pressure Cook on High, and set time to 10 minutes.

After cooking, perform a natural pressure release for 10 minutes, then a quick pressure release to let out remaining steam, and unlock the lid. Mix in lemon juice, artichoke, and vermicelli and cook further 5 minutes on Sauté. Dish soup and serve.

Thick Lentil Soup with Tortilla Chips

Serves: 2 | Ready in about: 50 minutes

Ingredients

2 cups vegetable broth
½ cups tomato sauce
½ small onion, chopped
½ cup dry red lentils

½ cup prepared salsa verde
1 garlic clove, minced
½ tbsp smoked paprika
1 tsp ground cumin

½ tsp chili powder
¼ tsp cayenne pepper
Salt and black pepper to taste
Crushed tortilla chips for garnish

Directions

Add in tomato sauce, broth, onion, salsa verde, cumin, cayenne pepper, chili powder, garlic, lentils, paprika, salt, and pepper. Seal the lid and cook for 20 minutes on High Pressure. Release pressure naturally for 10 minutes. Divide into serving bowls and add crushed tortilla topping. Serve.

Tomato & Lentil Soup

Serves: 2-4 | Ready in about: 20 minutes

Ingredients

2 cups red lentils, soaked overnight
1 carrot, cut into thin slices
3 tbsp tomato paste

3 garlic cloves, crushed
2 tbsp parsley, roughly chopped
1 onion, diced

½ tsp cumin, ground
Salt and black pepper to taste

Directions

Add all ingredients with 4 cup water to the IP. Seal the lid and cook on High for 7 minutes. Do a quick release. Serve.

Vegetable Corn Soup with Avocado

Serves: 2 | Ready in about: 25 minutes

Ingredients

1 ripe avocado
2 tbsp lemon juice
1 tbsp vegetable oil
3 oz canned sweet corn, drained

2 tomatoes, skinned and deseeded
1 garlic clove, crushed
1 leek, chopped
1 red chili, chopped

2 cups vegetable stock
4 oz soy milk
Shredded leek, to garnish

Directions

Peel the avocado and mash the flesh with a fork. Stir in the lemon juice and reserve until required. Heat the vegetable oil in your Instant Pot on Sauté and add corn, tomatoes, garlic, leek, and chili. Stir-fry for 4-5 minutes, until softened.

Put half of the vegetable mixture in a food processor, add the mashed avocado, and process until smooth. Transfer the contents to the pot. Pour in the stock, soy milk, and reserved vegetables, and seal the lid. Cook on Manual for 4 minutes on High. Once ready, and release the steam naturally for 10 minutes. Garnish with shredded leek and serve.

Spanish Chorizo Soup

Serves: 2 | Ready in about: 30 minutes

Ingredients

½ tbsp olive oil
½ shallot, chopped
1 cloves garlic, minced
Salt and black pepper to taste

2 cups beef broth
10 oz fire-roasted diced tomatoes
½ cup fresh ripe tomatoes
2 tbsp raw cashews

½ tbsp red wine vinegar
1 chorizo sausage, chopped
½ cup thinly chopped fresh basil

Directions

Warn oil jalapeno on Sauté and cook chorizo until crispy. Remove to a plate. Add in garlic and onion and cook for 5 minutes. Season with salt. Stir in red wine vinegar, broth, diced tomatoes, cashews, fire-roasted tomatoes, and pepper into the cooker.

Seal the lid and cook on High Pressure for 8 minutes. Release the pressure quickly. Pour the soup into a blender and process until smooth. Divide into bowls, top with chorizo, and decorate with basil. Serve.

Mexican Bean Soup with Cheddar & Tortillas

Serves: 2-4 | Ready in about: 35 minutes

Ingredients

4 boneless, skinless chicken thighs
4 cups chicken broth
14 oz canned whole tomatoes, chopped
2 jalapeno peppers, stemmed, chopped
2 tbsp tomato puree

3 cloves garlic, minced
1 tbsp chili powder
1 tbsp ground cumin
½ tsp dried oregano
1 (14.5-oz) can black beans, rinsed

2 cups frozen corn kernels, thawed
Crushed tortilla chips for garnish
¼ cup cheddar cheese, shredded
1 tbsp fresh cilantro, chopped

Directions

Add chicken, oregano, garlic, tomato puree, stock, cumin, tomatoes, chili, and jalapenos in your Instant Pot. Seal the lid and cook on High Pressure for 10 minutes. Once cooking is done, release the pressure quickly. Transfer the chicken to a plate.

Press Sauté and add corn and black beans. Shred the chicken with a pair of forks and return to the pot, stirring well. Simmer the soup for 5 minutes until heated through. Top with cilantro, cheddar cheese, and crushed tortilla chips and serve.

Sweet Potato Soup

Serves: 2-4 | Ready in about: 34 minutes

Ingredients

3 sweet potatoes, chopped
1 tsp sea salt
1 fennel bulb, chopped

16 oz pureed pumpkin
1 large onion, chopped
1 tbsp coconut oil

4 cups water
1 tbsp sour cream

Directions

Heat the oil on Sauté, and add onion and fennel bulbs. Cook for 3-5 minutes, until tender and translucent. Add the remaining ingredients and seal the lid. Cook on High Pressure for 25 minutes. Do a quick release, transfer the soup to a blender, and pulse for 20 seconds until creamy. Top with sour cream and serve.

Easy Chicken Soup with Quinoa

Serves: 2 | Ready in about: 30 minutes

Ingredients

1 tbsp butter
½ cup red onion, chopped
½ cup carrot, chopped
½ cup celery, chopped

2 chicken breasts, cubed
2 cups chicken broth
2 oz quinoa, rinsed
½ tbsp fresh parsley, chopped

Salt and black pepper to taste
2 oz mascarpone cheese, softened
⅓ cup milk
⅓ cup heavy cream

Directions

Melt butter on Sauté. Add carrot, onion, and celery and cook for 5 minutes until tender. Add broth, mix in parsley, quinoa, and chicken. Season with pepper and salt. Seal the lid and cook on High Pressure for 5 minutes. Release the pressure quickly.

Press Sauté. Add mascarpone cheese to the soup and stir well to melt completely; mix in heavy cream and milk. Simmer the soup for 3 to 4 minutes until thickened and creamy.

Coconut Squash Soup

Serves: 2 | Ready in about: 40 minutes

Ingredients

½ tbsp olive oil
½ small onion, diced
½ stalk celery, diced
½ carrot, diced

1 garlic clove, minced
½ lb acorn squash, peeled diced
3 cups chicken stock
Juice from 1 lemon

½ cup coconut milk
Salt and ground black pepper
1 tbsp cilantro leaves, chopped

Directions

Heat the olive oil in your Instant Pot on Sauté and stir-fry carrot, celery, garlic, salt, and onion for 4-5 minutes until soft. Mix acorn squash with the vegetables; cook for 1 more minute until tender. Seal the lid and cook on High Pressure for 20 minutes.

Release pressure naturally for about 10 minutes. Add in lemon juice and coconut milk and stir. Transfer the soup to a blender and process until smooth. Divide soup into serving plates. Garnish with cilantro, black pepper, and yogurt. Serve.

Leek Soup with Tofu

Serves: 2-4 | Ready in about: 25 minutes

Ingredients

3 large leeks
1 tbsp butter
1 onion, chopped
1 lb potatoes, chopped

5 cups vegetable stock
2 tsp lemon juice
¼ tsp nutmeg
¼ tsp ground coriander

1 bay leaf
5 oz silken tofu
Salt and white pepper
Freshly snipped chives, to garnish

Directions

Remove most of the green parts of the leeks. Slice the white parts very finely. Melt butter jalapeno in your Instant Pot on Sauté and stir-fry leeks and onion for 5 minutes. Add potatoes, stock, juice, nutmeg, ground coriander, and bay leaf; season.

Seal the lid. Press Manual/Pressure Cook and set the timer to 10 minutes. Cook on High Pressure. Do a quick release and discard the bay leaf. Process the soup in a food processor until smooth. Season to taste, add silken tofu. Serve the soup sprinkled with freshly snipped chives.

Easy Veggie Soup

Serves: 2-4 | Ready in about: 22 minutes

Ingredients

1 carrot, finely chopped
2 spring onions, finely chopped
1 red bell pepper, chopped,
2 celery stalks, finely chopped

½ cup celery leaves, chopped
½ tsp dried thyme
2 tbsp butter
1 tsp vegetable oil

4 cups vegetable broth
1 cup milk
1 tsp salt
¼ tsp black pepper

Directions

Melt butter in your Instant Pot on Sauté. Add carrot, onions, bell pepper, and celery. Cook for 5 minutes, stirring constantly. Pour in vegetable broth, seal the lid and cook on Manual/Pressure Cook mode for 5 minutes on High. Do a quick release. Stir in all remaining ingredients and cook for 2-3 minutes on Sauté. Serve warm.

Vegetable Winter Soup

Serves: 2-4 | Ready in about: 30 minutes

Ingredients

2 tbsp olive oil
1 onion, chopped
2 carrots, peeled and chopped
1 cup celery, chopped
2 cloves garlic, minced

5 cups chicken broth
2 turnips, peeled and chopped
28 oz canned tomatoes
15 oz canned garbanzo beans, rinsed
1 cup frozen green peas

2 bay leaves
1 sprig fresh sage
Salt and black pepper to taste
¼ cup Parmesan cheese, grated

Directions

In your Instant Pot warm the olive oil on Sauté. Stir in celery, carrots, garlic, and onion and cook for 4 minutes until soft. Add in vegetable broth, parsnip, garbanzo beans, bay leaves, tomatoes, pepper, salt, peas, and sage. Seal the lid and cook on High Pressure for 12 minutes. Allow natural pressure release for about 10 minutes. Serve topped with Parmesan cheese.

Homemade Borscht Soup

Serves: 2-4 | Ready in about: 30 minutes

Ingredients

2 tbsp olive oil
1 cup leeks, chopped
1 tsp garlic, smashed
2 beets, peeled and diced

1 tbsp cayenne pepper, finely minced
1 dried habanero pepper, crushed
4 cups beef stock
3 cups white cabbage, shredded

1 tsp salt
2 tsp red wine apple cider vinegar
¼ tsp paprika
Greek yogurt for garnish

Directions

Warm the olive oil in your Instant Pot on Sauté. Stir in the garlic and leeks and cook for 5 minutes until soft. Mix in the beef stock, paprika, salt, peppers, vinegar, beets, white cabbage, cayenne pepper, and crushed red pepper. Seal the lid and cook on High Pressure for 20 minutes. Do a quick release. Divide the soup between serving bowls and top with Greek yogurt to serve.

Celery & Carrot Soup

Serves: 2-4 | Ready in about: 10 minutes

Ingredients

1 carrot, finely chopped
3 oz celery root, finely chopped
½ cup green peas, soaked

2 tbsp butter
2 tbsp fresh parsley, finely chopped
2 tbsp cream cheese

¼ cup freshly squeezed lemon juice
Salt and black pepper to taste
4 cups beef broth

Directions

Add all ingredients to your Instant Pot and seal the lid. Cook on High Pressure for 5 minutes. When done, release the steam naturally for 10 minutes. Serve warm.

Flavorful Creamy White Bean Soup

Serves: 2 | Ready in about: 20 minutes

Ingredients

½ cup canned white beans
2 cups beef broth

1 potato, chopped
½ cup heavy cream

Salt and black pepper to taste
1 tsp garlic powder

Directions

Add all ingredients to your Instant Pot. Seal the lid and cook on Manual for 10 minutes on High. Release the steam naturally for 10 minutes. Transfer the ingredients to a blender. Pulse until smooth. Return the soup to the pot. Press Sauté and add a half cup of water. Cook for 5 more minutes or until desired thickness. Let it chill uncovered for a while before serving.

Noodle & Chicken Soup

Serves: 2-4 | Ready in about: 40 minutes

Ingredients

1 lb chicken breasts, chopped
½ cup egg noodles

4 cups chicken broth
1 tbsp fresh parsley, chopped

Salt and black pepper to taste

Directions

Season the filets with salt and place in the pot. Pour the broth and seal the lid. Cook on Soup/Broth for 20 minutes on High. Do a quick release. Add in the noodles and seal the lid again. Press the Manual/Pressure Cook and cook for 5 minutes on High Pressure. Release the pressure quickly, and sprinkle with freshly ground black pepper and parsley. Serve warm.

Collard Green Ramen Soup

Serves: 2-4 | Ready in about: 20 minutes

Ingredients

1 tbsp olive oil
½ tsp ground ginger
2 tbsp garlic, minced
2 cups chicken stock

1 tbsp soy sauce
1 tbsp chili powder
1 cup mushrooms, chopped
10 oz ramen noodles

1 lb fresh collard greens, trimmed
1 tbsp fresh cilantro, chopped
1 red chili, chopped

Directions

Warm the olive oil in your Instant Pot on Sauté. Stir in garlic and ginger and cook for 2 minutes until soft. Add in the chicken stock, chili powder, ramen noodles, and soy sauce. Seal the lid and cook on High Pressure for 10 minutes. Release pressure quickly. Stir in collard greens until wilted. Ladle the soup into serving bowls and add red chili and cilantro to serve.

Carrot & Black Bean Soup

Serves: 2 | Ready in about: 30 minutes

Ingredients

½ tsp olive oil
½ small onion, chopped
½ celery stalk, chopped
1 small carrot, chopped

1 serrano pepper, deseeded, chopped
2 cups vegetable broth
10 oz canned diced tomatoes
½ cup canned black beans, rinsed

¼ cup chopped fresh cilantro
½ tsp ground cumin
Sea salt and black pepper to taste

Directions

Warm oil on Sauté. Add in carrot, onion, serrano pepper, and celery and cook for 6 to 7 minutes until soft. Mix in water, sea salt, black beans, cumin, tomatoes, cilantro, and black pepper. Seal the lid and cook for 8 minutes on High Pressure. Release pressure naturally for 10 minutes. Serve.

Cilantro Squash Curry

Serves: 2-4 | Ready in about: 30 minutes

Ingredients

1 lb butternut squash, chopped
4 cups chicken stock
½ cup buttermilk

4 spring onions, chopped into lengths
1 tbsp curry powder
¼ tsp cayenne pepper

2 bay leaves
Salt and black pepper to taste
1 tbsp fresh cilantro, chopped

Directions

In the pot, stir in squash, buttermilk, curry, spring onions, stock, and cayenne pepper. Season with pepper and salt. Add bay leaves to the liquid and ensure they are submerged. Seal the lid, press Soup/Broth, and cook for 10 minutes on High.

Naturally release the pressure for 10 minutes. Remove and discard the bay leaves. Transfer the soup to a blender and process until smooth. Use a fine-mesh strainer to strain the soup. Divide into plates and garnish with cilantro before serving.

Carrot & Broccoli Chowder

Serves: 2-4 | Ready in about: 35 minutes

Ingredients

1 head broccoli, finely chopped
1 carrot, chopped
2 tbsp sesame oil

1 onion, peeled, chopped
2 garlic cloves
1 cup soy milk

2 cups vegetable broth
¼ cup crumbled tofu
A pinch of salt

Directions

Heat the sesame oil in your Instant Pot on Sauté. Add in onion and garlic and stir-fry for 2 minutes or until translucent. Pour in the broth, 1 cup of water, broccoli, and carrot. Seal the lid and cook on Manual/Pressure Cook mode for 5 minutes on High. Do a quick release. Let chill for a while, and transfer to a food processor. Pulse until creamy.

Mediterranean Minestrone

Serves: 2 | Ready in about: 15 minutes

Ingredients

½ cup chickpeas, soaked
1 carrot, chopped
½ onion, chopped

1 tomato, peeled and chopped
1 tbsp tomato paste
2 tbsp fresh parsley, chopped

2 cups vegetable broth
1 tbsp olive oil
Salt to taste

Directions

Add in chickpeas, oil, onion, carrot, and tomato. Pour in the broth and sprinkle salt. Stir in the paste and seal the lid. Cook on High Pressure for 6 minutes. Do a quick release and remove to a serving place. Sprinkle with chopped parsley to serve.

Chili & Sweet Potato Soup

Serves: 2 | Ready in about: 20 minutes

Ingredients

2 sweet potatoes, peeled and chopped
1 carrot, chopped
1 onion, chopped

2 cups chicken broth
2 garlic cloves, chopped
1 tsp salt

1 tbsp chili flakes
½ tsp black pepper, freshly ground
1 tbsp olive oil

Directions

Warm the olive oil in your Instant Pot on Sauté. Stir-fry the potatoes, onion, and garlic for 3-4 minutes. Mix in the remaining ingredients, seal the lid, and cook on High Pressure for 7 minutes. Do a natural release for 10 minutes. Serve in bowls.

Creamy Green Soup

Serves: 2 | Ready in about: 35 minutes

Ingredients

½ lb Brussels sprouts, chopped
6 oz baby spinach, torn, chopped
1 tsp sea salt

1 tbsp whole milk
2 tbsp sour cream
¼ cup celery, chopped

2 cups water
1 tbsp butter

Directions

Add all ingredients to the Instant Pot. Seal the lid, press Soup/Broth, and cook for 30 minutes on High. When ready, do a quick release. Transfer to a food processor and blend until smooth. Serve.

Pomodoro Soup with Farro

Serves: 2-4 | Ready in about: 25 minutes

Ingredients

1 cup tomato puree
¼ cup farro

¼ tsp salt
2 tbsp olive oil

4 cups vegetable broth

Directions

Add all ingredients to the pot and seal the lid. Set the steam release handle and cook on Soup/Broth mode for 30 minutes on High Pressure. Release the pressure naturally for about 10 minutes.

Potato & Spring Onion Creamy Soup

Serves: 2-4 | Ready in about: 30 minutes

Ingredients

2 tbsp butter
4 green onions, chopped
2 cloves garlic, minced

3 cups vegetable broth
3 potatoes, peeled and cubed
½ cup sour cream

2 tbsp rosemary
Salt and black pepper to taste
2 tbsp fresh chives, to garnish

Directions

Melt butter in your Instant Pot on Sauté. Stir in garlic and green onions and cook for 3 to 4 minutes until soft. Stir in the potatoes and broth. Seal the lid and cook on High Pressure for 15 minutes. Release pressure quickly. Transfer soup to a blender and puree soup to obtain a smooth consistency. Season with salt and pepper. Top with chives and sour cream. Serve.

Fast Chicken Rice Soup

Serves: 2-4 | Ready in about: 20 minutes

Ingredients

½ lb chicken breasts, cubed
1 carrot, chopped
1 onion, chopped

¼ cup rice
1 potato, finely chopped
½ tsp salt

1 tsp cayenne pepper
1 tbsp olive oil
4 cups chicken broth

Directions

Add all ingredients to your Instant Pot and seal the lid. Cook on Soup/Broth for 15 minutes on High. When ready, do a quick pressure release. Spoon onto individual soup bowls and serve hot.

Parsley Pork Soup

Serves: 2-4 | Ready in about: 65 minutes

Ingredients

1.5 lb pork ribs
1 large leek, chopped
1 onion, chopped

1 cup celery root, diced
½ cup parsley, chopped
4 cups vegetable broth

1 tsp salt
¼ tsp chili flakes
2 tbsp olive oil

Directions

Heat the olive oil in your Instant Pot on Sauté. Add the ribs and brown on all sides for 5-6 minutes. Add in the remaining ingredients. Seal the lid, press Meat/Stew, and cook on High for 30 minutes. When done, do a quick release. Serve hot.

Carrot & Turkey Soup

Serves: 2-4 | Ready in about: 55 minutes

Ingredients

6 oz turkey breast, chopped
4 cups chicken broth

1 onion, chopped
1 large carrot, chopped

Salt and white pepper to taste
1 tbsp cilantro, finely chopped

Directions

Add all ingredients in your Instant Pot. Seal the lid and set the steam release handle. Press Manual/Pressure Cook and cook for 35 minutes on High. Release the pressure naturally for 10 minutes and serve immediately.

Homemade Chicken Soup

Serves: 2-4 | Ready in about: 40 minutes

Ingredients

1 lb chicken breasts, chopped
1 onion, chopped
1 carrot, chopped

2 small potatoes, peeled, chopped
1 tsp cayenne pepper
2 egg yolks

1 tsp salt
4 cups chicken broth
2 tbsp olive oil

Directions

Add all ingredients to your Instant Pot and seal the lid. Select Soup/Broth and cook for 20 minutes on High. When done, release the pressure naturally for 10 minutes. Unlock the lid and spoon the soup onto individual bowls. Serve

Cheesy Cauliflower Soup

Serves: 2-4 | Ready in about: 20 minutes

Ingredients

2 tbsp butter
½ tbsp olive oil
1 onion, chopped

2 stalks celery, chopped
1 head cauliflower, cut into florets
1 potato, peeled and finely diced

3 cups vegetable broth
1 cup milk
4 oz blue cheese

Directions

Warm oil and butter in your Instant Pot on Sauté. Add celery and onion and sauté for 3 minutes until fragrant. Stir in the cauliflower and cook for 5 minutes until golden brown. Pour in the stock. Seal the lid and cook on High Pressure for 5 minutes. Release the pressure quickly. Place soup in a blender, add in milk, and puree until smooth. Top with blue cheese.

Spicy Beef Soup

Serves: 2-4 | Ready in about: 40 minutes

Ingredients

½ lb lean beef, cut into bite-sized pieces
1 onion, chopped

1 parsnip, chopped
1 tsp cayenne pepper

1 garlic clove, crushed
1 tbsp butter

Directions

Melt the butter your Instant Pot on Sauté. Add onion and garlic and stir-fry for 3 minutes or until translucent. Add in parsnip and spices and stir. Cook for 2 more minutes. Add the meat and pour in 4 cups of water. Seal the lid and cook on Manual/ Pressure Cook for 35 minutes on High. When ready, release the pressure quickly. Serve hot.

Autumn Pumpkin Soup

Serves: 2-4 | Ready in about: 20 minutes

Ingredients

1 lb pumpkin, chopped
1 onion, chopped
4 cups vegetable broth

1 tbsp ground turmeric
½ tbsp heavy cream
½ tsp salt

2 tbsp fresh parsley, chopped
2 tbsp olive oil

Directions

Add onion, pumpkin, turmeric, salt, broth, and oil to your Instant Pot. Seal the lid. Press Manual and cook for 15 minutes on High. Do a quick release. With an immersion blender, blend until smooth. Stir in heavy cream and top with parsley. Serve.

Delicious Pork Chop Soup

Serves: 2-4 | Ready in about: 60 minutes

Ingredients

2 pork chops, with bones
1 tbsp cayenne pepper
1 tsp chili powder
½ tsp garlic powder

2 bay leaves
4 cups vegetable broth
2 tbsp oil
1 large carrot, chopped

1 celery stalk, diced
1 onion, diced
1 tsp flour
2 tbsp soy sauce

Directions

Heat the olive oil in your Instant Pot on Sauté and stir-fry the onion for 3 minutes until translucent. Add in celery, carrot, cayenne and chili peppers and stir. Cook for 6-7 minutes. Add in pork chops, garlic, bay leaves, and soy sauce. Pour in the broth and seal the lid. Cook on Manual for 35 minutes on High. Do a quick release. Let chill for 5 minutes and serve.

Zucchini Two-Bean Soup

Serves: 2-4 | Ready in about: 35 minutes

Ingredients

1 tbsp olive oil
1 onion, chopped
2 cloves garlic, minced
4 cups vegetable broth

1 cup dried chickpeas
½ cup pinto beans, soaked overnight
½ cup navy beans, soaked overnight
3 carrots, chopped

1 large celery stalk, chopped
1 tsp dried thyme
16 oz zucchini noodles
Sea Salt and black pepper to taste

Directions

Warm oil on Sauté. Stir in garlic and onion and cook for 5 minutes until golden brown. Mix in pepper, broth, carrots, salt, celery, beans, and thyme. Seal the lid and cook for 15 minutes on High Pressure. Release the pressure naturally for 10 minutes. Mix zucchini noodles into the soup and stir until wilted. Taste and adjust the seasoning.

Lentil & Bell Pepper Soup

Serves: 2-4 | Ready in about: 35 minutes

Ingredients

1 cup red lentils, soaked overnight
1 red bell pepper, seeded and chopped
1 onion, chopped

½ cup carrot puree
Salt and black pepper to taste
½ tsp ground cumin

2 tbsp olive oil
2 tbsp fresh dill, chopped
4 cups vegetable stock

Directions

Heat the oil in your Instant Pot on Sauté. Stir-fry the onion for 4 minutes. Add the remaining ingredients. Seal the lid and cook on Soup/Broth mode for 30 minutes on High Pressure. Do a quick pressure release. Sprinkle with dill and serve.

Chicken & Cannellini Bean Soup

Serves: 2-4 | Ready in about: 40 minutes

Ingredients

2 tbsp olive oil
1 white onion, chopped
1 celery stalk, chopped
6 garlic clove, minced

2 tbsp thyme leaves
1 cup dried cannellini beans
2 chicken breasts, cut into 1-inch cubes
4 cups chicken stock

Salt and black pepper to taste
1 lemon, juiced
2 tbsp chopped parsley to garnish

Directions

Set your Instant Pot to Sauté and adjust to medium heat. Heat olive oil in the inner pot and sauté onion, celery, and garlic until softened, 3 minutes. Mix in thyme, beans, chicken breasts, stock, salt, and black pepper.

Seal the lid, select Manual on High, and cook for 13 minutes. After cooking, perform a natural pressure release for 10 minutes. Stir in lemon juice and adjust the taste with salt and pepper. Ladle the soup into bowls and garnish with parsley.

Quinoa & Mushroom Soup

Serves: 2-4 | Ready in about: 20 minutes

Ingredients

4 cups vegetable broth
1 carrot, peeled and chopped
1 stalk celery, diced
½ cup quinoa, rinsed

1 cup mushrooms, sliced
1 onion, chopped
2 garlic cloves, smashed
1 tsp salt

½ tsp dried thyme
2 tbsp butter
½ cup heavy cream

Directions

Melt the butter on Sauté. Add onion, garlic, celery, and carrot, and cook for 8 minutes until tender. Mix in broth, thyme, quinoa, mushrooms, and salt. Seal the lid and cook on High Pressure for 10 minutes. Release pressure quickly. Stir in heavy cream. Cook for 2 minutes to obtain a creamy consistency. Serve warm.

Mackerel & Bean Soup

Serves: 2-4 | Ready in about: 45 minutes

Ingredients

6 oz mackerel fillets
½ cup wheat groats, soaked
½ cup kidney beans, soaked

¼ cup sweet corn
1 lb tomatoes, peeled, chopped
4 cups fish stock

4 tbsp olive oil
1 tsp fresh rosemary, finely chopped
2 garlic cloves, crushed

Directions

Heat olive oil on Sauté, and stir-fry tomatoes and garlic for 5 minutes. Add rosemary, stock, corn, kidney beans, and wheat groats. Seal the lid and cook on High Pressure for 25 minutes.

Do a quick release and add mackerel fillets. Seal the lid and cook on Steam for 8 minutes on High. Do a quick release, open the lid and serve immediately drizzled with lemon juice.

Chili Bean Soup

Serves: 2-4 | Ready in about: 45 minutes

Ingredients

14.5 oz canned red kidney beans, rinsed
14.5 oz canned tomatoes
2 tbsp olive oil

4 cups water
2 cloves garlic, crushed
2 small fresh red chilies, finely chopped

1 green bell pepper, diced
½ cup tomato sauce

Directions

Heat the olive oil in your Instant Pot on Sauté and stir-fry garlic, chili, and onion for 3 minutes, or until translucent. Add the remaining ingredients and seal the lid. Cook on Manual/Pressure Cook mode for 25 minutes on High Pressure. Press Cancel and release the steam naturally for 10 minutes and serve immediately.

Gingered Squash Soup

Serves: 2-4 | Ready in about: 35 minutes

Ingredients

4 leeks, washed and trimmed
2 cups butternut squash, chopped
Salt and black pepper to taste

1 tsp ginger, grated
1 garlic clove, crushed
4 cups vegetable broth

2 tbsp olive oil
1 tsp cumin
1 tsp ginger powder

Directions

Heat the oil in your Instant Pot on Sauté. Stir-fry leeks and garlic for about 5 minutes. Add in ginger powder and cumin. Give it a good stir and continue to cook for 1 more minute. Pour in the remaining ingredients and seal the lid. Cook on Soup/Broth mode for 10 minutes on High. Release the pressure naturally for about 10 minutes.

Potato Soup with Broccoli

Serves: 2-4 | Ready in about: 50 minutes

Ingredients

1 lb broccoli, chopped into florets
1 potato, chopped
4 cups chicken broth

2 tbsp fresh parsley, chopped
Salt and black pepper to taste
¼ cup cooking cream

¼ cup sour cream
1 cup milk

Directions

Add the veggies to your Instant Pot and pour in the broth. Seal the lid and cook on High Pressure for 20 minutes. When ready, do a quick release. Let chill and transfer to a blender. Pulse until well-combined. Serve.

Rosemary Broccoli Soup

Serves: 2-4 | Ready in about: 45 minutes

Ingredients

1 lb broccoli, cut into florets
2 potatoes, peeled, chopped

4 cups vegetable broth
½ tsp dried rosemary

½ tsp salt
½ cup sour cream

Directions

Place broccoli and potatoes in the pot. Pour the broth and seal the lid. Cook on Soup/Broth for 20 minutes on High. Do a quick release and remove to a blender. Pulse to combine. Stir in sour cream and add salt. Serve.

Wax Bean & Veggie Soup

Serves: 2-4 | Ready in about: 18 minutes

Ingredients

1 cup green beans, chopped
1 carrot, peeled, chopped
2 red bell peppers, chopped

1 cup wax beans, chopped
1 tomato, roughly chopped
2 cups vegetable broth

2 tbsp olive oil
Salt and black pepper to taste
1 shallot, chopped

Directions

Heat the olive oil in your Instant Pot on Sauté. Stir-fry shallot, red peppers, and carrot for about 5 minutes. Add in the ingredients. Seal the lid and cook on High pressure for 8 minutes. When done, do a quick release. Serve hot.

Basil Chicken Chili

Serves: 2 | Ready in about: 35 minutes

Ingredients

½ lb chicken thighs, with skin and bones
⅓ tbsp chili powder
⅓ tsp fresh basil

Salt and black pepper to taste
2 cups chicken broth
⅓ tbsp ginger, freshly grated

⅓ tbsp coriander seeds
1 garlic clove, crushed

Directions

Season the meat with salt, and place it in the Instant Pot. Add the remaining ingredients, and cook on Meat/Stew mode for 25 minutes on High. Do a natural release for about 10 minutes. Serve immediately.

Homemade Tomato Soup

Serves: 2-4 | Ready in about: 40 minutes

Ingredients

2 lb tomatoes, diced
1 cup white beans, pre-cooked
1 small onion, diced

2 garlic cloves, crushed
1 cup heavy cream
1 cup vegetable broth

2 tbsp fresh parsley, chopped
Salt and black pepper to taste
2 tbsp olive oil

Directions

Warm oil in your Instant Pot on Sauté. Stir-fry onion and garlic for 2 minutes. Add tomatoes, beans, broth, 3 cups of water, parsley, salt, pepper, and a little bit of sugar to balance the bitterness. Seal the lid and cook on Soup/Broth for 30 minutes on High Pressure. Release the pressure naturally for 10 minutes. Top with a dollop of sour cream and chopped parsley to serve.

Asparagus Cream Soup

Serves: 2-4 | Ready in about: 40 minutes

Ingredients

2 lb fresh asparagus, trimmed
1 onion, chopped
1 cup heavy cream

4 cups vegetable broth
2 tbsp butter
½ tsp salt

½ tsp dried oregano
½ tsp paprika

Directions

Melt butter in your Instant Pot on Sauté. Stir-fry the onion for 2 minutes, until translucent. Add asparagus, oregano, salt, and paprika. Stir well and cook until asparagus soften for a few minutes. Pour the broth and mix well to combine. Seal the lid and cook on Soup/Broth for 20 minutes on High. Do a quick release and whisk in 1 cup of heavy cream. Serve.

Chicken & Navy Bean Chili with Buffalo Sauce

Serves: 2 | Ready in about: 45 minutes

Ingredients

5 oz canned diced tomatoes with green chilies

½ tbsp olive oil
½ shallot, diced
2 tbsp fennel, chopped
2 tbsp minced garlic

⅓ tbsp smoked paprika
1 tsp chili powder
1 tsp ground cumin
Salt and white pepper to taste

9 oz canned crushed tomatoes
½ lb chicken sausage, chopped
4 tbsp Buffalo wing sauce
½ cup canned navy beans, drained

Directions

Warm oil on Sauté. Add the sausages and brown for 5 minutes, turning frequently. Set aside on a plate. In the same fat, sauté onion, roasted red peppers, fennel, and garlic for 4 minutes until soft. Season with paprika, cumin, pepper, salt, and chili.

Stir in crushed tomatoes, diced tomatoes with green chilies, buffalo sauce, and navy beans. Return the sausages to the pot. Seal the lid and cook on High Pressure for 30 minutes. Do a quick pressure release. Spoon chili into bowls and serve warm.

Spicy Chicken & Chickpea Chili

Serves: 2-4 | Ready in about: 25 minutes

Ingredients

1 tbsp olive oil
3 large serrano peppers, diced
1 onion, diced
1 jalapeño pepper, diced
½ lb chicken breasts, cubed

1 tsp ground cumin
1 tsp minced fresh garlic
1 tsp salt
2 (14.5 oz) cans chickpeas, drained
2 ½ cups water

2 tbsp chili powder
½ cup chopped fresh cilantro
½ cup shredded Monterey Jack cheese
1 lime, cut into wedges

Directions

Warm oil in your Instant Pot on Sauté. Add in onion, serrano jalapeno peppers and cook for 5 minutes until tender. Season with salt, cumin, and garlic. Stir chicken with vegetable mixture; cook for 3 minutes until no longer pink.

Add 2 cups water and chickpeas. Mix well. Seal the lid and cook for 5 minutes on High Pressure. Release pressure naturally for 10 minutes. Stir chili powder with remaining ½ cup water. Press Sauté.

Boil the chili as you stir and cook until slightly thickened. Divide chili into plates; garnish with Monterey Jack cheese and cilantro. Over the chili, squeeze a lime wedge. Serve.

Yogurt Zucchini Sauce

Serves: 2 | Ready in about: 10 minutes

Ingredients

1 zucchini, chopped
½ cup Greek yogurt
½ cup sour cream

1 tsp garlic powder
¼ cup shallots, minced
1 tbsp ground dried parsley

1 tsp salt
1 tsp ground black pepper

Directions

In a bowl, mix zucchini, sour cream, garlic, shallots, parsley, salt, and pepper. Stir until well combined. Transfer the mixture to the pot, and seal the lid. Cook on High Pressure for 3 minutes. Do a quick release. Remove the sauce to a bowl and stir in the yogurt. Serve chilled.

Tomato & Mushroom Sauce

Serves: 2-4 | Ready in about: 45 minutes

Ingredients

1 lb mushrooms, chopped
2 cups canned tomatoes, diced
1 carrot, chopped
1 onion, chopped

1 celery stalk, chopped
1 tbsp olive oil
2 garlic cloves
1 tsp salt

½ tsp paprika
1 tsp fish sauce
1 cup water

Directions

Heat oil in your Instant Pot on Sauté. Stir-fry carrot, onion, celery, and paprika for 5 minutes. Add in the remaining ingredients, except for the tomatoes, and cook for 5-6 more minutes. Seal the lid. Cook on High Pressure for 20 minutes. When done, release the steam naturally for 10 minutes. Hit Sauté and cook for 7-8 minutes to thicken the sauce.

Homemade Granberry Sauce

Serves: 2-4 | Ready in about: 15 minutes

Ingredients

2 cups cranberries
1 tsp orange zest, freshly grated

½ cup orange juice, freshly juiced
¼ cup brown sugar

1 cup water
2 tbsp maple syrup

Directions

Combine maple syrup, water, cranberries, and orange juice in the Instant Pot. Sprinkle with orange zest. Seal the lid, and cook on High Pressure for 5 minutes. When done, release the pressure naturally for about 10 minutes. Press Sauté, add brown sugar, and stir until thick sauce mixture is formed. Turn off the heat and transfer the sauce to the serving dish. Serve.

Creamy Onion Gravy

Serves: 2-4 | Ready in about: 10 minutes

Ingredients

1 onion, chopped
1 tsp onion powder

3 cups vegetable broth
2 cups cream cheese

2 tsp dried parsley, chopped
1 tbsp olive oil

Directions

Heat oil on Sauté, and stir-fry the onions for 5 minutes, or until translucent. Stir in the remaining ingredients. Seal the lid and cook on High Pressure for 5 minutes. Do a quick pressure release and serve immediately.

Hot Sauce

Serves: 2-4 | Ready in about: 8 minutes

Ingredients

4 oz green jalapeno peppers, chopped
1 green bell pepper, chopped

2 garlic cloves, crushed
½ cup white vinegar

1 tbsp apple cider vinegar
1 tsp sea salt

Directions

Add all ingredients to the Instant Pot. Seal the lid and cook on High for 2 minutes. Do a quick release. Transfer to a blender, pulse until combined.

Tomato Sauce with Goat Cheese

Serves: 2-4 | Ready in about: 15 minutes

Ingredients

1 cup goat cheese, crumbled
1 cup tomatoes, diced
3 tbsp tomato paste

1 onion, finely chopped
3 tbsp apple cider vinegar
3 garlic cloves, chopped

¼ cup mozzarella cheese
2 cups vegetable broth

Directions

Add all ingredients to your Instant Pot. Seal the lid and cook on High Pressure for 6 minutes. Do a quick pressure release.

Beet & Squash Sauce

Serves: 2 | Ready in about: 40 minutes

Ingredients

2 beets, trimmed, peeled, cubed
2 carrots, peeled, cubed
2 cups butternut squash, peeled, cubed

3/4 cup red wine
½ tsp dried basil, ground
½ tbsp dried parsley, ground

½ tsp dried oregano, ground
½ tsp garlic powder
Salt and black pepper to taste

Directions

Add all vegetables in your Instant Pot. Pour in 2 cups water and seal the lid. Press Manual and cook for 10 minutes on High. Do a quick pressure release. Transfer to a food processor and pulse until smooth and creamy. Add the remaining ingredients and blend for 1 minute. Return to the pot, press Sauté, and cook for 10 minutes, stirring occasionally. Serve.

Two-Cheese Carrot Sauce

Serves: 2-4 | Ready in about: 15 minutes

Ingredients

1 carrot, shredded
1 cup cream cheese
½ cup gorgonzola cheese

3 cups vegetable broth
1 cup gruyere cheese, crumbled
Salt and black pepper to taste

1 tsp garlic powder
1 tbsp fresh parsley, finely chopped

Directions

Combine all ingredients in a large bowl. Pour in the Instant Pot. Seal the lid and cook on High Pressure for 8 minutes. Do a natural release for 10 minutes. Store for up to 5 days.

Pimiento Rojo Salsa

Serves: 2 | Ready in about: 15 minutes

Ingredients

2 red peppers, seeds removed, chopped
1 cup cherry tomatoes, diced
½ onion, chopped

1 tsp garlic powder
½ cup sour cream
2 cups vegetable broth

1 tbsp balsamic vinegar
1 tbsp cayenne pepper
1 tsp salt

Directions

Combine all ingredients in a mixing bowl. Add the mixture to your Instant Pot, seal the lid, and cook on High Pressure for 6 minutes. Do a quick release. Transfer to your food processor and purée until the mixture is smooth. Serve.

Delicious Tomato Sauce

Serves: 2-4 | Ready in about: 15 minutes

Ingredients

2 cups tomatoes, diced
½ cup tomato sauce
½ cup sun-dried tomatoes

1 medium onion, chopped
3 tbsp balsamic vinegar
3 garlic cloves, chopped

1 tbsp olive oil
Salt and black pepper to taste

Directions

Combine all ingredients in a mixing bowl and give it a good stir. Transfer to the Instant Pot and seal the lid. Cook on High Pressure for 6 minutes. When done, remove to serving bowls and serve with pasta or rice.

Basil Parmesan Sauce

Serves: 2-4 | Ready in about: 10 minutes

Ingredients

1 cup fresh basil, torn
1 cup cream cheese

2 tbsp Parmesan cheese, shredded
1 tbsp olive oil

Salt and black pepper to taste
2 cups vegetable broth

Directions

In a bowl, stir in all ingredients. Transfer the mixture to the Instant Pot. Seal the lid and cook on High Pressure for 5 minutes. Do a quick pressure release.

Cheese Broccoli Sauce

Serves: 2-4 | Ready in about: 15 minutes

Ingredients

1 cup broccoli, chopped
1 cup cream cheese

1 cup cheddar cheese, shredded
3 cups chicken broth

Salt and black pepper to taste
1 tsp garlic powder

Directions

Mix all ingredients in a large bowl. Pour the mixture in the Instant Pot. Seal the lid and cook on High Pressure for 8 minutes. Do a quick release. Store for up to 5 days.

Classic Bolognese Sauce

Makes: 4-6 serves | Ready in about: 45 minutes

Ingredients

4 slices bacon, chopped
1 tbsp olive oil
1 onion, minced
2 celery stalks, minced

1 carrot, chopped
1½ lb ground beef
3 tbsp red wine
28 oz canned tomatoes, crushed

2 bay leaves
Salt and black pepper to taste
½ cup yogurt
¼ cup chopped fresh basil

Directions

Set on Sauté, and cook bacon until crispy for 4 to 5 minutes. Mix in celery, butter, carrots, and onion, and continue cooking for about 5 minutes until vegetables are softened. Mix in ¼ teaspoon pepper, ½ teaspoon salt, and beef, and cook for 4 minutes until golden brown. Stir in the wine and allow to soak for 4 more minutes.

Add in bay leaves, tomatoes, and remaining pepper and salt. Seal the lid and cook for 15 minutes on High Pressure. Release pressure naturally for 10 minutes. Add yogurt and stir. Serve alongside noodles and basil.

Chili Mexican Dipping Sauce

Serves: 2 | Ready in about: 15 minutes

Ingredients

½ cup sour cream
1 cup tomato sauce

¼ tsp dried oregano, ground
½ cup cream cheese

½ tsp cayenne pepper, ground
¼ tsp chili pepper, ground

Directions

In a mixing bowl, add all ingredients and stir well to combine. Pour the mixture in the pot. Cook on High Pressure for 8 minutes. When ready, do a natural pressure release for 10 minutes. Transfer the dip into the serving bowl. Serve.

Homemade Spinach Dip Sauce

Serves: 2 | Ready in about: 10 minutes

Ingredients

1 cup cream cheese
½ cup baby spinach

½ cup mozzarella cheese, shredded
½ tsp Italian seasoning mix

¼ cup scallions
½ cup vegetable broth

Directions

Place all ingredients in a mixing bowl. Stir well and transfer to your Instant Pot. Seal the lid and cook on High Pressure for 5 minutes. Release the steam naturally for 10 minutes. Serve with celery sticks or chips.

FISH & SEAFOOD

Oregano & Chili Salmon

Serves: 2-4 | Ready in about: 60 minutes

Ingredients

1 lb fresh salmon fillets, skin on
¼ cup olive oil
½ cup lemon juice

2 garlic cloves, crushed
1 tbsp fresh oregano leaves, chopped
1 tsp sea salt

¼ tsp chili flakes
2 cups fish stock

Directions

In a bowl, mix oil, lemon juice, garlic, oregano leaves, salt, and flakes. Brush the fillets with the mixture and refrigerate for 30 minutes. Pour the stock in your Instant Pot and insert the trivet. Pat dry the salmon and place it on the steamer rack. Seal the lid, and cook on Steam for 10 minutes on High. Do a quick release and serve.

Tangy Salmon & Rice

Serves: 2-4 | Ready in about: 20 minutes

Ingredients

½ cup rice
1 cup vegetable stock
1 lb skinless salmon fillets
¼ cup green peas

2 tbsp olive oil
Salt and black pepper to taste
1 lime, juiced
1 tsp honey

1 tsp sweet paprika
2 jalapeño peppers, seeded and diced
2 garlic cloves, minced
¼ cup canned corn kernels, drained

Directions

Add rice, stock, and salt in your Instant Pot. Place a trivet over the rice. In a bowl, mix oil, lime juice, honey, paprika, jalapeño, and garlic. Coat the fish with the honey sauce while reserving a little for garnishing. Lay the salmon fillets on the trivet.

Seal the lid and cook on High Pressure for 8 minutes. Do a quick release. Fluff the rice with a fork and mix in the green peas and corn kernels. Transfer to a serving plate and top with the salmon. Drizzle with the remaining honey sauce and serve.

Lemon-Garlic Salmon Steak

Serves: 2 | Ready in about: 65 minutes

Ingredients

2 salmon steaks
½ tsp garlic powder
¼ tsp rosemary powder

1 cup olive oil
½ cup apple cider vinegar
½ tsp salt

¼ cup lemon juice
¼ tsp white pepper

Directions

In a bowl, mix garlic, rosemary, olive oil, apple cider vinegar, salt, lemon juice, and pepper. Pour the mixture into a Ziploc bag along with the salmon. Seal the bag and shake to coat well. Refrigerate for 30 minutes. Pour in 1 cup of water in the instant pot and insert the trivet. Remove the fish from the Ziploc bag and place it on top. Reserve the marinade. Seal the lid.

Cook on Steam for 15 minutes on High Pressure. When ready, do a quick release and remove the steaks. Discard the liquid and wipe clean the pot. Grease with some of the marinade and hit Sauté. Brown salmon steaks on both sides for 3-4 minutes.

Paprika Salmon with Dill Sauce

Serves: 2 | Ready in about: 15 minutes

Ingredients

2 salmon fillets
Juice from 1 lemon

¼ tsp paprika
Salt and black pepper to taste

¼ cup fresh dill
¼ cup extra virgin olive oil

Directions

In a food processor, blend dill, half of the lemon juice, extra virgin olive oil, and salt until creamy. Set aside. To your Instant Pot, add 1 cup of water and place a steamer basket. Arrange salmon fillets skin-side down on the basket.

Drizzle the remaining lemon juice over salmon and sprinkle with paprika, salt, and pepper. Seal the lid and cook for 3 minutes on High Pressure. Release the pressure quickly. Transfer the fillets to a serving plate and top with the dill sauce.

Salmon with Sweet Chili Sauce

Serves: 2 | Ready in about: 15 minutes

Ingredients

2 salmon fillets
Salt and black pepper to taste
1 tbsp chili garlic sauce

½ lemon, juiced
1 tbsp honey
1 tbsp olive oil

1 tbsp hot water
1 tbsp chopped cilantro
½ tsp cumin

Directions

In a bowl, combine chili garlic sauce, lemon juice, honey, olive oil, 1 tbsp hot water, cumin, and cilantro and mix well. Pour 1 cup of water in your Instant Pot and fit in a trivet. Place salmon on the trivet and sprinkle with salt and pepper.

Seal the lid, select Steam, and set the cooking time to 5 minutes on High. When done, perform a quick pressure release. Transfer the salmon to a plate. Drizzle with the sweet chili sauce and serve.

Green Lemon Salmon

Serves: 2-4 | Ready in about: 30 minutes

Ingredients

1 lb salmon fillets, boneless
1 lb fresh spinach, torn
2 tbsp olive oil

2 garlic cloves, chopped
2 tbsp lemon juice
1 tbsp fresh dill, chopped

1 tsp sea salt
¼ tsp black pepper

Directions

Place spinach in your Instant Pot, cover with water, and lay the trivet on top. Rub the salmon fillets with half of the olive oil, dill, salt, pepper, and garlic. Lay on the trivet. Seal the lid and cook on Steam for 5 minutes on High. Do a quick release. Remove salmon to a plate. Drain the spinach. Serve the fish on a bed of spinach. Season with salt and drizzle of lemon juice.

Dilled Salmon

Serves: 2-4 | Ready in about: 15 minutes

Ingredients

4 salmon fillets
1 cup lemon juice

2 tbsp butter, softened
2 tbsp dill

¼ tsp salt
¼ tsp black pepper

Directions

Sprinkle the fillets with salt and pepper. Insert the steamer tray and place the salmon on top. Pour in the lemon juice and 2 cups of water. Seal the lid. Cook on Steam mode for 5 minutes on High.

When done, release the pressure naturally for 10 minutes. Set aside the salmon and discard the liquid. Wipe the pot clean and Press Sauté. Add butter and briefly brown the fillets on both sides – for 3-4 minutes. Sprinkle with dill to serve.

Creamy Polenta with Cajun Salmon

Serves: 2-4 | Ready in about: 20 minutes

Ingredients

1 cup corn grits polenta
½ cup coconut milk

3 cups chicken stock
2 tbsp butter, melted

3 tbsp Cajun seasoning
4 salmon fillets, skin removed

Directions

Combine polenta, milk, chicken stock, and some butter in your Instant Pot. Stir and press Sauté. Bring the mixture to a boil. Brush the fillets with remaining butter and season with Cajun seasoning. Insert a trivet and arrange the fillets on top. Seal the lid and cook on High Pressure for 9 minutes. Do a natural pressure release for 10 minutes. Stir and serve with the salmon.

Herby Trout & Green Beans

Serves: 2-4 | Ready in about: 20 minutes

Ingredients

½ cup farro
1 lb skinless trout fillets
8 oz green beans

1 tbsp olive oil
Salt and black pepper to taste
2 tbsp melted butter

½ tbsp lemon juice
½ tsp dried rosemary
2 garlic cloves, minced

Directions

Pour the farro and water in your Instant Pot and season with salt and pepper. In a bowl, toss the green beans with olive oil, pepper, and salt. In another bowl, mix black pepper, salt, butter, lemon juice, rosemary, and garlic.

Coat the trout with the buttery herb sauce. Insert a trivet in the pot and lay the trout fillets on the trivet. Seal the lid and cook on High Pressure for 12 minutes. Do a quick release and serve immediately.

Salmon with Orange Zest

Serves: 2 | Ready in about: 20 minutes

Ingredients

2 salmon fillets

1 cup orange juice, freshly squeezed

2 tbsp cornstarch

Salt and black pepper to taste

½ tsp garlic, minced

½ tsp orange zest, freshly grated

Directions

Add all ingredients and seal the lid. Cook on High Pressure for 10 minutes. Do a quick pressure release.

Spinach & Trout with Red Sauce

Serves: 2 | Ready in about: 25 minutes + marinating time

Ingredients

½ lb trout fillets

1 cup fresh spinach, torn

2 tomatoes, peeled, diced

2 cups fish stock

½ tsp dried thyme

2 tbsp olive oil

¼ cup lime juice

½ tsp sea salt

2 garlic cloves, crushed

Directions

Sprinkle the fillets with sea salt. In a bowl, mix olive oil, thyme, and lime juice. Stir well and submerge fillets in the mixture. Refrigerate for 30 minutes. Pour the trout with the marinade and stock in your Instant Pot. Seal the lid.

Cook on Steam for 8 minutes on High. Do a quick release. Remove the fish to a plate. Hit Sauté and add the tomatoes and spinach to the pot. Stir and cook until soft. Drizzle the sauce over the fish and serve warm.

Trout Fillets with Squid Ink Pasta

Serves: 2-4 | Ready in about: 25 minutes

Ingredients

1 lb squid ink pasta

6 oz trout fillet

1 cup olive oil

½ cup lemon juice

1 tsp fresh rosemary, chopped

3 garlic cloves, crushed, halved

Sea salt to taste

2 tbsp fresh parsley, finely chopped

Olives and capers for serving

Directions

In a bowl, mix oil, lemon juice, rosemary, 2 garlic cloves, and salt. Stir well and submerge fillets in this mixture. Refrigerate for 30 minutes. Remove from the fridge and drain, reserving the liquid. Grease the pot with some of the marinade.

Add fillets, 1 cup water, and 3 tbsp marinade. Seal the lid and cook on High Pressure for 4 minutes. Do a quick release. Add in the pasta and 1 cup water. Seal the lid. Cook for 3 minutes on High Pressure. Do a quick release. Serve with capers and olives.

Cherry Tomato Tilapia

Serves: 2 | Ready in about: 30 minutes

Ingredients

2 tilapia fillets

Salt and black pepper to taste

4 sprigs fresh thyme

1 lemon, sliced

2 tbsp butter

2 garlic cloves, thinly sliced

16 cherry tomatoes, halved

2 tsp green olives, sliced

Directions

Rub the fish with salt and pepper on both sides. Transfer to a foil-lined baking dish and top each fillet with 2 sprigs of thyme and 2 slices of lemon. Set your Instant Pot to Sauté and melt the butter. Cook the garlic for 30 seconds until slightly pale and fragrant. Stir in the tomatoes and green olives and sauté for 3 minutes. Pour the tomato mixture over the fish.

Wipe inner pot clean. Pour in 1 cup of water and fit in a trivet. Place the baking dish on the trivet. Seal the lid, select Manual/Pressure Cook mode on High, and cook for 10 minutes. When done, perform a quick pressure release to let out the steam. Unlock the lid and remove the fish to a plate. Top with the sauce to serve.

Herby Trout with Garlic

Serves: 2 | Ready in about: 30 minutes

Ingredients

1 lb fresh trout (2 pieces)
1 cup fish stock
1 tbsp fresh mint, chopped

¼ tsp dried thyme, ground
1 tbsp fresh parsley, chopped
3 garlic cloves, chopped

3 tbsp olive oil
2 tbsp fresh lemon juice
1 tsp sea salt

Directions

In a bowl, mix mint, thyme, parsley, garlic, olive oil, lemon juice, chili, and salt. Stir to combine. Spread the abdominal cavity of the fish and brush with the marinade. Insert a trivet in your Instant Pot. Pour in the stock and place the fish on top. Seal the lid and cook on Steam for 15 minutes on High Pressure. Do a quick release and serve immediately.

Dill & Rosemary Trout

Serves: 2 | Ready in about: 20 minutes + marinating time

Ingredients

2 trout fillets, skin on
2 tbsp olive oil
2 tbsp apple cider vinegar

⅓ red onion, chopped
1 garlic clove, crushed
⅓ tbsp fresh rosemary, chopped

⅓ tbsp dill sprigs, chopped
Sea salt and black pepper to taste
1 cup fish stock

Directions

In a bowl, mix the olive oil, apple cider, onion, garlic, rosemary, dill, sea salt, and pepper. Submerge the fillets into the mixture and refrigerate for 1 hour. Grease the bottom of the pot with 4 tbsp of the marinade and pour in the stock. Add the fish, seal the lid, and cook on High Pressure for 4 minutes. Do a quick release. Serve.

Rosemary & Tuna Pizza

Serves: 2-4 | Ready in about: 25 minutes

Ingredients

1 cup canned tuna, flaked
½ cup mozzarella cheese, shredded
¼ cup goat's cheese

3 tbsp olive oil
1 tbsp tomato paste
½ tsp dried rosemary

14 oz pizza crust
1 cup olives, optional

Directions

Grease a baking dish with some olive oil. Line some parchment paper. Flour the working surface and roll out the pizza dough to the approximate size of your instant pot. Gently fit the dough in the previously prepared baking dish.

In a bowl, mix oil, tomato paste, and rosemary. Spread the mixture over the crust. Sprinkle with goat cheese, mozzarella, and tuna. Place a trivet in the pot and pour in 1 cup water. Seal the lid and cook for 15 minutes on High Pressure. Do a quick release.

Mediterranean Tuna Steaks

Serves: 2 | Ready in about: 10 minutes

Ingredients

4 tbsp olive oil
2 tuna steaks

Salt and black pepper to taste
1 lemon, zested and lemon juice

1 tbsp chopped thyme
3 tbsp drained capers

Directions

Pour 1 cup of water in your Instant Pot and fit in a trivet. Rub the tuna with salt, black pepper, and some olive oil and arrange on the trivet. Seal the lid, select Manual/Pressure Cook, and set the cooking time to 6 minutes on High.

After cooking, do a quick pressure release. Remove fish to a serving platter. Clean the inner pot. Set it to Sauté and heat the remaining oil. Sauté lemon zest, lemon juice, thyme, capers, and 2 tbsp water for 3 minutes. Top tuna with sauce and thyme.

Garlic Cod with Lemon Sauce

Serves: 2 | Ready in about: 20 minutes

Ingredients

2 cod fillets, skinless and boneless
1 tbsp maple syrup

¼ cup soy sauce
2 garlic cloves, chopped

1 lemon, juiced
1 tbsp butter, melted

Directions

In a bowl, mix maple syrup, soy sauce, garlic, and lemon juice. Stir until combined and set aside. Grease your Instant Pot with butter. Place the fillets at the bottom and pour over the maple sauce. Seal the lid and cook on Steam for 8 minutes on High. Release the pressure naturally for about 10 minutes. Serve.

Bell Pepper & Cod with Millet

Serves: 2-4 | Ready in about: 20 minutes

Ingredients

1 tbsp olive oil
½ cup millet
1 yellow bell pepper, diced

1 red bell pepper, diced
1 cup vegetable broth
1 cup breadcrumbs

4 tbsp melted butter
¼ cup minced fresh cilantro
1 lb cod fillets

Directions

Combine olive oil, millet, yellow and red bell peppers in your Instant Pot and cook for 1 minute on Sauté. Mix in the vegetable broth. Insert a trivet. In a bowl, mix breadcrumbs, butter, cilantro, lemon zest, and juice.

Spread the breadcrumb mixture evenly on the cod fillets. Lay the fish on the trivet. Seal the lid and cook on High for 6 minutes. Do a quick release and serve with millet and bell peppers.

Mediterranean Cod with Olives

Serves: 2 | Ready in about: 20 minutes

Ingredients

½ lb cherry tomatoes, halved
1 tbsp fresh thyme, chopped
½ lb cod fillets

1 tsp olive oil
1 garlic clove, pressed
Salt and black pepper to taste

½ cup white rice
1 cup kalamata olives
1 tbsp olive oil

Directions

Line a parchment paper on a baking pan. Place half of the tomatoes in a single layer on the pan. Sprinkle with thyme. Arrange cod fillets on top. Sprinkle with a little bit of olive oil. Spread the garlic, pepper, salt, and remaining tomatoes over the fish.

Mix rice and 1 cup of water in your Instant Pot. Insert a trivet and lay the baking pan onto the trivet. Seal the lid and cook for 7 minutes on Low Pressure. Release the pressure quickly. Remove the fish to a plate. Use a fork to fluff rice. Garnish the cod with olives and drizzle with the remaining olive oil. Serve with the rice.

Mint & Rosemary Mackerel with Potatoes

Serves: 2-4 | Ready in about: 32 minutes

Ingredients

4 mackerels, skin on
1 lb of fresh spinach, torn
5 potatoes, peeled and chopped

¼ cup olive oil,
2 garlic cloves, crushed
1 tsp dried rosemary, chopped

2 sprigs of fresh mint leaves, chopped
1 lemon, juiced
Sea salt to taste

Directions

Grease the pot with 4 tbsp olive oil. Stir-fry garlic and rosemary on Sauté for 1 minute. Stir in spinach, a pinch of salt and cook for 4-5 minutes, until soft. Remove the spinach from the cooker and set aside. Add the remaining oil.

Make a layer of potatoes. Top with fish and drizzle with lemon juice, olive oil, and salt. Pour in 1 cup of water, seal the lid and cook on Steam for 7 minutes on High. When ready, do a quick release. Plate the fish and potatoes with spinach and serve.

Lemon & Herb Stuffed Tench

Serves: 2 | Ready in about: 20 minutes

Ingredients

1 tench, cleaned and gutted
1 lemon, sliced

2 tbsp olive oil
1 tsp fresh rosemary, chopped

¼ tsp fresh thyme, chopped
½ tsp sea salt

Directions

In a bowl, mix olive oil, rosemary, thyme, and salt. Stir to combine. Brush the fish with the mixture and stuff with lemon slices. Pour 1 cup of water into your Instant Pot, set a steamer tray, and place the fish on top. Seal the lid and cook on Steam for 15 minutes on High Pressure. Do a quick release. Briefly brown the fish in a preheated grill pan. Serve.

Potato & Haddock Fillets

Serves: 2-4 | Ready in about: 25 minutes

Ingredients

8 oz beer
2 eggs
1 cup flour

½ tbsp cayenne powder
1 tbsp cumin powder
Salt and black pepper to taste

1 lb haddock fillets
4 potatoes, cut into matchsticks
2 tbsp olive oil

Directions

In a bowl, whisk beer and eggs. In another bowl, combine flour, cayenne, cumin, black pepper, and salt. Coat each fish piece in the egg mixture, then dredge in the flour mixture, coating all sides well. Place the fish fillets on a greased baking dish.

Pour in ¼ cup water. Add in the potatoes and cover with water. Place a trivet on top. Lay the baking dish on the trivet. Seal the lid. Cook on High Pressure for 15 minutes. Do a quick release. Drain and crush potatoes with olive oil. Serve with the fish.

Tasty Steamed Sea Bass Dinner

Serves: 2-4 | Ready in about: 15 minutes

Ingredients

1½ cups water
1 lemon, chopped
4 sea bass fillets

4 sprigs thyme
1 white onion, chopped into thin rings
2 turnips, chopped

Salt and black pepper to taste
2 tsp olive oil

Directions

Add water and set a rack into the pot. Line a parchment paper to the bottom of the steamer basket. Place lemon slices in a single layer on the rack. Arrange fillets on the top of the lemons, cover with onion and thyme sprigs. Top with turnip slices.

Drizzle pepper, salt, and olive oil over the mixture. Put the steamer basket onto the rack. Seal lid and cook on Low pressure for 8 minutes. Release the pressure quickly. Serve over the delicate onion rings and thinly turnips.

Simple Fish Stew

Serves: 2 | Ready in about: 30 minutes

Ingredients

½ lb different fish and seafood
1 tbsp olive oil

½ onion, chopped
½ carrot, grated

1 tbsp fresh parsley, chopped
1 garlic clove, crushed

Directions

Heat olive oil in your Instant Pot on Sauté. Stir-fry onion and garlic for 3-4 minutes or until translucent. Add the remaining ingredients and 1 cup of water. Seal the lid and cook on High Pressure for 10 minutes. Do a quick release. Serve

Tomato & Red Pollock Stew

Serves: 2-4 | Ready in about: 50 minutes

Ingredients

1 lb pollock fillet
4 cloves, crushed
1 lb tomatoes, peeled and chopped

2 bay leaves, whole
2 cups fish stock
1 tsp ground black pepper

1 onion, peeled and finely chopped
½ cup olive oil
1 tsp sea salt

Directions

Heat 2 tbsp olive oil on Sauté. Add onion and Sauté until translucent, stirring constantly, for about 3-4 minutes. Add tomatoes and cook until soft. Press Cancel. Add the remaining ingredients and seal the lid. Cook on High Pressure for 15 minutes. When ready, do a quick release and serve warm.

Fish Packs

Serves: 2 | Ready in about: 15 minutes

Ingredients

2 tilapia fillets
2 tbsp olive oil

2 garlic cloves, minced
2 tomatoes, chopped

Salt and black pepper to taste
¼ cup white wine

Directions

Cut out 2 heavy-duty foil papers to contain each tilapia. Place each fish on each foil and arrange on top olive oil, garlic, tomatoes, salt, black pepper, and drizzle with white wine. Wrap foil tightly to secure fish well.

Pour 1 cup of water in the inner pot, fit in a trivet with slings, and lay fish packs on top. Seal the lid, select Manual/Pressure Cook mode on High, and set the cooking time to 3 minutes. When done cooking, perform a quick pressure release to let out steam, and carefully remove fish packs using tongs. Place on serving plates and serve.

Mustardy Steamed Catfish Fillets

Serves: 2 | Ready in about: 50 minutes + marinating time

Ingredients

½ lb catfish fillets	½ onion, finely chopped	1 ½ tbsp Dijon mustard
1 lemon, juiced	½ tbsp fresh basil, chopped	3/4 cup extra virgin olive oil
2 garlic cloves, crushed	½ cup white wine	½ cup fish stock

Directions

In a bowl, mix lemon juice, garlic, onion, basil, white wine, mustard, and extra virgin olive oil. Stir well to combine. Add in the fillets and cover with a tight lid. Refrigerate for 1 hour. Insert the trivet in your Instant Pot.

Remove the fish from the fridge and place it on the trivet. Pour in stock along with the marinade and seal the lid. Cook on Steam for 8 minutes on High. Release the pressure quickly and serve.

Squid in Wine Sauce

Serves: 2 | Ready in about: 45 minutes

Ingredients

½ lb fresh squid rings	1 garlic clove, crushed	¼ tsp red pepper flakes
3 tbsp dry white wine	1 lemon, juiced	¼ tsp dried oregano
2 tbsp olive oil	1 ¼ cups fish stock	¼ tbsp fresh rosemary, chopped

Directions

In a bowl, mix wine, olive oil, lemon juice, garlic, flakes, oregano, and rosemary. Submerge squid rings in this mixture and cover with a lid. Refrigerate for 1 hour. Remove the squid from the fridge and place them in the pot.

Add in the stock and half of the marinade. Seal the lid. Cook on High Pressure for 6 minutes. Release the pressure naturally for 10 minutes. Transfer the rings to a plate and drizzle with some marinade to serve.

Chickpea & Olive Seafood Pot

Serves: 2 | Ready in about: 25 minutes

Ingredients

⅓ cup scallions, cleaned and chopped	⅓ cup chickpeas, soaked	Sea Salt and black pepper to taste
⅓ carrot, chopped	1 cup fish broth	¼ tsp Italian seasoning mix
⅓ lb shrimp, cleaned and deveined	5-6 olives, pitted	

Directions

Add all ingredients in your instant pot. Seal the lid and cook on High Pressure for 12 minutes. Release the pressure naturally for 10 minutes. Serve warm.

Shrimp & Chorizo Boil

Serves: 2-4 | Ready in about: 30 minutes

Ingredients

2 red potatoes	2 chorizo sausages, chopped	Salt to taste
2 ears corn, cut into rounds	1 lb shrimp, peeled and deveined	1 lemon, cut into wedges
1 cup white wine	1 tbsp seafood seasoning	¼ cup butter, melted

Directions

Add all ingredients and 2 cups of water, except butter and lemon wedges in your Instant Pot. Do not stir. Seal the lid and cook for 2 minutes on High Pressure. Release the pressure quickly. Drain the mixture through a colander. Transfer to a serving platter. Serve with melted butter and lemon wedges.

Brussels Sprout Shrimp

Serves: 2 | Ready in about: 45 minutes

Ingredients

¼ lb large shrimp, cleaned, rinsed
2 oz Brussels sprouts, outer leaves removed
1 oz whole okra
2 carrots, chopped
1 cup chicken broth

1 tomato, diced
½ tbsp tomato paste
1/8 tsp cayenne pepper, ground
Sea salt and black pepper to taste
¼ cup olive oil

2 tbsp balsamic vinegar
½ tbsp fresh rosemary, chopped
¼ small celery stalk, for decoration
½ tbsp sour cream

Directions

Mix half of the oil, balsamic vinegar, rosemary, salt, and pepper in a large bowl. Stir and submerge the shrimp into the mixture. Toss to coat and refrigerate for 20 minutes. Heat remaining olive oil in your Instant Pot on Sauté. Add in the shrimp, tomato, tomato paste, and cayenne pepper. Cook for 5 minutes. Remove to a bowl, cover, and set aside.

Pour the broth, Brussels sprouts, carrots, and okra in the pot. Sprinkle with salt and black pepper and seal the lid. Cook on High Pressure for 15 minutes. Then, do a quick release. Remove the vegetables and add shrimp in the remaining broth.

Seal the lid again and cook on Steam for 3 minutes on High. Do a quick release. Add in the cooked vegetables. Cook for 2-3 minutes on Sauté. Remove to a bowl. Top with sour cream and drizzle with shrimp marinade. Serve.

Spinach Shrimp Farfalle

Serves: 2-4 | Ready in about: 20 minutes

Ingredients

1¼ lb shrimp, peeled and deveined
1 tbsp melted butter
2 garlic cloves, minced

¼ cup white wine
10 oz farfalle
⅓ cup tomato puree

½ tsp red chili flakes
½ lemon, juiced and zested
10 oz spinach, torn

Directions

Set your Instant Pot to Sauté and pour in the white wine. Bring to simmer for 2 minutes to reduce the liquid by half. Stir in the farfalle, 1 cup water, salt, garlic, puréed tomato, shrimp, melted butter, and chili flakes. Seal the lid. Cook for 5 minutes on High Pressure. Do a quick release. Stir in lemon zest, juice, and spinach until wilted and soft. Serve.

Spanish Seafood Paella

Serves: 2-4 | Ready in about: 25 minutes

Ingredients

2 tbsp olive oil
1 onion, chopped
1 red bell pepper, diced
2 garlic cloves, minced

1 tsp paprika
1 tsp turmeric
½ cup Spanish rice
¼ cup frozen green peas

1 cup fish broth
1 lb frozen shrimp, peeled and deveined
2 tbsp fresh parsley, chopped
1 lemon, cut into wedges

Directions

Warm the olive oil in your Instant Pot on Sauté. Add in bell pepper, garlic, and onion and cook for 5 minutes until fragrant. Stir in paprika and turmeric and cook for 1 minute. Stir in fish broth and rice. Add shrimp to the rice mixture.

Seal the lid and cook on High Pressure for 5 minutes. Release the pressure quickly. Stir in green peas and let sit for 5 minutes until green peas are heated through. Serve garnished with parsley and lemon wedges.

Easy White Wine Mussels

Serves: 2-4 | Ready in about: 15 minutes

Ingredients

1 cup white wine
½ cup water

1 tsp garlic powder
1 lb mussels, cleaned and debearded

Juice from 1 lemon

Directions

In the pot, mix garlic powder, water, and wine. Put the mussels into the steamer basket, rounded-side should be placed facing upwards to fit as many as possible. Insert a rack into the cooker and lower steamer basket onto the rack.

Seal the lid and cook on Low Pressure for 1 minute. Release the pressure quickly. Remove unopened mussels. Coat the mussels with the wine mixture. Serve with a side of French fries or slices of toasted bread.

Pancetta & Mussel Chowder with Oyster Crackers

Serves: 2-4 | Ready in about: 20 minutes

Ingredients

20 oz canned mussels, drained, liquid reserved

2 cups low carb oyster crackers
2 tbsp olive oil
¼ cup grated pecorino romano cheese
½ tsp garlic powder
Salt and black pepper to taste

2 pancetta slices
2 celery stalks, chopped
1 medium onion, chopped
1 tbsp flour
¼ cup white wine

1 lb potatoes, peeled and cut chunks
1 tsp dried rosemary
1 bay leaf
1 ½ cups heavy cream
2 tbsp chopped fresh chervil

Directions

Set your Instant Pot to Sauté and fry the pancetta for 5 minutes, until crispy. Remove to a paper towel–lined plate and set aside. Sauté the celery and onion in the same fat for 1 minute, stirring, until the vegetables soften. Mix in the flour to coat the vegetables. Pour in the wine and cook until it is reduced by about one-third. Pour in 1 cup of water and mussel liquid.

Stir in potatoes, salt, rosemary, and bay leaf. Seal the lid and cook on High Pressure for 4 minutes. Do a natural pressure release for 10 minutes. Stir in the mussels and heavy cream. Press Sauté and bring the soup to a simmer to heat the mussels through. Discard the bay leaf. Crumble the pancetta over the top. Garnish with the chervil and crackers on the side.

Spicy Penne with Seafood

Serves: 2-4 | Ready in about: 20 minutes

Ingredients

1 tbsp olive oil
1 onion, diced
16 oz penne

24 oz arrabbiata sauce
3 cups chicken broth
Salt and black pepper to taste

16 oz scallops
¼ cup parmesan cheese, grated
Basil leaves for garnish

Directions

Heat oil on Sauté and stir-fry onion for 5 minutes. Add the garlic and cook until fragrant, for about 1 minute. Stir in penne, arrabbiata sauce, and 2 cups of broth. Season with black pepper and salt. Seal the lid and cook for 6 minutes on High.

Do a quick release. Remove to a plate. Pour the remaining broth and add scallops. Stir to coat, seal the lid and cook on High Pressure for 4 minutes. Do a quick release. Mix in the pasta and serve topped with parmesan cheese and basil leaves.

Collard Greens Octopus & Shrimp

Serves: 2-4 | Ready in about: 35 minutes

Ingredients

1 lb collard greens, chopped
1 lb shrimp, whole
6 oz octopus, cut into bite-sized pieces

1 large tomato, peeled, chopped
3 cups fish stock
4 tbsp olive oil

3 garlic cloves
2 tbsp fresh parsley, chopped
1 tsp sea salt

Directions

Place shrimp and octopus in the pot. Add tomato and fish stock. Seal the lid and cook on High Pressure for 15 minutes. Do a quick release. Remove shrimp and octopus, drain the liquid. Heat olive oil on Sauté and add garlic and parsley. Stir-fry for 3 minutes. Add collard greens and simmer for 5 minutes. Season with salt. Serve with shrimp and octopus.

Tasty Steamed Sea Bream

Serves: 2-4 | Ready in about: 50 minutes

Ingredients

2 pieces sea bream (2 lb), cleaned
¼ cup freshly squeezed lemon juice
1 tbsp fresh thyme sprigs

1 tbsp Italian seasoning mix
½ tsp sea salt
1 tsp garlic powder

4 cups fish stock
¼ cup olive oil

Directions

In a bowl, mix oil, lemon juice, thyme, Italian seasoning, sea salt, and garlic powder. Brush onto fish and wrap tightly with a plastic foil. Refrigerate for 30 minutes. Pour fish stock in your Instant Pot. Set the steamer rack and place the fish on top.

Seal the lid. Cook on Steam mode for 8 minutes on High. Do a quick release, open the lid, and unwrap the fish. Serve immediately with steam vegetables.

Clam & Prawn Paella

Serves: 2-4 | Ready in about: 30 minutes

Ingredients

2 tbsp olive oil
1 onion, chopped
2 garlic cloves, minced
½ cup dry white wine

½ cup Spanish rice
1 cup chicken stock
1 tsp turmeric powder
Salt and black pepper to taste

½ lb small clams, scrubbed
1 lb fresh prawns, peeled and deveined
1 red bell pepper, diced
1 lemon, cut into wedges

Directions

Heat 1 tbsp of the olive oil in your Instant Pot on Sauté. Fry the onion and garlic for 3 minutes. Pour in wine, scraping the bottom of the pot of any brown. Cook for 2 minutes until the wine is reduced by half. Add in rice and stock. Season with turmeric, salt, and pepper. Seal the lid and cook on High Pressure for 18 minutes. Do a quick release. Remove to a plate. Wwipe the pot clean. Heat the remaining oil on Sauté. Cook clams and prawns for 6 minutes, until the clams have opened and the shrimp are pink. Discard unopened clams. Arrange seafood and lemon wedges over paella to serve.

Asparagus & Broccoli Crabmeat Pilaf

Serves: 2-4 | Ready in about: 20 minutes

Ingredients

½ lb asparagus, trimmed and chopped
½ lb broccoli florets
Salt to taste

2 tbsp olive oil
1 small onion, chopped
1 cup rice

⅓ cup white wine
3 cups vegetable stock
8 oz lump crabmeat

Directions

Heat oil in your Instant Pot on Sauté. Cook onion for 3 minutes. Stir in rice for 1 minute. Pour in the wine. Cook for 2 to 3 minutes, stirring until the liquid has almost evaporated. Add vegetable stock and salt; stir to combine. Place a trivet atop.

Arrange the broccoli and asparagus on the trivet. Seal the lid and cook on High Pressure for 8 minutes. Do a quick release. Remove the vegetables to a bowl. Fluff the rice with a fork and add in the crabmeat, heat for a minute. Taste and adjust the seasoning. Serve immediately topped with broccoli and asparagus.

Hot Shrimp & Potato Chowder

Serves: 2-4 | Ready in about: 20 minutes

Ingredients

4 slices pancetta, chopped
4 tbsp minced garlic
1 onion, chopped
2 potatoes, chopped

16 oz canned corn kernels
4 cups vegetable stock
1 tsp dried rosemary
Salt and black pepper to taste

1 lb jumbo shrimp, peeled, deveined
1 tbsp olive oil
½ tsp red chili flakes
¾ cup heavy cream

Directions

Set your Instant Pot to Sauté. Fry the pancetta for 5 minutes until crispy; set aside. Add 2 tbsp of garlic and onion in the pot and stir-fry for 3 minutes. Add in potatoes, corn, stock, rosemary, salt, and pepper. Seal the lid and cook on High Pressure for 10 minutes. Do a quick pressure release. Remove to a serving bowl.

In a bowl, toss the shrimp in the remaining garlic, salt, pepper, oil, and flakes. Wipe the pot clean and fry shrimp for 5 minutes until pink. Mix in heavy cream and cook for 2 minutes. Add in shrimp, garnish with the pancetta, and serve.

Seafood Squid Ink Pasta

Serves: 2-4 | Ready in about: 30 minutes

Ingredients

1 lb fresh seafood mix
2 tbsp olive oil
4 garlic cloves, crushed

1 tbsp fresh parsley, chopped
1 tsp fresh rosemary, chopped
½ tbsp white wine

1 tsp salt
1 lb squid ink pasta

Directions

Heat the olive oil in your Instant Pot on Sauté. Stir-fry the garlic for 1 minute until fragrant. Stir in seafood, parsley, rosemary, and salt. Add in the white wine, squid link pasta, and 4 cups of water. Seal the lid and cook on High Pressure for 4 minutes. When ready, do a quick pressure release. Serve hot.

Andouille Sausage Shrimp Gumbo

Serves: 2-4 | Ready in about: 25 minutes

Ingredients

1 lb jumbo shrimp
¼ cup olive oil
⅓ cup flour
1 tsp Cajun seasoning

1 onion, chopped
1 cup red bell pepper, chopped
1 celery stalk, chopped
2 garlic cloves, minced

1 serrano pepper, seeded and minced
4 cups chicken broth
6 oz andouille sausage, sliced
2 green onions, finely sliced

Directions

Heat the olive oil in your Instant Pot on Sauté. Stir in the flour and cook 3 minutes, stirring constantly. Add in Cajun seasoning, onion, bell pepper, celery, garlic, and serrano pepper and cook for about 5 minutes. Pour in the chicken broth.

Add in andouille sausage. Seal and cook for 6 minutes on High Pressure. Do a natural pressure for 10 minutes. Stir in the shrimp for 3 minutes. Adjust the seasoning. Ladle the gumbo into bowls and garnish with the green onions.

Mustard Rice & Marinated Smelt

Serves: 2-4 | Ready in about: 35 minutes

Ingredients

1 lb fresh smelt, cleaned, heads removed
1 cup extra virgin olive oil
½ cup freshly squeezed lemon juice
¼ cup freshly squeezed orange juice
1 tbsp Dijon mustard

1 tsp fresh rosemary, finely chopped
2 garlic cloves, crushed
1 tsp sea salt
½ tbsp rice
5 oz okra

1 carrot, chopped
¼ cup green peas, soaked overnight
5 oz cherry tomatoes, halved
4 tbsp vegetable oil
2 cups fish stock

Directions

In a bowl, mix oil, juices, dijon, garlic, salt, and rosemary. Stir well and submerge fish in this mixture. Refrigerate for 1 hour.

Meanwhile, heat oil on Sauté and stir-fry carrot, peas, cherry tomatoes, and okra, for 10 minutes. Add rice and fish stock.

Seal the lid and cook on Rice for 8 minutes on High. Do a quick release and add in the fish along with half of the marinade. Seal the lid again and cook on Steam for 4 minutes on High. Release the pressure naturally for 10 minutes. Serve immediately.

Mussels & Anchovy with Rice

Serves: 2-4 | Ready in about: 40 minutes

Ingredients

1 cup rice
6 oz mussels
1 onion, finely chopped

1 garlic clove, crushed
1 tbsp dried rosemary
¼ cup capers

Salt and chili pepper to taste
2 tbsp olive oil
2 anchovies

Directions

Add rice to the pot and pour 2 cups of water. Seal the lid and cook on Rice mode for 8 minutes on High. Do a quick release. Remove the rice and set aside. Grease the pot with oil, and stir-fry garlic and onions, for 2 minutes, on Sauté. Add mussels and rosemary. Cook for 10 more minutes. Stir in rice and season with salt and chili pepper. Serve with anchovies and capers.

Seafood with Garlic & Brown Rice

Serves: 2-4 | Ready in about: 30 minutes

Ingredients

1 lb frozen seafood mix
1 cup brown rice
1 tbsp calamari ink

2 tbsp extra virgin olive oil
2 garlic cloves, crushed
1 tbsp chopped rosemary

½ tsp salt
3 cups fish stock
Freshly squeezed lemon juice

Directions

Add in all ingredients, Seal the lid and cook on Rice mode for 10 minutes on High. Release the pressure naturally for 10 minutes. Squeeze lemon juice and serve.

SNACKS & APPETIZERS

Mushroom & Gouda Cheese Pizza

Serves: 2 | Ready in about: 25 minutes

Ingredients

¾ cup all-purpose flour
1 cup whole wheat flour
½ tsp brown sugar
1 tsp garlic powder

2 tsp dried yeast
¼ tsp salt
1 tbsp olive oil
1 cup lukewarm water

1 cup button mushrooms, sliced
¼ cup gouda cheese, grated
2 tbsp tomato paste, sugar-free
½ tsp dried oregano

Directions

In a bowl fitted with a dough hook attachment, combine all-purpose flour with whole wheat flour, brown sugar, dried yeast, and salt and mix well. Gradually add lukewarm water and oil. Continue to beat on high speed until smooth dough. Transfer to a lightly floured surface and knead until smooth. Form into a tight ball and wrap with plastic foil. Let sit for 1 hour.

Roll out the dough with a rolling pin and transfer to a lined with parchment paper baking dish. Brush with tomato paste and sprinkle with oregano, gouda, and mushrooms. Add a trivet inside the pot and pour in 1 cup water. Seal the lid, and cook for 15 minutes on High Pressure. Do a quick release. Remove the pizza from the pot using a parchment paper. Cut and serve.

Mac & Cheese with Greek Yogurt

Serves: 2 | Ready in about: 15 minutes

Ingredients

8 oz elbow macaroni
½ tsp mustard powder
1 tbsp butter

1 tsp cayenne pepper
1 cup milk
¼ cup Greek yogurt

1 ½ cups cheddar cheese, shredded
¼ cup Parmesan cheese, grated
Salt to taste

Directions

Place the macaroni and salt in your Instant Pot and cover with water. Seal the lid, select Manual, and cook for 4 minutes on High. When done, perform a quick pressure release. Drain the pasta and return to the pot. Mix in the milk, mustard powder, butter, cayenne pepper, Greek yogurt, and the cheeses. Stir for 1 minute until the cheeses melt. Serve.

Turkey Meatballs with Tomato Sauce

Serves: 2 | Ready in about: 50 minutes

Ingredients

½ lb ground turkey
½ carrot, shredded
½ celery stalk, minced
2 tbsp cotija queso, crumbled

1 tbsp hot sauce
¼ cup bread crumbs
1 egg, beaten
1 tbsp olive oil

¼ cup water
1 tomato, chopped
Salt and pepper to taste
1 tsp fresh basil, chopped

Directions

In a bowl, combine turkey, carrot, celery, cotija cheese, hot sauce, breadcrumbs, and egg. Season with salt and pepper. Shape the mixture into 12 meatballs. Heat oil on Sauté and fry the meatballs in batches until lightly golden. Pour in water, tomatoes, and salt. Seal the lid and cook on High Pressure for 5 minutes. Do a quick release. Sprinkle with basil and serve.

Baba Ganoush with Nachos

Serves: 2 | Ready in about: 20 minutes

Ingredients

1 lb eggplants, sliced
¼ cup olive oil
2 tbsp tahini

1 garlic clove
1 ¼ tbsp lemon juice
1 tsp parsley, chopped

Salt and black pepper to taste
Nacho Tortilla Chips

Directions

Pour 1 cup of water into your Instant Pot and fit in a trivet. Place the eggplants on the trivet. Seal the lid, select Steam on High, and cook for 6 minutes. When done, do a quick pressure release. In a food processor, blend the eggplants and the remaining ingredients, except for the parsley, until smooth. Season to taste and sprinkle with parsley. Serve with tortilla chips.

Sticky Chicken Wings

Serves: 2 | Ready in about: 30 minutes

Ingredients

½ tbsp honey
½ cup teriyaki sauce

1 lb chicken wings
1 tbsp cornstarch

1 tbsp cold water
½ tsp sesame seeds

Directions

In the pot, combine honey and teriyaki sauce until the honey dissolves completely. Toss in chicken to coat. Seal the lid, press Poultry, and cook for 10 minutes on High. Release the pressure quickly. Transfer chicken to a platter.

Mix cold water with the cornstarch. Press Sauté, stir cornstarch slurry into the sauce, and cook for 4 to 6 minutes until thickened. Top the chicken with the sauce. Add a garnish of sesame seeds.

Cheesy Rice Balls

Serves: 2 | Ready in about: 60 minutes

Ingredients

1 ½ tbsp olive oil
½ white onion, diced
1 garlic clove, minced
2 cups chicken stock

¼ cup apple cider vinegar
½ cup short grain rice
½ cups grated cheddar cheese
1 tbsp grated Parmesan cheese

½ cup canned sweet corn, drained
Salt and black pepper to taste
1 cup fresh bread crumbs
1 egg, beaten

Directions

On Sauté, heat ½ tbsp of oil and Sauté onion for 2 minutes until translucent. Add the garlic and cook for a minute. Stir in the stock and rice. Seal the lid and cook on High Pressure for 7 minutes. Do a natural pressure release for 10 minutes. Stir in cheddar cheese, corn, salt, and pepper. Spoon into a bowl and let cool completely. Wipe clean the pot.

Form balls out of the rice mixture. Dip each into the beaten egg and coat in the breadcrumb mixture. Heat remaining oil on Sauté and fry arancini until crispy and golden brown. Sprinkle with Parmesan cheese and serve.

Paprika Chicken Wings

Serves: 2 | Ready in about: 15 minutes

Ingredients

1 lb chicken wings
2 tbsp olive oil
2 garlic cloves, crushed

Salt and white pepper to taste
1 tsp paprika
½ tbsp fresh thyme, chopped

1 tbsp freshly grated ginger
2 tbsp lime juice
1 tbsp apple cider vinegar

Directions

In a bowl, mix olive oil, garlic, thyme, white pepper, paprika, ginger, lime juice, and apple cider vinegar. Submerge wings into the mixture and cover. Refrigerate for one hour. Remove the wings from the marinade and pat dry.

In your Instant Pot, insert a steaming rack and add in 1 cup of water. Place the chicken on the rack. Seal the lid and cook on High Pressure for 8 minutes. Release the steam naturally for about 10 minutes. Serve.

Dill Duo-Cheese Spinach Tart

Serves: 2-4 | Ready in about: 30 minutes

Ingredients

1 lb spinach, chopped
½ cup mascarpone cheese
½ cup feta cheese, shredded

3 eggs, beaten
½ cup goat's cheese
3 tbsp butter

½ cup milk
1 pack (6 sheets) pie dough
1 tbsp olive oil

Directions

In a bowl, mix spinach, eggs, mascarpone, feta, and goat cheese. Dust a clean surface with flour and unfold the pie sheets onto it. Using a rolling pin, roll the dough to fit your Instant Pot. Repeat with the other five sheets. Combine milk and butter in a skillet. Bring it to a boil and melt the butter completely. Remove from the heat. Grease a baking pan with oil.

Place in 2 pie sheets and brush with milk mixture. Make the first layer of spinach mixture and cover with another two pie sheets. Again, brush with butter and milk mixture, and repeat until you have used all ingredients.

Pour 1 cup water in your Instant Pot and insert a trivet. Lower the pan on the trivet and seal the lid. Cook on High Pressure for 6 minutes. Do a quick release. Place parchment paper under the pie to use it as a lifting method to remove the pie. Serve cold.

Pickled Cucumbers

Serves: 2 | Ready in about: 5 minutes

Ingredients

1 cucumber, sliced
1 cup white vinegar
1/8 cup green garlic, minced
1 tbsp dill pickle seasoning
½ tsp salt
¼ tsp cumin

Directions

Into the pot, add cucumber, vinegar, sugar, cumin, dill pickle seasoning, salt, and ½ cup water. Stir well to dissolve the sugar. Seal the lid and cook for 4 minutes on High Pressure. Release the pressure quickly. Spoon into a large storage container and pour cooking liquid over. Chill for one hour.

Prosciutto & Beef with Horseradish Sauce

Serves: 2 | Ready in about: 40 minutes

Ingredients

½ lb beef fillets, center-cut
½ small onion, finely chopped
1 tbsp horseradish sauce
1 tbsp butter
⅓ cup red wine
1 cup beef stock
2 oz prosciutto, chopped
Salt and black pepper to taste

Directions

Melt butter in your Instant Pot on Sauté and stir-fry the onion for 2 minutes. Add in the beef and brown it on both sides for 6 minutes; season. Pour in the wine and stock. Seal the lid and cook on High Pressure for 30 minutes. Do a quick release and remove the fillets to a platter. In a saucepan, mix horseradish sauce with prosciutto. Warm-up and drizzle over the meat.

Parmesan & Garlic Leeks

Serves: 2 | Ready in about: 15 minutes

Ingredients

3 leeks, cut into 2-inches long pieces
2 garlic cloves, crushed
1 tsp sea salt
¼ cup extra virgin olive oil
3 tbsp freshly squeezed lemon juice
½ cup Parmesan cheese, grated

Directions

Pour 1 cup of water in your Instant Pot and insert the trivet. In a baking pan, combine leeks, oil, garlic, and salt. Lower the pan on the trivet. Cook on High Pressure for 3 minutes. Do a quick pressure release. Transfer to a plate and sprinkle with freshly squeezed lemon juice and Parmesan cheese. Serve.

Avocado Chicken Dip

Serves: 2-4 | Ready in about: 25 minutes

Ingredients

2 chicken breasts, boneless and skinless
¼ cup chicken broth
Salt and black pepper to taste
1 large avocado, peeled and diced
1 shallot, finely chopped
2 tbsp chopped cilantro
1 tbsp lemon juice
2 tbsp sour cream
½ tsp garlic powder
¼ tsp cumin powder
¼ tsp hot sauce

Directions

Add chicken, broth, salt, and pepper to your Instant Pot and. Seal the lid, select Manual on High, and cook for 10 minutes. After cooking, perform a quick pressure release, and unlock the lid. Using two forks, shred chicken into small strands.

Add avocado, shallot, cilantro, lemon juice, sour cream, garlic powder, cumin powder, hot sauce, salt, and black pepper. Stir ingredients until well-combined. Adjust taste and spoon food into serving bowls. Serve with pretzel chips.

Buttered Hot Chicken Wings

Serves: 2 | Ready in about: 25 minutes

Ingredients

4 chicken wings
¼ cup cayenne hot pepper sauce
1 ½ tbsp oil
3 tbsp butter
1 ½ tbsp Worcestershire sauce
½ tsp tabasco
½ tsp salt
2 cups chicken broth

Directions

Pour broth, olive oil, and cayenne hot pepper sauce in your Instant Pot. Seal the lid and cook on Poultry for 15 minutes on High. Do a quick release and remove the wings from broth; set aside. In the pot, melt the butter on Sauté on High. Brown the wings for 3-4 minutes, turning once. Add the Worcestershire sauce and tabasco. Stir and remove from heat. Serve hot.

Baked Turnips with Cheese

Serves: 2-4 | Ready in about: 20 minutes

Ingredients

4 small turnips, scrubbed clean
¼ cup whipping cream
¼ cup sour cream
½ cup chopped roasted red bell peppers
1 tsp Italian seasoning mix
1½ cups shredded Monterey Jack cheese
4 green onions, chopped
⅓ cup grated Parmesan cheese

Directions

Pour 1 cup of water into the pot and insert a trivet. Place the turnips on top. Seal the lid and cook on High and for 10 minutes. Do a quick pressure release. Remove the turnips to a cutting board and allow cooling. Cut the turnips in half. Scoop out the pulp into a bowl, mix in the whipping cream and sour cream using a potato mash until smooth.

Stir in bell peppers, Cajun seasoning, and Monterey Jack. Fetch out 2 tbsp green onions and stir the remaining into the turnips. Fill the turnip skins with the mashed mixture and sprinkle with Parmesan cheese. Arrange on a greased baking dish and place it on the trivet. Seal the lid and cook on High for 3 minutes. Do a quick pressure release. Garnish with the remaining onions.

Rosemary Beef Meatballs with Yogurt Dip

Serves: 2-4 | Ready in about: 35 minutes

Ingredients

1 lb ground beef
3 garlic cloves, crushed
¼ cup flour
1 tbsp fresh rosemary, crushed
1 egg, beaten
½ tsp salt
3 tbsp olive oil
1 cup Greek yogurt
2 tbsp fresh dill

Directions

In a bowl, mix ground beef, half of the garlic, rosemary, egg, and salt. Lightly dampen hands and shape into balls. Grease the Instant Pot with oil. Transfer the balls to the pot. Add 1 cup of water. Seal the lid and cook on High Pressure for 13 minutes. Do a quick release. Mix Greek yogurt, dill, and remaining garlic. Stir well and drizzle over meatballs.

Herby Garlic Shrimp

Serves: 2-4 | Ready in about: 15 minutes

Ingredients

1 lb shrimp, whole
½ cup olive oil
1 tsp garlic powder
1 tsp dried rosemary, crushed
1 tsp dried thyme
½ tsp dried basil
½ tsp dried sage
½ tsp salt
1 tsp chili pepper

Directions

Pour 1 ½ cups of water in the inner pot. In a bowl, mix oil, garlic, rosemary, thyme, basil, sage, salt, and chili. Brush the marinade over the shrimp. Insert the steamer rack, and arrange the shrimp on top. Seal the lid and cook on Steam for 3 minutes on High. Release the steam naturally for 10 minutes. Press Sauté and stir-fry for 2 minutes, or until golden brown.

Cheese & Turkey Pepperoni Pizza

Serves: 2-4 | Ready in about: 25 minutes

Ingredients

1 whole-wheat Italian pizza crust
1 cup fire-roasted tomatoes, diced
1 tsp oregano
½ cup turkey pepperoni, chopped
7 oz gouda cheese, grated
2 tbsp olive oil

Directions

Grease a baking pan with oil. Line some parchment paper and place the pizza crust in it. Spread the fire-roasted tomatoes over the pizza crust and sprinkle with oregano and basil. Make a layer with cheese and top with pepperoni.

Add a trivet inside the pot and pour in 1 cup of water. Seal the lid, and cook for 15 minutes on High Pressure. Do a quick release. Remove the pizza from the pot using a parchment paper.

Easy Vegan Green Dip

Serves: 2-4 | Ready in about: 20 minutes

Ingredients

10 oz canned green chiles, drained, liquid reserved

2 cups broccoli florets | ¼ cup raw cashews | ½ tsp sea salt
¾ cup green bell peppers, chopped | 2 tbsp soy sauce | ¼ tsp chili powder

Directions

In your Instant Pot, add cashews, broccoli, green bell peppers, and 1 cup water. Seal the lid and cook for 5 minutes on High Pressure. Release the pressure quickly. Drain water from the pot.

Add reserved liquid from canned green chilies, salt, garlic powder, chili powder, soy sauce, and cumin. Use an immersion blender to blend the mixture until smooth. Set aside in a mixing bowl. Stir chilies through the dip.

Delicious Beef Meatballs

Serves: 2-4 | Ready in about: 20 minutes

Ingredients

1 lb ground beef | 1 tbsp Italian seasoning mix | 2 wheat bread slices
2 tbsp milk | 1 onion, chopped | Salt and black pepper to taste
3 tbsp oil | 2 eggs

Directions

Place two slices of bread in a bowl. Add ¼ cup water and let soak for 5 minutes. Mix the ground beef, milk, oil, Italian seasoning mix, onion, eggs, salt, and pepper. Add soaked bread and shape balls with an approximately ¼ cup of the mixture.

Flatten each ball with hand and place it on a lightly floured surface. Grease the stainless steel insert with oil. Add the meatballs to the Instant Pot and fry for 3 minutes per side, on Sauté. Serve immediately with garlic sauce.

Turkey Lettuce Cups

Serves: 2-4 | Ready in about: 45 minutes

Ingredients

¾ cup olive oil | 1 cup coconut milk | 1 lb turkey breast, cut into strips
4 cloves garlic, minced | 3 tbsp rice wine vinegar | 1 romaine lettuce, leaves separated
3 tbsp maple syrup | 3 tbsp soy sauce | ⅓ cup chopped peanuts
2 tbsp pineapple juice | 1 tbsp Thai-style chili paste | ¼ cup chopped fresh cilantro leaves

Directions

In the pot, mix peanut butter, garlic, rice wine vinegar, soy sauce, pineapple juice, honey, coconut milk, and chili paste until smooth; add turkey strips and ensure they are submerged in the sauce. Seal the lid and cook on High Pressure for 12 minutes. Release the pressure quickly. Place the turkey at the center of each lettuce leaf. Top with cilantro and chopped peanuts.

Sriracha Chicken Wings

Serves: 2-4 | Ready in about: 30 minutes

Ingredients

½ cup sriracha sauce | 2 tbsp butter, melted | 2 lb chicken vignettes
¼ cup ranch salad dressing mix | Juice from ½ lemon | ½ tsp paprika

Directions

Mix the chicken, sriracha, butter, lemon, and 1 cup water in your Instant Pot. Seal the lid and cook on High Pressure for 5 min minutes. Do a quick pressure release. Serve with the paprika and ranch dressing. Serve.

Beef Pie

Makes 4-6 servings | Ready in about: 35 minutes

Ingredients

1 lb lean ground beef | 1 (16 oz) pack pie dough | 1 tbsp sour cream
Salt and black pepper to taste | ½ tbsp butter, melted | 3 cups liquid yogurt

Directions

In a bowl, mix beef, salt, and pepper, until fully incorporated. Lay a sheet of dough on a flat surface and brush with melted butter. Line with the meat mixture and roll-up. Repeat the process until you have used all the ingredients.

Grease a baking dish and carefully place the rolls inside. In your Instant Pot, Pour in 1 ½ cups of water and place the trivet. Lay the baking dish on the trivet. Seal the lid and cook on High Pressure for 15 minutes. Do a quick pressure release, and transfer the pie to a serving plate. Mix sour cream and yogurt. Spread the mixture over the pie and serve cold.

Spinach Tarts with Camembert

Serves: 2-4 | Ready in about: 45 minutes

Ingredients

2 tbsp butter
1 small white onion, sliced
2 cups spinach, chopped

Salt and black pepper to taste
¼ cup dry white wine
1 pie pastry, thawed

1 cup Camembert cheese, cubed
1 tbsp thinly sliced fresh green onions

Directions

Melt 1 tbsp of butter on Sauté and cook onion and spinach for 5 minutes, or until tender. Season with salt and black pepper, then pour in white wine and cook until evaporated, about 2 minutes. Set aside.

Unwrap the pie pastry and cut into 4 squares. Prink the dough with a fork and brush both sides with the remaining butter. Share half of the cheese over the pie pastry squares. Cover with the spinach and top with the remaining cheese.

Arrange the tarts in a buttered baking dish. Pour 1 cup of water in the pot. Insert a trivet and lower the baking dish on top. Seal the lid and cook on High Pressure for 30 minutes. Do a quick release. Serve with green onions.

Pizza Quatro Formaggi

Serves: 2-4 | Ready in about: 25 minutes

Ingredients

1 pizza crust
½ cup tomato paste
1 tsp dried oregano

1 oz cheddar cheese
5-6 slices mozzarella
¼ cup grated gouda

¼ cup grated Parmesan cheese
½ cup grated gouda cheese
2 tbsp olive oil

Directions

Grease the bottom of a baking dish with 1 tbsp of olive oil. Line some parchment paper. Flour the working surface and roll out the pizza dough to the approximate size of your Instant Pot. Fit the dough in the baking dish.

In a small bowl, combine tomato paste with ¼ cup water and oregano. Spread the mixture over the dough and finish with cheeses. Add a trivet inside your the pot and pour in 1 cup of water. Seal the lid, and cook for 15 minutes on High Pressure. Do a quick release. Remove the pizza from the pot using a parchment paper. Cut and serve.

Brunch Burrito Bowls

Serves: 2-4 | Ready in about: 30 minutes

Ingredients

2 tbsp olive oil
1 onion, chopped
2 garlic cloves, minced
1 tbsp chili powder
2 tsp ground cumin
2 tsp paprika

Salt and black pepper to taste
¼ tsp cayenne pepper
1 cup quinoa, rinsed
1 (14.5-oz) can diced tomatoes
1 (14.5-oz) can black beans
1 ½ cups vegetable stock

1 cup frozen corn kernels
2 tbsp chopped cilantro
1 tbsp roughly chopped fresh coriander
Cheddar cheese, grated for garnish
1 avocado, chopped

Directions

Warm the olive oil in your Instant Pot on Sauté. Add in onion and stir-fry for 3 to 5 minutes until fragrant. Add garlic and sauté for 1 more minute until soft and golden brown. Add in chili powder, paprika, cayenne pepper, salt, cumin, and black pepper.

Cook for 1 minute until spices are soft. Pour quinoa into onion and spice mixture and stir to coat quinoa completely in spices. Add diced tomatoes, black beans, vegetable stock, and corn; stir to combine.

Seal the lid and cook for 7 minutes on High Pressure. Release the pressure quickly. Open the lid and let sit for 6 minutes until flavors combine. Use a fork to fluff quinoa and season with pepper and salt. Stir in cilantro and divide into plates. Top with cheese and avocado slices.

MEATLESS RECIPES

Carrot Soup

Serves: 2 | Ready in about: 25 minutes

Ingredients

2 tbsp butter
1 large red onion, diced
6 large carrots, peeled and chopped

2 cups lemongrass, chopped
2 tsp ginger puree
3 cups chicken broth

1 cup coconut cream
Salt to taste
4 basil leaves, chopped

Directions

Set your Instant Pot to Sauté. Melt butter and sauté onion, carrots, and lemongrass until softened, 5 minutes. Stir in ginger and pour in chicken broth. Seal the lid, select Manual/Pressure Cook on High, and set the cooking time to 1 minute.

After cooking, do a natural pressure release for 10 minutes. Unlock the lid, add coconut cream, and using an immersion blender, puree ingredients until smooth. Season with salt. Spoon soup into serving bowls and garnish with basil. Serve warm.

Veggie Quinoa Bowls with Pesto

Serves: 2 | Ready in about: 30 minutes

Ingredients

1 cup quinoa, rinsed
Salt and black pepper to taste
1 small beet, peeled and cubed

1 cup broccoli florets
1 carrot, peeled and chopped
½ lb Brussels sprouts

2 eggs
1 avocado, chopped
¼ cup pesto sauce

Directions

In your Instant Pot, mix 2 cups water, salt, quinoa, and pepper. Set trivet over quinoa and set steamer basket on top. To the steamer basket, add eggs, Brussels sprouts, broccoli, beet cubes, carrot, pepper, and salt. Seal the lid and cook for 1 minute on High Pressure. Release pressure naturally for 10 minutes. Remove steamer basket and trivet from the pot.

Set the eggs to a bowl of ice water. Peel and halve the eggs. Use a fork to fluff the quinoa. Divide quinoa, broccoli, avocado, carrots, beet, Brussels sprouts, and eggs between two bowls and top with a dollop of pesto. Serve.

Spinach Mashed Potatoes

Serves: 2 | Ready in about: 30 minutes

Ingredients

4 potatoes, quartered
Salt and black pepper to taste

2 tbsp milk
2 tbsp butter

½ tbsp chopped fresh chives
½ cup spinach, chopped

Directions

In the cooker, cover the potatoes with salted water. Seal the lid and cook on High Pressure for 8 minutes. Release the pressure quickly. Drain the potatoes and reserve the liquid in a bowl. In a bowl, mash the potatoes. Mix in butter and milk; season.

With reserved cooking liquid, thin the potatoes to attain the desired consistency. Put the spinach in the remaining potato liquid and stir until wilted. Drain and serve with potato mash. Garnish with chives.

Farro & Braised Greens

Serves: 2 | Ready in about: 15 minutes

Ingredients

2 oz kale, chopped
2 oz spinach, chopped
2 oz collard greens, chopped

1 oz Swiss chard, chopped
⅓ medium-sized leek, chopped
½ cup farro

1 tbsp olive oil
2 cups vegetable broth
⅓ tsp sea salt

Directions

In the Instant Pot, pour farro and vegetable broth. Season with salt and seal the lid. Cook on Rice mode for 9 minutes on High. Do a quick release and open the lid. Remove farro and wipe the pot clean.

Pour 1 cup water, insert the steamer basket and place the chopped greens on the basket. Seal the lid. Cook on Steam mode for 2 minutes on High. Do a quick release and remove the greens to a large bowl. Toss in farro and drizzle with olive oil to serve.

Vegan Indian Curry

Serves: 2 | Ready in about: 25 minutes

Ingredients

1 tbsp vegan butter
½ onion, chopped
2 cloves garlic, minced
½ tsp ginger, grated
½ tsp ground cumin

½ tsp red chili powder
½ tsp salt
½ tsp ground turmeric
1 cup canned chickpeas, drained
1 tomato, diced

⅓ cup water
5 cups collard greens, chopped
½ tsp garam masala
1 tsp lemon juice

Directions

Melt butter on Sauté. Toss in the onion to coat. Seal the lid and cook for 2 minutes until soft. Mix in ginger, cumin powder, turmeric, red chili powder, garlic, and salt and cook for 30 seconds until crispy. Stir in tomatoes. Into the cooker, mix in ⅓ water, tomato, and chickpeas. Seal the lid and cook on High Pressure for 4 minutes. Release the pressure quickly. Press Sauté.

Into the chickpea mixture, stir in lemon juice, collard greens, and garam masala, until well coated. Cook for 2 to 3 minutes until collard greens wilt on Sauté. Serve over rice or naan.

Parsnips & Cauliflower Mash

Serves: 2 | Ready in about: 15 minutes

Ingredients

½ lb parsnips, peeled and cubed
¼ head cauliflower, cut into florets
1 garlic cloves

Salt and black pepper to taste
2 tbsp sour cream
2 tbsp grated Parmesan cheese

½ tbsp butter
½ tbsp minced chives

Directions

In your Instant Pot, mix parsnips, garlic, ½ cup water, salt, cauliflower, and pepper. Seal the lid and cook on High Pressure for 4 minutes. Release the pressure quickly. Drain parsnips and cauliflower and return to pot.

Add Parmesan, butter, and sour cream. Use a potato masher to mash until the desired consistency is attained. Into the mashed parsnip, add half of the chives, and place to a serving plate. Garnish with remaining chives and.

Stuffed Potatoes with Feta

Serves: 2 | Ready in about: 60 minutes

Ingredients

4 whole potatoes, washed
2 tbsp olive oil
2 garlic cloves, crushed

¼ cup feta cheese
½ tsp fresh rosemary, chopped
½ tsp dried thyme

2 oz button mushrooms, chopped
½ tsp salt

Directions

Rub the potatoes with salt and place them in the Instant Pot. Add enough water to cover and seal the lid. Cook on High Pressure for 30 minutes. Do a quick release and remove the potatoes. Let chill for a while. Clean the pot.

Press Sauté and mix in olive oil, garlic, rosemary, thyme, and mushrooms. Sauté for 5 minutes. Remove from the cooker and stir in feta. Cut the top of each potato and spoon out the middle. Fill with cheese mixture and serve.

Gingered Palak Paneer

Serves: 2-4 | Ready in about: 20 minutes

Ingredients

¼ cup milk
2 tbsp butter
1 tsp cumin seeds
1 tsp coriander seeds

1 tomato, chopped
1 tsp minced fresh ginger
1 tsp minced fresh garlic
1 red onion, chopped

1 lb spinach, chopped
1 tsp salt, or to taste
2 cups paneer, cubed
1 tsp chili powder

Directions

Warm butter on Sauté. Add in garlic, cumin seeds, coriander, chili powder, ginger, and garlic and fry for 1 minute until fragrant. Add onion and cook for 2 minutes until crispy. Add in salt, 1 cup water, and spinach.

Seal the lid and cook for 1 minute on High Pressure. Release the pressure quickly. Add spinach mixture to a blender and blend to obtain a smooth paste. Mix paneer and tomato with spinach mixture.

Vegetarian Chipotle Stew

Serves: 2 | Ready in about: 45 minutes

Ingredients

½ cup canned diced tomatoes
⅓ cup cashews, chopped
¼ cup onions, chopped
¼ cup red lentils

¼ cup red quinoa
1 chipotle pepper, chopped
1 garlic clove, minced
½ tbsp chili powder

1 tsp salt
½ cup carrots, chopped
¼ cup canned black beans, rinsed
2 tbsp fresh parsley, chopped

Directions

In the pot, mix tomatoes, onion, chipotle pepper, chili powder, lentils, walnuts, carrots, quinoa, garlic, and salt. Stir in 1 cup water. Seal the lid, Press Soup/Stew, and cook for 30 minutes on High. Release the pressure quickly. Into the chili, add black beans and simmer on Sauté until heated through. Top with a garnish of parsley. Serve.

Chili Cauliflower & Pea Rice

Serves: 2 | Ready in about: 15 minutes

Ingredients

1 head cauliflower, cut into florets
2 tbsp olive oil

Salt to taste
1 tsp chili powder

¼ cup green peas
1 tbsp chopped fresh parsley

Directions

Add 1 cup water, set a rack over water, and place the steamer basket onto the rack. Add cauliflower into the steamer basket. Seal the lid and cook on High Pressure for 1 minute. Release the pressure quickly. Remove rack and steamer basket.

Drain water from the pot, pat dry, and return to pressure cooker base. Press Sauté and warm oil. Add in cauliflower and stir to break into smaller pieces. Stir in chili powder, peas, and salt. Garnish with parsley and serve.

Spinach Omelet with Potatoes

Serves: 2 | Ready in about: 30 minutes

Ingredients

4 eggs, beaten
1 cup spinach, torn, rinsed

1 potato, steamed and chopped
1 cup heavy cream

Salt and black pepper to taste
1 tbsp olive oil

Directions

In a bowl, mix eggs, heavy cream, and potato. Sprinkle with salt and pepper and stir to combine. Heat the olive oil in your Instant Pot on Sauté. Cook the spinach for 3-5 minutes until wilted. Remove the spinach to the egg mixture and stir well.

Transfer all to an oven-safe dish. Add 1 cup of water, insert a trivet, and place the oven-safe dish on top. Seal the lid and cook on High Pressure for 12 minutes. Release the steam naturally for 10 minutes. Serve.

Feta & Nut Green Beans

Serves: 2 | Ready in about: 15 minutes

Ingredients

Juice from ½ lemon
½ cup green beans, trimmed

⅓ cup chopped toasted pine nuts
⅓ cup feta cheese, crumbled

2 tbsp olive oil
Salt and black pepper to taste

Directions

Add 1 cup water and set the rack over the water and the steamer basket on the rack. Loosely heap green beans into the steamer basket. Seal lid and cook on High Pressure for 5 minutes. Release pressure quickly. Drop green beans into a salad bowl. Top with olive oil, feta cheese, pepper, and pine nuts. Serve.

Parmesan & Veggie Mash

Serves: 2 | Ready in about: 15 minutes

Ingredients

1 lb Yukon gold potato, chopped
½ cup cauliflower, broken into florets
⅓ carrot, chopped

⅓ cup Parmesan cheese, shredded
2 tbsp butter, melted
2 tbsp milk

Salt to taste
1 garlic clove, minced
1 tbsp fresh parsley, chopped

Directions

Into your Instant Pot, add veggies and salt and cover with enough water. Seal the lid and cook on High Pressure for 10 minutes. Release the pressure quickly. Drain the vegetables and mash them with a potato masher. Add garlic, butter, and milk, and whisk until everything is well incorporated. Serve topped with Parmesan cheese and chopped parsley.

Veggie Pilau Rice

Serves: 2-4 | Ready in about: 30 minutes

Ingredients

3 tbsp olive oil

1 tbsp ginger, minced

1 cup onion, chopped

1 cup green peas

1 cup carrot, chopped

1 cup mushroom, chopped

1 cup broccoli, chopped

1 tbsp chili powder

½ tbsp ground cumin

1 tsp garam masala

½ tsp turmeric powder

1 cup basmati rice, rinsed and drained

2 cups vegetable broth

1 tbsp lemon juice

2 tbsp chopped fresh cilantro

Directions

Warm 1 tbsp of tholive oil in your Instant Pot on Sauté. Add in onion and ginger and cook for 3 minutes until soft. Stir in broccoli, green peas, mushrooms, and carrots; cook for 1 more minute. Add turmeric powder, chili powder, garam masala, and cumin; cook for 1 minute until soft. Add ¼ cup water to deglaze; scrape the bottom to get rid of any browned bits.

To the vegetables, add the remaining water and rice. Seal the lid and cook for 1 minute on High Pressure. Release the pressure quickly. Use a fork to fluff rice, sprinkle with lemon juice. Divide into plates and garnish with cilantro.

Blue Cheese Spinach with Leeks

Serves: 2 | Ready in about: 10 minutes

Ingredients

9 oz fresh spinach

2 leeks, chopped

2 garlic cloves, crushed

½ cup blue cheese, crumbled

2 tbsp olive oil

1 tsp salt

Directions

Heat the olive oil in your Instant Pot on Sauté. Stir-fry leeks and garlic for about 5 minutes on Sauté. Add spinach and give it a good stir. Season with salt and cook for 3 more minutes, stirring constantly. Press Cancel, transfer to a serving dish, and sprinkle with blue cheese. Serve right away.

Vegan Green Peas

Serves: 2 | Ready in about: 35 minutes

Ingredients

1 cup green peas

1 tomato, roughly chopped

½ onion, peeled, chopped

1 carrot, peeled, chopped

1 potato, peeled, chopped

½ celery stalk, chopped

2 tbsp parsley, chopped

1 garlic clove, crushed

3 tbsp tomato sauce, canned

1 ½ tbsp olive oil

2 cups vegetable stock

Directions

Add all the ingredients in the Instant Pot and seal the lid. Cook on High Pressure for 15 minutes. Do a natural pressure release for 10 minutes. Serve warm.

Parmesan Lentil Spread

Serves: 2 | Ready in about: 15 minutes

Ingredients

½ cup lentils, rinsed

⅓ cup sweet corn

1 tomato, diced

1 tbsp tomato paste

½ tbsp Parmesan cheese, chopped

Salt and black pepper to taste

¼ tsp red pepper flakes

1 tbsp olive oil

2 tbsp red wine

Directions

Heat oil your Instant Pot on Sauté and add tomatoes, tomato paste, and 2 tbsp water. Sprinkle with salt and pepper and stir-fry for 5 minutes. Add in lentils, sweet corn, wine, and 1 cup water. Seal the lid. Cook on High Pressure for 10 minutes. Do a quick release. Set aside to cool completely and refrigerate for 30 minutes. Sprinkle with Parmesan cheese before serving.

Scallion & Cauliflower Rice

Serves: 2 | Ready in about: 20 minutes

Ingredients

2 tbsp olive oil

2 scallions, sliced

1 garlic clove, minced

2 cups cauliflower rice

Salt and black pepper to taste

¼ tsp hot sauce

Directions

Set your Instant Pot to Sauté and heat the oil. Place in the scallions and garlic and cook for 2-3 minutes, stirring often. Stir in cauliflower rice and butter. Cook for 7-8 minutes. Add in the hot sauce and mix well. Season with salt and pepper and serve.

Bean & Carrot Stew

Serves: 2 | Ready in about: 30 minutes

Ingredients

½ cup cranberry beans, soaked, rinsed

½ onion, chopped

1 carrot, chopped

1 tomato, peeled, diced

1 tbsp olive oil

½ tbsp fresh parsley, ch

Directions

Heat the olive oil in your Instant Pot on Sauté and stir-fry the onion for 3-4 minutes until translucent. Add carrot and tomato. Stir well and cook for 5 minutes. Stir in beans and ½ cup water. Seal the lid. Cook on High Pressure for 15 minutes. Do a quick release and serve hot sprinkled with fresh parsley. Serve.

Rice with Red Beans

Serves: 2-4 | Ready in about: 1 hour

Ingredients

1 cup red beans

½ cup rice

½ tsp cayenne pepper

1 ½ cups vegetable broth

1 onion, diced

1 red bell pepper, diced

1 stalk celery, diced

1 tbsp fresh thyme leaves

Salt and black pepper to taste

Directions

Add beans and water to cover about 1-inch. Seal the lid and cook for 1 minute on High Pressure. Release the pressure quickly. Drain the beans and set aside. Rinse and pat dry the inner pot. Return the inner pot to the cooker, add oil to the pot, and press Sauté. Add onion to the oil and Sauté for 3 minutes until soft. Add celery and pepper and cook for 1 to 2 minutes.

Add garlic and cook for 30 seconds until soft. Add the rice, return the beans back to the pot, and top with broth. Stir black pepper, thyme, cayenne pepper, and salt into the mixture. Seal the lid and cook for 15 minutes on High Pressure. Release the pressure quickly. Season with more thyme, black pepper, and salt. Serve.

Broccoli Leeks Green Soup

Serves: 2-4 | Ready in about: 30 minutes

Ingredients

2 tbsp olive oil

1 head broccoli, cut into florets

4 celery stalks, chopped thinly

1 leek, chopped thinly

1 zucchini, chopped

1 cup green beans

2 cups vegetable broth

Salt to taste

2 cups chopped kale

Directions

Add broccoli, leek, beans, salt, zucchini, and celery. Mix in vegetable broth, oil, and cover with water. Seal the lid and cook on High Pressure for 4 minutes. Release pressure naturally for 10 minutes, then release the remaining pressure quickly. Stir in kale, set to Sauté, and cook until tender, about 3-4 minutes. Serve.

Carrot Vegan Gazpacho

Serves: 2-4 | Ready in about: 2 hours 30 minutes

Ingredients

1 lb trimmed carrots

1 lb tomatoes, chopped

1 cucumber, peeled and chopped

¼ cup olive oil

2 tbsp lemon juice

1 red onion, chopped

2 cloves garlic

2 tbsp white wine vinegar

Salt and black pepper to taste

Directions

Add carrots and salt and cover with enough water. Seal the lid and cook for 20 minutes on High Pressure. Do a quick release. Remove, drain, and let them cool. In a blender, add carrots, cucumber, red onion, pepper, garlic, oil, tomatoes, lemon juice, vinegar, and salt. Blend until very smooth. Place gazpacho in a serving bowl. Chill while covered for 2 hours. Serve.

Potatoes & Braised Swiss Chard

Serves: 2-4 | Ready in about: 15 minutes

Ingredients

1 lb Swiss chard, torn   ¼ tsp oregano
2 potatoes, peeled, chopped   1 tsp salt

Directions

Add Swiss chard and potatoes to the pot. Pour water to cover all and sprinkle with salt. Seal the lid and select Manual/ Pressure Cook. Cook for 3 minutes on High. Release the steam naturally for 5 minutes. Transfer to a serving plate. Sprinkle with oregano or Italian seasoning to serve.

Potatoes & Braised Swiss Chard

Serves: 2-4 | Ready in about: 15 minutes

Ingredients

1 lb Swiss chard, torn   ¼ tsp oregano
2 potatoes, peeled, chopped   1 tsp salt

Directions

Add Swiss chard and potatoes to the pot. Pour water to cover all and sprinkle with salt. Seal the lid and select Manual/ Pressure Cook. Cook for 3 minutes on High. Release the steam naturally for 5 minutes. Transfer to a serving plate. Sprinkle with oregano or Italian seasoning to serve.

Cilantro-Flavored Aloo Gobi

Serves: 2-4 | Ready in about: 40 minutes

Ingredients

1 tbsp vegetable oil   1 onion, minced   1 tsp ground turmeric
1 head cauliflower, cut into florets   4 garlic cloves, minced   ½ tsp chili pepper
1 potato, peeled and diced   1 tomato, cored and chopped   Salt to taste
1 tbsp ghee   1 jalapeño pepper, deseeded and minced   1 tbsp fresh cilantro, chopped
2 tsp cumin seeds   1 tbsp curry paste

Directions

Warm the olive oil in your Instant Pot on Sauté. Add in potato and cauliflower and cook for 8 to 10 minutes until lightly browned; season with salt. Set the vegetables to a bowl. Add ghee to the pot. Mix in cumin seeds and cook for 10 seconds until they start to pop; add onion and cook for 3 minutes until softened. Mix in garlic; cook for 30 seconds.

Add in tomato, curry paste, chili pepper, jalapeño pepper, and turmeric; cook for 4 to 6 minutes until the tomato starts to break down. Return potato and cauliflower to the pot. Pour 1 cup of water over the vegetables. Seal the lid and cook on High Pressure for 4 minutes. Quick-release the pressure. Top with cilantro.

Lentil & Carrot Chili

Serves: 2-4 | Ready in about: 30 minutes

Ingredients

1 tbsp olive oil   2 garlic cloves, chopped   2 carrot, halved lengthwise
1 onion, chopped   2 cups vegetable stock   1 tbsp harissa sauce
1 celery, chopped   ½ cup dried lentils, rinsed   1 tbsp fresh parsley, chopped

Directions

Warm the olive oil in your Instant Pot on Sauté. Add in onion, garlic, and celery and sauté for 5 minutes until onion is soft. Mix in lentils, carrots, and vegetable stock. Seal the lid and cook on High Pressure for 10 minutes. Release the pressure quickly. Mix lentils with harissa sauce and serve topped with parsley.

Steamed Artichokes with Aioli

Serves: 2-4 | Ready in about: 20 minutes

Ingredients

4 artichokes, trimmed
1 lemon, halved
1 tsp lemon zest

1 tbsp lemon juice
3 cloves garlic, crushed
½ cup mayonnaise

Salt to taste
1 tbsp fresh parsley, chopped

Directions

On artichokes' cut ends, rub with lemon. Add 1 cup water into in your Instant Pot. Set steamer rack over water and set steamer basket on top. Place artichokes into the basket with the points upwards; sprinkled with salt.

Seal lid and cook on High Pressure for 10 minutes. Release the pressure quickly. In a mixing bowl, combine mayonnaise, garlic, lemon juice, and lemon zest. Season to taste with salt. Serve with steamed artichokes sprinkled with parsley.

Garlic Potatoes with Herbs

Serves: 2-4 | Ready in about: 30 minutes

Ingredients

1 lb potatoes
3 tbsp butter
2 cloves garlic, chopped

2 tbsp fresh rosemary, chopped
½ tsp fresh thyme, chopped
½ tsp fresh parsley, chopped

¼ tsp ground black pepper
½ cup vegetable broth

Directions

Use a small knife to pierce each potato to ensure there are no blowouts when placed under pressure. Melt butter in your Instant Pot on Sauté. Add in potatoes, rosemary, parsley, pepper, thyme, and garlic, and cook for 10 minutes until browned.

In a bowl, mix miso paste and vegetable stock. Stir into the mixture in the Instant Pot. Seal the lid and cook for 5 minutes on High Pressure. Release the pressure quickly.

Sweet Potato Mash with Tahini

Serves: 2-4 | Ready in about: 25 minutes

Ingredients

2 lb sweet potatoes, peeled and cubed
2 tbsp tahini

1 tbsp sugar
¼ tsp ground nutmeg

2 tbsp chopped fresh chives
Sea salt to taste

Directions

Into the cooker, add 1 cup water, and insert a steamer basket. Add in the sweet potatoes. Seal the lid and cook for 18 minutes at High Pressure. Release the pressure quickly. In a bowl, add sweet potatoes and slightly mash. Using a hand mixer, whip in nutmeg, sugar, and tahini until the potatoes attain the desired consistency. Add salt to taste and top with chives to serve.

Feta & Asparagus Appetizer

Serves: 2-4 | Ready in about: 15 minutes

Ingredients

1 cup water
1 lb asparagus spears, ends trimmed

1 tbsp olive oil
Salt and black pepper to taste

1 lemon, cut into wedges
1 cup feta cheese, cubed

Directions

Into the pot, add water and set trivet over the water. Place the steamer basket on the trivet. Place the asparagus into the steamer basket. Seal the lid and cook on High Pressure for 1 minute. Release the pressure quickly. Add olive oil in a bowl and toss in asparagus until well coated. Season with pepper and salt. Serve alongside feta cheese and lemon wedges.

Traditional Thai Stew

Serves: 2-4 | Ready in about: 30 minutes

Ingredients

1 tbsp coconut oil
1 cup onion, chopped
1 tbsp fresh ginger, minced

1 carrot, peeled and chopped
1 red bell pepper, chopped
1 orange bell pepper, chopped

1 (14-oz) can coconut milk
1 cup bok choy, chopped
2 tbsp red curry paste

Directions

Melt coconut oil in your Instant Pot on Sauté. Add in onion and cook for 3 minutes until soft; add ginger and cook for 30 more seconds. Mix in orange bell peppers and carrot; cook for 4 minutes until the peppers become tender.

Add curry paste, bok choy, coconut milk, and ½ cup water and stir well to obtain a consistent color of the sauce. Press Cancel and seal lid. Cook for 1 minute on High Pressure. Release the pressure quickly. Serve hot.

Sage Cauliflower Mash

Serves: 2-4 | Ready in about: 15 minutes

Ingredients

1 head cauliflower
1 tbsp butter

¼ tsp celery salt
¼ cup heavy cream

1 tbsp fresh sage, chopped
½ tsp ground black pepper

Directions

In your Instant Pot, add 1 cup water, and set trivet on top. Lay cauliflower head onto the trivet. Seal the lid and cook for 8 minutes on High Pressure. Release the pressure quickly. Remove and drain the cauliflower. Use an immersion blender to blend the cauliflower to the pot alongside the pepper, heavy cream, salt, and butter until smooth. Top with sage and serve.

Tofu & Peanut Noodles

Serves: 2-4 | Ready in about: 20 minutes

Ingredients

1 (14-oz) package tofu, cubed
8 oz egg noodles
2 bell peppers, chopped
¼ cup soy sauce

¼ cup orange juice
1 tbsp fresh ginger, minced
2 tbsp vinegar
1 tbsp sesame oil

1 tbsp sriracha
¼ cup roasted peanuts
3 scallions, chopped

Directions

In the Instant Pot, mix tofu, bell peppers, orange juice, sesame oil, ginger, egg noodles, soy sauce, vinegar, and sriracha. Cover with enough water. Seal the lid and cook for 2 minutes on High Pressure. Release the pressure quickly. Place the mixture into 4 plates; top with scallions and peanuts to serve.

Maple-Glazed Acorn Squash

Serves: 2-4 | Ready in about: 30 minutes

Ingredients

2 tbsp maple syrup
1 lb acorn squash, cut into 2-inch chunks

2 tbsp butter
1 tbsp dark brown sugar

1 tbsp cinnamon
Salt and black pepper to taste

Directions

In your Instant Pot, mix 1 tbsp maple syrup and ½ cup water. Add in squash, seal the lid and cook on High Pressure for 4 minutes. Release the pressure quickly. Transfer the squash to a serving dish. Set to Sauté.

Mix sugar, cinnamon, remaining maple syrup and the liquid in the pot. Cook as you stir for 4 minutes to obtain a thick consistency and starts to turn caramelized and golden. Spread honey glaze over squash; add pepper and salt to taste.

Coconut Lime Yogurt

Makes: 3-5 serves | Ready in about: 10 hours 30 minutes

Ingredients

2 cans coconut milk
1 tbsp gelatin

1 tbsp honey
1 tsp probiotic powder

Zest from 1 lime

Directions

Into the pot, stir in gelatin and coconut milk until well dissolved. Seal the lid, press the Yogurt button until the display is reading "Boil". Once complete, the screen will then display "Yogurt." Ensure milk temperature is at 180°F. Remove the steel pot from the pressure cooker's base and place it into a large ice bath to cool milk for 5 minutes to reach 112°F.

Remove pot from ice bath and wipe the outside dry. Into the coconut milk mixture, add probiotic powder, honey, and lime zest, and stir to combine. Return steel pot to the base of the Instant Pot. Seal the lid, press Yogurt and cook for 10 hours. Once done, spoon yogurt into clean glass canning jars with rings and lids; place in the refrigerator to chill for 4 hours to thicken.

Easy Lasagna Soup

Serves: 2-4 | Ready in about: 30 minutes

Ingredients

1 tsp olive oil	1 cup tomatoes, chopped	2 tsp Italian seasoning
1 cup leeks, chopped	1 carrot, chopped	Salt to taste
2 garlic cloves minced	½ lb broccoli, chopped	2 cups vegetable broth
1 cup tomato paste	¼ cup dried green lentils	3 lasagna noodles

Directions

Warm the olive oil in your Instant Pot on Sauté. Add garlic and leeks and cook for 2 minutes until soft. Add in tomato paste, carrot, Italian seasoning, broccoli, tomatoes, lentils, and salt. Stir in vegetable broth and lasagna pieces. Seal the lid and cook on High Pressure for 3 minutes. Release pressure naturally for 10 minutes. Divide soup into serving bowls and serve.

Sweet Potato Medallions with Rosemary

Serves: 2-4 | Ready in about: 25 minutes

Ingredients

1 tbsp fresh rosemary	4 sweet potatoes	Salt to taste
1 tsp garlic powder	2 tbsp butter	

Directions

Add 1 cup water and place steamer rack over the water into your Instant Pot. Use a fork to prick sweet potatoes all over and set onto steamer rack. Seal the lid and cook on High Pressure for 12 minutes. Release the pressure quickly. Transfer sweet potatoes to a cutting board and slice into ½-inch medallions and ensure they are peeled. Remove the water from the pot.

Melt butter in the cooker on Sauté. Add in the medallions and cook each side for 2 to 3 minutes until browned. Season with salt and garlic powder. Serve topped with fresh rosemary.

Steamed Artichoke with Garlic Mayo Sauce

Serves: 2-4 | Ready in about: 20 minutes

Ingredients

2 large artichokes	½ cup mayonnaise	Juice of 1 lime
2 garlic cloves, smashed	Salt and black pepper to taste	

Directions

Using a serrated knife, trim about 1 inch from the artichokes' top. Into your Instant Pot, add 1 cup water, and set trivet over. Lay the artichokes on the trivet. Seal lid and cook for 14 minutes on High Pressure. Release the pressure quickly. Mix the mayonnaise with garlic and lime juice. Season with salt and pepper. Serve artichokes in a platter with garlic mayo on the side.

Easy Vegetarian Paella

Serves: 2-4 | Ready in about: 30 minutes

Ingredients

¼ cup frozen green peas	1 cup zucchini, finely chopped	Salt and black pepper to taste
1 carrot, finely chopped	½ tbsp celery root, finely chopped	1 cup vegetable broth
1 cup fire-roasted tomatoes	1 tbsp turmeric	½ cup long grain rice

Directions

Place all ingredients, except for the rice, in the Instant Pot. Stir well and seal the lid. Cook on Rice mode for 8 minutes on High. Do a quick release, open the lid, and stir in the rice. Seal the lid and cook on High Pressure for 3 minutes. When ready, release the pressure naturally for about 10 minutes. Serve.

Low-Carb Eggplant Lasagna

Serves: 2-4 | Ready in about: 35 minutes

Ingredients

1 large eggplant, chopped	3 oz mascarpone cheese, softened	¼ cup olive oil
4 oz mozzarella cheese, chopped	2 tomatoes, chopped	Salt and black pepper to taste

Directions

Grease a baking dish with olive oil. Slice the eggplant and make a layer in the dish. Cover with mozzarella and tomato slices. Top with mascarpone cheese. Repeat the process until you run out of ingredients.

In a bowl, mix olive oil, salt, and pepper. Pour the mixture over the lasagna, and add ½ cup of water. In your inner pot, Pour 1 ½ cups of water and insert a trivet. Lower the baking dish on the trivet, Seal the lid and cook on High Pressure for 4 minutes. When ready, do a natural release for 10 minutes.

Onion & Chickpea Stew

Serves: 2-4 | Ready in about: 35 minutes

Ingredients

1 cup chickpeas, soaked	2 tbsp fresh parsley, chopped	1 tbsp butter
1 purple onion, chopped	3 cups vegetable broth	2 tbsp olive oil
2 tomatoes, roughly chopped	1 tbsp paprika	Salt and black pepper to taste

Directions

Warm oil on Sauté and stir-fry the onions for 3 minutes. Add the rest of the ingredients. Seal the lid and cook on the Meat/Stew for 30 minutes on High. Do a quick release and serve warm.

Spinach & Mushroom Cannelloni

Serves: 2-4 | Ready in about: 40 minutes

Ingredients

8 oz of cannelloni	3 oz ricotta cheese	¼ tsp salt
12 oz spinach, torn	¼ cup milk	1 tbsp sour cream
6 oz button mushrooms, chopped	3 oz butter	

Directions

Melt butter on Sauté and add mushrooms. Stir well and cook until soft. Add spinach and milk, and continue to cook for 6 minutes, stirring constantly. Stir in the cheese, season to taste. Line a baking dish with parchment paper.

Fill the cannelloni with spinach mixture. Gently place them on the baking sheet. Pour 2 cups of water in the Instant Pot and insert a trivet. Lay the baking sheet on the trivet. Seal the lid, and cook on High Pressure for 20 minutes. Do a quick release. Remove the cannelloni and chill for a while. Top with sour cream and serve.

Parsley Chickpea Stew

Serves: 2-4 | Ready in about: 45 minutes

Ingredients

6 oz chickpeas, soaked overnight	1 tbsp cumin seeds	2 tbsp butter
1 tomato, peeled and chopped	2 cups vegetable broth	2 tbsp fresh parsley, chopped
1 red onion, chopped	2 tbsp olive oil	

Directions

Add in the tomato, onion, cumin seeds, chickpeas, and pour in the broth. Seal the lid and set the steam handle. Cook on Soup/Broth for 30 minutes on High. Do a quick release and set aside to cool for a while. Transfer the soup to a food processor. Process until pureed and spoon to a serving dish. Stir in 2 tbsp of butter. Top with freshly chopped parsley. Serve.

Split Pea & Potato Stew

Serves: 2-4 | Ready in about: 40 minutes

Ingredients

2 cups split yellow peas	2 potatoes, chopped	1 tsp chili pepper
1 cup onions, chopped	2 tbsp butter	½ tsp salt
1 carrot, chopped	2 garlic cloves, crushed	4 cups vegetable stock

Directions

Melt butter in your Instant Pot on Sauté and stir-fry the onions for 3 minutes. Add the remaining vegetables and cook for 5-6 minutes, until tender. Stir in chili pepper and season with salt. Pour in the stock and seal the lid. Cook on High on Meat/Stew for 25 minutes. Do a quick release and serve.

Spinach & Potato Balls with Marinara Sauce

Serves: 2-4 | Ready in about: 30 minutes

Ingredients

2 potatoes, peeled
2 onions, chopped
1 lb fresh spinach, torn
¼ cup mozzarella cheese, shredded
2 eggs, beaten
Salt and black pepper to taste

1 tsp dried oregano, crushed
1 cup whole milk
¼ cup flour
1 lb tomatoes, peeled and chopped
1 large onion, peeled, chopped
2 garlic cloves, peeled, crushed

3 tbsp olive oil
¼ cup white wine
1 tsp sugar
1 tbsp dried rosemary, crushed
1 tbsp tomato paste

Directions

Place the potatoes in your Instant Pot and add enough water to cover. Seal the lid and cook on High Pressure for 13 minutes. Do a quick release. Drain and add the milk and mash with a potato masher. Whisk in eggs. Add in half of the onions, spinach, mozzarella cheese, oregano, flour, salt, and pepper and mix with hands. Shape into balls and set aside.

Press Sauté on the pot, warm olive oil, and stir-fry the remaining onions and garlic for 3 minutes. Stir in tomatoes and cook for 10 minutes. Pour in the wine, sugar, rosemary, tomato paste, and salt. Cook for 5 more minutes. Place the potato balls in the cooker and seal the lid. Cook on High Pressure for 5 minutes. Do a natural release for 5 minutes. Serve.

Primavera Noodles with Parmesan

Serves: 2-4 | Ready in about: 20 minutes

Ingredients

1 bunch asparagus, trimmed
2 cups broccoli florets
3 tbsp olive oil
3 tsp salt

10 oz egg noodles
3 garlic cloves, minced
2 ½ cups vegetable stock
½ cup heavy cream

1 cup small tomatoes, halved
¼ cup chopped basil
½ cup grated Parmesan cheese

Directions

Pour 2 cups of water, add the noodles, 2 tbsp of olive oil, garlic, and salt. Place a trivet over the water. Combine asparagus, broccoli, remaining olive oil, and salt in a bowl. Place the vegetables on the trivet.

Seal the lid and cook on Steam for 12 minutes on High. Do a quick release. Remove the vegetables to a plate. Stir the heavy cream and tomatoes in the pasta. Press Sauté and simmer the cream until desired consistency. Gently mix in the asparagus and broccoli. Garnish with basil and Parmesan cheese and to serve.

Chickpea & Raisin Boil

Serves: 2-4 | Ready in about: 20 minutes

Ingredients

1 cup canned chickpeas
1 onion, chopped
A handful of string beans, trimmed
1 apple, chopped into 1-inch cubes

½ cup raisins
½ tbsp button mushrooms, chopped
1 carrot, chopped
2 garlic cloves, crushed

4 cherry tomatoes
½ tbsp fresh mint, chopped
½ cup orange juice
½ tsp salt

Directions

Place all ingredients in the Instant Pot. Pour enough water to cover. Cook on High Pressure for 8 minutes. Do a natural release for 10 minutes.

Flavorful Vegetable Mix

Serves: 2-4 | Ready in about: 15 minutes

Ingredients

1 head broccoli, cut into florets
16 asparagus, trimmed

1 head cauliflower, cut into florets
5 oz green beans

2 carrots, cut on bias
Salt to taste

Directions

Add 1 cup water and set trivet on top of the water in your Instant Pot. Place a steamer basket on the trivet. In an even layer, spread green beans, broccoli, cauliflower, asparagus, and carrots in the steamer basket. Seal the lid and cook on Steam for 3 minutes on High. Release the pressure quickly. Remove the basket from the pot and season with salt. Serve.

Pasta with Tofu & Broccoli

Serves: 2-4 | Ready in about: 25 minutes

Ingredients

8 oz orecchiette pasta

16 oz broccoli, roughly chopped

2 garlic cloves

2 tbsp olive oil

1 tbsp grated tofu

Salt and black pepper to taste

Directions

Place the orecchiette and broccoli in your Instant Pot. Cover with water and seal the lid. Cook on High Pressure for 10 minutes. Do a quick release. Drain the broccoli and orecchiette. Set aside. Heat the olive oil on Sauté. Stir-fry garlic for 2 minutes. Stir in broccoli, orecchiette, salt, and pepper. Cook for 2 more minutes. Stir in grated tofu and serve.

Tomato & Lentil Quinoa Stew

Serves: 2-4 | Ready in about: 25 minutes

Ingredients

1 cup quinoa, rinsed

1 cup tomatoes, diced

1 cup lentils

¼ cup sun-dried tomatoes, chopped

1 tsp garlic, minced

4 cups beef broth

1 tsp salt

1 tsp red pepper flakes

Directions

Add all ingredients in your Instant Pot. Seal the lid and adjust the steam release handle. Cook on High Pressure for 20 minutes. Release the steam naturally for 5 minutes. Serve.

Tasty Vegetable Stew

Serves: 2-4 | Ready in about: 25 minutes

Ingredients

3 zucchini, peeled, chopped

1 eggplant, peeled, chopped

3 red bell peppers, chopped

½ cup fresh tomato juice

2 tsp Italian seasoning

2 tbsp olive oil

Directions

Add all ingredients and give it a good stir. Pour 1 cup of water. Seal the lid and cook on High Pressure for 15 minutes. Do a quick release. Set aside to cool completely. Serve as a cold salad or a side dish.

South Asian Stew

Serves: 2-4 | Ready in about: 35 minutes

Ingredients

2 cups green peas, frozen

1 large onion, chopped

4 cloves garlic, chopped

3 oz of olives, pitted

1 tbsp ginger, shredded

1 tbsp turmeric

1 tbsp salt

4 cups beef stock

3 tbsp olive oil

Directions

Heat oil on Sauté. Stir-fry the onions and garlic for 2-3 minutes, stirring constantly. Add the remaining ingredients and seal the lid. Cook on High Pressure for 20 minutes. Do a quick release and serve.

Mac & Goat Cheese

Serves: 2-4 | Ready in about: 20 minutes

Ingredients

1 lb elbow macaroni

2 oz goat's cheese, crumbled

½ cup skim milk

1 tsp Dijon mustard

1 tsp sea salt

1 tsp Italian seasoning

2 tbsp olive oil

1 tbsp vegetable oil

5 olives

Directions

Add macaroni in the Instant Pot and pour in 4 cups of water. Add 1 tablespoon of oil. Seal the lid and cook on High Pressure for 3 minutes. Do a quick release. Drain the macaroni in a colander and set aside.

Press Sauté, add olive oil, mustard, milk, salt, and Italian seasoning mix. Stir-fry for 5 minutes. Stir in macaroni and cook for 2 minutes. Remove from the pot and top with some fresh goat's cheese and olives.

Kidney Bean Stew

Serves: 2-4 | Ready in about: 30 minutes

Ingredients

6 oz canned red beans, drained
1 carrot, chopped
1 celery stalk, chopped

1 onion, chopped
2 tbsp tomato paste
2 cups vegetable broth

3 tbsp olive oil
1 tsp salt
2 tbsp fresh parsley, chopped

Directions

Warm oil in your Instant Pot on Sauté and stir-fry the onion for 3 minutes until soft. Add celery and carrot. Cook for 5 minutes, adding some broth at the time. Add the red beans, salt, parsley, and tomato paste and pour in the remaining broth. Seal the lid and cook on High Pressure for 5 minutes. Do a natural release for 10 minutes. Sprinkle with parsley and serve.

Indian Lentil Dhal

Serves: 2-4 | Ready in about: 35 minutes

Ingredients

1 cup lentils
2 tbsp almond butter
1 carrot, peeled, chopped
1 potato, peeled, chopped

1 bay leaf
¼ tbsp parsley, chopped
½ tbsp chili powder
2 tbsp ground cumin

1 tbsp garam masala
3 cups vegetable stock
Salt to taste

Directions

Melt the almond butter in your Instant Pot on Sauté. Add carrot, potato, and parsley. Stir and cook for 10 minutes. Press Cancel and add the remaining ingredients. Cook on High Pressure for 15 minutes. Do a quick release and serve hot.

Garlic & Leek Cannellini Beans

Serves: 2-4 | Ready in about: 45 minutes

Ingredients

1 lb cannellini beans, soaked overnight
1 onion, peeled, chopped
1 leek, finely chopped

2 garlic cloves, whole
Salt and black pepper to taste
2 tbsp vegetable oil

2 tbsp flour
1 tbsp cayenne pepper

Directions

Add beans, onion, leek, garlic, salt, and pepper in your Instant Pot. Press Manual/Pressure Cook and cook for 20 minutes on High. Heat the vegetable oil in a skillet. Add in flour and cayenne pepper. Stir-fry for 2 minutes and set aside. When you hear the cooker's end signal, do a quick release. Pour in the cayenne mixture and stir. Let it sit for 15 minutes before serving.

Hearty Vegetable Stew

Serves: 2-4 | Ready in about: 55 minutes

Ingredients

1 lb potatoes, peeled, chopped
1 carrot, peeled, chopped
2 celery stalk, chopped
1 onion, peeled, chopped

1 zucchini, chopped into ½ -inch slices
1 tbsp fresh celery leaves, chopped
1 tbsp butter
2 tbsp olive oil

2 cups vegetable broth
1 tbsp paprika
Salt and black pepper to taste

Directions

Warm oil in your Instant Pot on Sauté and stir-fry the onion for 3 minutes, until translucent. Add carrot, celery, zucchini, and ¼ cup of broth. Continue to cook for 10 minutes, stirring constantly. Stir in potatoes, cayenne pepper, salt, pepper, bay leaves, and remaining broth. Seal the lid and cook on Meat/Stew for 30 minutes on High. Do a quick release and stir in butter.

Homemade Greek Dolmades

Serves: 2-4 | Ready in about: 60 minutes

Ingredients

10 wine leaves
½ cup long-grain rice, rinsed

2 tbsp olive oil
2 garlic cloves, crushed

¼ cup lemon juice
Salt and black pepper to taste

Directions

In a bowl, mix rice with 1 tbsp of olive oil, garlic, salt, and pepper. Place 1 wine leaf at a time on a working surface and add 1 tsp of filling at the bottom. Fold the leaf over the filling towards the center. Bring the 2 sides in towards the center and roll them up tightly. Grease the Instant Pot with the remaining olive oil. Make a layer of wine leaves.

Transfer the previously prepared rolls. Add the remaining olive oil, 1 cup of water, and lemon juice. Seal the lid and cook on High Pressure for 30 minutes. Do a natural release for 10 minutes. Remove the dolmades from the pot and chill overnight.

Spinach & Mushroom Tagliatelle

Serves: 2-4 | Ready in about: 25 minutes

Ingredients

1 lb spinach tagliatelle	¼ cup feta cheese	¼ cup heavy cream
6 oz frozen mixed mushrooms	¼ cup grated Parmesan cheese	1 tbsp Italian seasoning mix
3 tbsp butter, unsalted	2 garlic cloves, crushed	

Directions

Melt butter on Sauté, and stir-fry the garlic for a minute. Stir in feta and mushrooms. Add tagliatelle and 2 cups of water. Cook on High Pressure for 4 minutes. Quick-release the pressure and top with Parmesan cheese. Serve.

Easy Homemade Pizza

Serves: 2-4 | Ready in about: 20 minutes

Ingredients

1 pizza crust	1 tsp dried oregano	2 tbsp olive oil
½ cup tomato paste	4 oz button mushrooms, chopped	12 olives
1 tsp sugar	½ cup grated gouda cheese	1 cup arugula

Directions

Flour the working surface and roll out the pizza dough to the approximate size of your Instant Pot. Gently fit the dough in a greased baking dish. In a bowl, combine tomato paste, ¼ cup water, sugar, and oregano. Spread the mixture over the dough, make a layer with button mushrooms and grated gouda.

Add a trivet inside the Instant Pot and pour in 1 cup of water. Place the baking dish on the trivet. Seal the lid and cook for 15 minutes on High Pressure. Do a quick release. Remove the pizza from the pot. Sprinkle with olives and arugula. Serve.

Penne with Shiitake & Veggies

Serves: 2-4 | Ready in about: 25 minutes

Ingredients

6 oz penne pasta	6 oz zucchini, cut into strips	2 tbsp soy sauce
6 oz shiitake mushrooms, chopped	1 chopped leek	1 tsp ground ginger
2 garlic cloves, crushed	4 oz baby spinach	½ tsp salt
1 carrot, cut into strips	2 tbsp oil	

Directions

Heat oil on Sauté and stir-fry carrot and garlic for 3-4 minutes. Add the remaining ingredients and pour in 2 cups of water. Cook on High Pressure for 4 minutes. Quick-release the pressure and serve.

Carrot & Sweet Potato Chowder

Serves: 2-4 | Ready in about: 50 minutes

Ingredients

3 sweet potatoes, cut into bite-sized pieces	6 tbsp olive oil	1 tbsp parsley, finely chopped
2 carrots, chopped	2 tbsp tomato sauce	Salt and pepper
1 onion, peeled, chopped	1 tbsp celery, finely chopped	

Directions

Heat olive oil in your Instant Pot on Sauté. Add in onion, carrots, celery, and potatoes. Stir-fry for 2 minutes. Cover with water and stir in tomato sauce. Seal the lid and cook for 25 minutes on High Pressure. Do a quick release. Open the pot and add the remaining ingredients. Seal again and cook for 5 minutes on High. Do a quick release. Serve.

Greek Dill-Lemon Pilaf

Serves: 2-4 | Ready in about: 35 minutes

Ingredients

1 tbsp olive oil	2 garlic cloves, minced	½ cup jasmine rice
1 tbsp Greek seasoning	1 tbsp dried dill	Salt and black pepper to taste
1 white onion, chopped	2 lemons, zested and juiced	1 tbsp fresh chopped dill

Directions

Set your Instant Pot to Sauté. Heat olive oil in the inner pot. Mix in onion and garlic and cook for 3 minutes or until fragrant. Stir in dill, lemon zest, rice, salt, black pepper, and 1 cup of water.

Seal the lid, select Manual/Pressure Cook on High, and cook for 5 minutes. Perform a quick pressure release to let out steam. Mix in lemon juice and dish food onto serving plates. Garnish with dill and serve warm.

Pea & Mushroom Stew

Serves: 2-4 | Ready in about: 65 minutes

Ingredients

6 oz portobello mushrooms, sliced	½ cup celery, chopped	1 tsp rosemary
1 cup green peas	2 garlic cloves, crushed	Salt and black pepper to taste
1 pearl onion, chopped	2 potatoes, chopped	2 tbsp butter
2 carrots, chopped	1 tbsp apple cider vinegar	4 cups vegetable stock

Directions

Melt butter in your Instant Pot on Sauté and stir-fry onions, carrots, celery, and garlic for 2-3 minutes. Season with salt, pepper, and rosemary. Add the remaining ingredients and seal the lid. Cook on High Pressure for 30 minutes. When ready, release the pressure naturally for about 10 minutes. Serve.

Rice & Mushroom Stuffed Bell Peppers

Serves: 2-4 | Ready in about: 35 minutes

Ingredients

5 bell peppers, seeds and stems removed	4 garlic cloves, peeled, crushed	¼ tbsp rice
6 oz button mushrooms, chopped	2 tbsp olive oil	½ tbsp paprika
1 onion, chopped	Salt and black pepper to taste	2 cups vegetable stock

Directions

Warm the olive oil in your Instant Pot on Sauté. Add onion and garlic and stir-fry until fragrant and translucent, about 2 minutes. Stir in rice and mushrooms. Season with salt, pepper, and paprika. Stuff each bell pepper with the mixture.

Place them in the pot, filled side up, and pour in broth. Seal the lid and cook on High Pressure for 15 minutes. Release the pressure naturally for 10 minutes. Serve warm.

Potato & Zucchini with Mushrooms

Serves: 2-4 | Ready in about: 45 minutes

Ingredients

1 lb shiitake mushrooms	1 tsp garlic powder	1 cup onions
2 potatoes, chopped	1 tbsp cumin seeds	2 cups vegetable stock
3 garlic cloves, crushed	½ tsp chili powder	1 cup tomato sauce
2 tbsp oil	1 large zucchini, chopped	

Directions

Warm olive oil on Sauté. Stir-fry cumin seeds for one minute. Add onions, chili powder, garlic, and garlic powder. Cook for 3 minutes, stirring constantly. Add mushrooms and continue to cook on Sauté for 3 more minutes.

Add the remaining ingredients, seal the lid, and cook on High for 20 minutes. When done, release the pressure naturally for 10 minutes. Serve.

GRAINS & PASTA

Chickpea Chicken Stew

Serves: 2 | Ready in about: 40 minutes

Ingredients

½ lb boneless, skinless chicken legs
1 tsp ground cumin
Salt and black pepper to taste
¼ tsp cayenne pepper
1 tbsp olive oil

½ onion, minced
1 jalapeño pepper, deseeded and minced
1 garlic clove, crushed
⅓ tsp freshly grated ginger
¼ cup chicken stock

10 oz canned crushed tomatoes
½ cup chickpeas, drained and rinsed
¼ cup coconut milk
2 tbsp fresh parsley, chopped
½ cup hot cooked basmati rice

Directions

Season the chicken with salt, cayenne pepper, and cumin. Set on Sauté and warm the oil. Add in jalapeño pepper and onion and cook for 5 minutes until soft. Mix in ginger and garlic and cook for 3 minutes until tender. Add the stock into the cooker to ensure the pot is deglazed. From the pan's bottom, scrape any browned bits of food.

Mix the onion mixture with chickpeas, tomatoes, and salt. Stir in the chicken to coat in the sauce. Seal the lid and cook on High Pressure for 20 minutes. Release the pressure quickly. Remove the chicken and slice into chunks. Into the remaining sauce, mix in coconut milk, and simmer for 5 minutes on Keep Warm. Top with chicken, sauce, and cilantro and serve.

Easy Wild Rice Pilaf

Serves: 2 | Ready in about: 25 minutes

Ingredients

1 cup vegetable broth
½ cup wild rice, rinsed and drained

½ tbsp butter
Zest and juice from ½ lemon

Salt and black pepper to taste

Directions

Place rice, lemon zest, butter, and broth in your Instant Pot. Stir, seal the lid, and cook on High Pressure for 20 minutes. Once ready, release pressure naturally for 10 minutes. Sprinkle salt, lemon juice, and pepper over the pilaf and serve.

Quinoa & Brown Rice with Mushrooms

Serves: 2 | Ready in about: 35 minutes

Ingredients

½ cup mixed quinoa and brown rice, rinsed
2 tbsp olive oil
1 onion, chopped

1 cup button mushrooms, sliced
1 cup vegetable stock

1 tbsp butter
½ cup Parmesan shavings

Directions

Set your Instant Pot to Sauté and heat the olive oil. Place in the onion and mushrooms and sauté for 5 minutes, until softened. Stir in the quinoa, brown rice, and vegetable stock. Seal the lid, select Rice, and set the cooking time to 12 minutes. When done, perform a natural pressure release for 10 minutes. Stir in the butter to melt. Scatter over the Parmesan and serve.

Green Farro with Parmesan

Serves: 2 | Ready in about: 35 minutes

Ingredients

1 tbsp butter
1 small onion, diced
1 cup pearl barley, rinsed and drained

2 garlic cloves, smashed
2 cups vegetable broth
½ cup grated Parmesan cheese

1 cup kale, chopped
½ lemon, juiced
Salt and black pepper to taste

Directions

Warm the butter your Instant Pot on Sauté. Add in onion and cook for 3 minutes until soft. Stir in garlic and barley and continue cooking for 1 minute. Mix in broth. Seal the lid and cook for 9 minutes on High Pressure.

Release pressure naturally for 10 minutes. Add Parmesan cheese into barley mixture and stir until fully melted. Just before serving, add lemon juice and kale into the barley mixture. Add pepper and salt for seasoning. Serve.

Pesto Veggie Quinoa Bowls

Serves: 2 | Ready in about: 30 minutes

Ingredients

1 cup quinoa, rinsed and drained
2 cups vegetable broth
Salt and black pepper to taste
1 potato, peeled, cubed

1 head broccoli, cut into small florets
1 bunch baby heirloom carrots, peeled
¼ cabbage, chopped
2 eggs

1 avocado, sliced
¼ cup pesto sauce
Lemon wedges, for serving

Directions

In the pot, mix broth, pepper, quinoa, and salt. Set trivet to the inner pot on top of quinoa and add a steamer basket to the top of the trivet. Mix carrots, potato, eggs, and broccoli in the steamer basket. Add pepper and salt. Seal the lid and cook for 1 minute on High Pressure. Quick-release the pressure.

Take away the trivet and steamer basket from the pot. Set the eggs in a bowl of ice water. Then peel and halve the eggs. Use a fork to fluff the quinoa. Adjust the seasonings. In two bowls, equally divide avocado, quinoa, broccoli, eggs, carrots, sweet potatoes, and a dollop of pesto. Serve alongside a lemon wedge.

Pumpkin & Rice Chicken

Serves: 2 | Ready in about: 45 minutes

Ingredients

2 chicken thighs, skinless
Salt and ground red pepper to taste
¼ tsp onion powder
⅓ tsp cajun seasoning

1/8 tsp smoked paprika
1 tbsp olive oil
⅓ cup pumpkin, peeled and cubed
½ celery stalk, diced

½ onion, diced
1 garlic clove, crushed
1 cup chicken broth
½ cup wild rice

Directions

Season the chicken with salt, onion powder, cajun seasoning, white pepper, red pepper, and paprika. Warm oil in your Instant Pot on Sauté. Stir in celery and pumpkin and cook for 5 minutes until tender; set the vegetables on a plate.

In batches, sear the chicken in oil for 3 minutes each side until golden brown; set aside. Into the cooker, add ¼ cup chicken stock to deglaze the pan, scrape away any browned bits from the bottom and add garlic and onion. Cook for 2 minutes.

Take back the celery and pumpkin the cooker; add the wild rice and remaining chicken stock. Place the chicken over the rice mixture. Seal the lid and cook for 10 minutes on High Pressure. Release the pressure quickly. Plate and serve.

Jalapeno Lentil Dhal

Serves: 2 | Ready in about: 35 minutes

Ingredients

1 tbsp olive oil
½ red jalapeño, seeded and minced
½ cup spinach, chopped
1 clove garlic, minced
⅓ tsp fresh ginger, peeled and grated

⅓ tbsp cumin seeds
⅓ tbsp coriander seeds
⅓ tsp ground turmeric
1/8 tsp cayenne pepper
½ cup red lentils

½ tomato, diced
1/8 cup lemon juice
Salt to taste
1 tbsp fresh cilantro, chopped
Natural yogurt for garnish

Directions

Heat oil in your instant pot on Sauté and add cayenne, jalapeño pepper, ginger, turmeric, cumin, and garlic, and coriander seeds. Cook for 2 minutes until seeds begin to pop. Pour in 1 cup water, tomato, and lentils into the pot and stir.

Seal the lid and cook on High Pressure for 10 minutes. Release pressure naturally for 10 minutes. Stir in spinach for 3-4 minutes until wilted. Add lemon juice and season to taste. Divide lentils between bowls and garnish with yogurt and cilantro.

Asian Yellow Lentils

Serves: 2 | Ready in about: 30 minutes

Ingredients

½ tbsp ghee
1 tsp cumin seeds
½ onion, chopped
1 garlic clove, minced

A ½-inch piece of ginger, peeled, minced
Sea salt salt
½ tomato, chopped
½ cup split yellow lentils, soaked

½ tbsp garam masala
¼ tsp ground turmeric
¼ tsp cayenne pepper
½ tbsp fresh cilantro, finely chopped

Directions

Warm the ghee in your Instant Pot on Sauté. Add cumin seeds and cook for 10 seconds until they begin to pop. Stir in onion and cook for 2 to 3 minutes until softened. Mix in ginger, salt, and garlic and cook for 1 minute as you stir.

Mix in tomato and cook for 3 to 5 minutes until the mixture breaks down. Stir in the turmeric, lentils, garam masala, and cayenne and cover with water. Seal the lid and cook for 8 minutes on High Pressure. Release the pressure quickly. Serve in bowls sprinkled with fresh cilantro.

Parsley Mushroom Pilaf

Serves: 2 | Ready in about: 35 minutes

Ingredients

½ tbsp olive oil

1 clove garlic, minced

½ yellow onion, finely chopped

1 cup button mushrooms, sliced

1 cup vegetable stock

½ cup white rice

½ tsp salt

2 sprigs parsley, chopped

Directions

Select Sauté and heat oil. Add mushrooms, onion, and garlic, and stir-fry for 5 minutes until tender. Mix in rice, stock, and salt. Seal the lid and cook on High Pressure for 20 minutes. Release the pressure naturally for 10 minutes. Use a fork to fluff the rice. Garnish with parsley and serve.

Avocado & Black Bean Tacos

Serves: 2 | Ready in about: 40 minutes

Ingredients

1 tbsp olive oil

½ cup black beans, soaked overnight

½ shallot, chopped

½ tbsp dried oregano

½ tsp chili powder

2 soft taco tortillas

½ avocado, chopped

Salt to taste

1 tbsp fresh cilantro, chopped

Directions

Add the black beans to your Instant Pot. Mix in the onion, olive oil, oregano, and chili powder. Top with water. Seal the lid and cook on High Pressure for 30 minutes. When ready, do a quick release. Allow to cool for a few minutes. Serve with taco tortillas, avocado slices, and cilantro. Serve warm.

Pancetta & Baked Garbanzo Beans

Serves: 2 | Ready in about: 50 minutes

Ingredients

1 strips pancetta

½ small onion, diced

½ cup canned garbanzo beans

⅓ cup apple cider

1 garlic clove, minced

2 tbsp ketchup

½ tsp mustard powder

Salt and black pepper to serve

1 tbsp fresh parsley, chopped

Directions

Cook pancetta for 5 minutes, until crispy on Sauté. Add onion and garlic, and cook for 3 minutes until soft. Mix in garbanzo beans, ketchup, salt, apple cider, mustard powder, 1 cup water, and pepper. Seal the lid, press Bean/Chili, and cook on High Pressure for 30 minutes. Release the pressure naturally for 10 minutes. Serve in bowls garnished with parsley.

Chicken & Broccoli Bulgur

Serves: 2 | Ready in about: 20 minutes

Ingredients

½ cup bulgur

1 head broccoli, cut into florets

2 tbsp butter

Salt and black pepper to taste

2 boneless, skinless chicken tenders

2 tbsp sliced green onions

Directions

On your Instant Pot, select Sauté. Melt the butter and cook the chicken for 5 minutes in total. Add in the bulgur and stir for 2 minutes, then pour in 1 cup of water. Season with salt and pepper. Seal the lid, select Manual/Pressure Cook on High, and set the cooking time to 10 minutes. When done cooking, perform a quick pressure release and unlock the lid.

Place a trivet over the rice and put the broccoli on top. Seal the lid, select Manual, and cook for 3 minutes on High. Once ready, do a quick pressure release. Spoon the bulgur into serving plates and top with broccoli. Sprinkle with green onions and serve.

Kale & Black-Eyed Peas

Serves: 2 | Ready in about: 30 minutes

Ingredients

1 tbsp olive oil
½ onion, chopped
1 garlic clove, minced
⅓ cup fire-roasted red peppers, diced

¼ tsp allspice
¼ tsp red pepper, crushed
Salt to taste
½ cup black-eyed peas, soaked

½ cup vegetable broth
1 small bay leaf
10 oz canned fire-roasted tomatoes
1 cup chopped kale

Directions

Warm the olive oil in your Instant Pot on Sauté. Add onion, garlic, and fire-roasted red peppers and cook for 5 minutes until fragrant. Season with salt, crushed red pepper, and allspice. Add broth, bay leaf, and black-eyed peas to the pot.

Seal the lid and cook on High Pressure for 5 minutes. Do a quick pressure release. Remove the bay leaf and discard it. Mix the peas with kale and tomatoes. Seal the lid and cook on High Pressure for 1 minute. Adjust the seasoning and serve.

Yogurt Chicken Pilaf with Quinoa

Serves: 2 | Ready in about: 60 minutes

Ingredients

1 lb chicken breasts
½ cup quinoa

1 cup chicken broth
Salt and black pepper to taste

Greek yogurt for topping

Directions

Add chicken and broth to the pot. Seal the lid and cook on Poultry for 15 minutes. Do a quick release and remove the chicken. Add quinoa to the pot and seal the lid. Cook on Manual for 10 minutes on High. Do a quick release. Cut the chicken meat into bite-sized pieces and place it in the cooker. Stir, season with black pepper, and top with greek yogurt to serve.

Corn & Pinto Bean Stew

Serves: 2 | Ready in about: 1 hour 5 minutes

Ingredients

1 tbsp olive oil
½ onion, chopped
½ red bell pepper, chopped
¼ tbsp dried oregano

¼ tbsp ground cumin
¼ tsp red pepper flakes
1 cup vegetable stock
½ cup dried pinto beans, rinsed

10 oz canned tomatoes, chopped
¼ tsp sea salt
¼ cup fresh chives, chopped
2 tbsp fresh corn kernels

Directions

Warm the oil in your Instant Pot on Sauté. Stir in the bell pepper, pepper flakes, oregano, onion, salt, and cumin. Cook for 3 minutes until soft. Mix in pinto beans, vegetable stock, and tomatoes. Seal the lid, select Bean/Chili, and cook for 30 minutes on High Pressure. Release the pressure naturally for 10 minutes. Top with corn and fresh chives and serve.

Brown Rice with Sunflower Seeds

Serves: 2 | Ready in about: 30 minutes

Ingredients

½ cup brown rice
1 cup chicken broth

⅓ tsp lemon juice
1 tsp olive oil

½ tbsp toasted sunflower seeds

Directions

Add broth and brown rice your Instant Pot. Seal the lid, press Manual, and cook for 15 minutes. Release the pressure quickly. Use a fork to fluff the rice. Top with lemon juice, sunflower seeds, and olive oil and serve.

Grana Padano Risotto

Serves: 2 | Ready in about: 25 minutes

Ingredients

1 tbsp olive oil
½ white onion, chopped
½ tbsp butter

½ cup Carnaroli rice, rinsed
¼ cup dry white wine
2 cups chicken stock

Salt and ground white pepper to taste
1 tbsp Grana Padano cheese, grated
¼ tbsp Grana Padano cheese, flakes

Directions

Warm oil on Sauté. Stir-fry onion for 3 minutes until soft and translucent. Add in butter and rice and cook for 5 minutes, stirring occasionally. Pour wine into the pot to deglaze, scrape away any browned bits of food from the pan.

Stir in stock, pepper, and salt to the pot. Seal the lid, press Rice and cook on High for 15 minutes. Release the pressure quickly. Sprinkle with grated Parmesan and stir well. Top with flaked cheese for garnish before serving.

Onion & Carrot Quinoa

Serves: 2 | Ready in about: 15 minutes

Ingredients

½ cup quinoa, rinsed
1 carrot, cut into sticks
½ small onion, chopped
1 tbsp olive oil
Salt to taste
1 tbsp fresh cilantro, chopped

Directions

Heat oil in your Instant Pot on Sauté. Add in onion and carrot and stir-fry for about 10 minutes until tender and crispy. Remove to a plate and set aside. Add 1 cup water, salt, and quinoa in the pot. Seal the lid and cook on High Pressure for 1 minute. Do a quick release. Fluff the cooked quinoa with a fork. Top with the carrots and onion. Serve scattered with cilantro.

Rice & Lentil Chicken

Serves: 2-4 | Ready in about: 45 minutes

Ingredients

1 tsp olive oil
1 garlic clove, minced
1 small yellow onion, chopped
3 cups chicken broth,
4 boneless, skinless chicken thighs
1 cup white rice
½ cup dried lentils
Salt and black pepper to taste
Chopped fresh parsley for garnish

Directions

Warm oil on Sauté. Stir-fry onion and garlic for 3 minutes until soft. Add in broth, rice, lentils, chicken, pepper, and salt. Seal the lid and cook on High Pressure for 15 minutes. Do a quick release. Remove and shred the chicken in a large bowl. Set the lentils and rice into serving plates. Top with shredded chicken and parsley and serve.

Chicken & Zucchini Pilaf

Serves: 2-4 | Ready in about: 40 minutes

Ingredients

2 tsp olive oil
1 zucchini, chopped
1 cup leeks, chopped
1 cup rice, rinsed
2 garlic cloves, minced
1 tbsp chopped fresh rosemary
2 tsp chopped fresh thyme leaves
Salt and black pepper to taste
2 cups chicken stock
1 lb boneless, skinless chicken legs

Directions

Warm oil on Sauté, add in zucchini and cook for 5 minutes until tender. Stir in thyme, leeks, rosemary, pepper, salt, and garlic. Cook the mixture for 3-4 minutes. Add ½ cup chicken stock into the pot to deglaze.

Scrape the bottom to get rid of any browned bits of food. When liquid stops simmering, add in the remaining stock, rice, and chicken with more pepper and salt. Seal the lid and cook on High Pressure for 5 minutes. Do a quick release. Serve.

Mushroom Risotto with Pumpkin Seeds

Serves: 2-4 | Ready in about: 30 minutes

Ingredients

2 tbsp olive oil
1 onion, chopped
2 cups Swiss chard, chopped
1 cup risotto rice
⅓ cup white wine
2 cups vegetable stock
½ cup mushrooms
4 tbsp pumpkin seeds, toasted
⅓ cup grated Pecorino Romano cheese

Directions

Heat the olive oil in your Instant Pot on Sauté. Cook onion and mushrooms for 5 minutes, stirring, until tender. Add the rice and cook for a minute. Stir in wine and cook for 2 to 3 minutes until almost evaporated. Pour in stock and season with salt.

Seal the lid and cook on High Pressure for 10 minutes. Do a quick release. Stir in chard for 3-5 minutes until wilted and mix in cheese to melt. Serve scattered with pumpkin seeds.

Cajun Chicken with Rice & Green Peas

Serves: 2-4 | Ready in about: 30 minutes

Ingredients

2 chicken breasts, chopped
1 garlic clove, minced
½ tsp paprika
¼ tsp dried oregano
¼ tsp dried thyme

1 tsp cayenne pepper
Salt and white pepper to taste
1 tbsp oil olive
1 onion, chopped
1 tbsp tomato puree

2 cups chicken broth
1 cup long-grain rice
1 celery stalk, diced
1 cup frozen green peas

Directions

Season chicken with garlic powder, oregano, white pepper, thyme, paprika, cayenne pepper, and salt. Warm the oil in your Instant Pot on Sauté. Add in onion and cook for 4 minutes until fragrant. Mix in tomato puree to coat. Add ¼ cup chicken stock into the cooker to deglaze the pan, scrape the pan's bottom to get rid of browned bits of food.

Mix in celery, rice, and seasoned chicken. Add in the remaining broth to the chicken mixture. Seal the lid and cook on High Pressure for 8 minutes. Do a quick release. Mix in green peas, cover with the lid, and let sit for 5 minutes. Serve warm.

Hainanese Chicken Rice

Serves: 2-4 | Ready in about: 35 minutes

Ingredients

2 tbsp sesame oil
1 lb boneless, skinless chicken breasts
½ cup Thai sweet chili sauce
2 tbsp soy sauce

1 tsp minced fresh ginger
1 garlic clove, minced
1 lime, juiced
1 tsp habanero hot sauce

1 tbsp peanut butter
½ cup white rice
½ cup chicken broth
1 cup coconut milk

Directions

Set your Instant Pot to Sauté and warm the sesame oil. Place in the chicken and brown for 6 minutes on all sides. Remove to a plate. In a bowl, mix sweet chili sauce, soy sauce, ginger, garlic, lime juice, habanero sauce, and peanut butter. Stir to combine. Place the rice in the pot, top with the chicken, and pour the sauce over. Add in broth and coconut milk.

Seal the lid, select Manual on High, and cook for 10 minutes. When done, perform a natural pressure release for 10 minutes. Remove the chicken to a plate. Shred-it with a fork. Fluff the rice and ladle it into bowls. Top with the chicken and serve.

Vegetable Chicken Risotto

Serves: 2-4 | Ready in about: 65 minutes

Ingredients

10 oz chicken breasts, cut into pieces
6 oz button mushrooms, stems removed
1 red bell pepper, halved, seeds removed
1 green bell pepper, halved, seeds removed
1 yellow bell pepper, halved, seeds removed

6 oz broccoli, cut into florets
2 carrots, peeled and chopped
½ cup sweet corn
1 cup rice
2 tbsp olive oil

1 tbsp butter
Salt and black pepper to taste
1 tsp fresh basil, finely chopped
Parmesan cheese for topping

Directions

Add rice and pour in 3 cups of water. Stir in butter, pepper and salt and seal the lid. Cook on Rice mode for 8 minutes on High. Do a quick release and remove the rice. Heat oil on Sauté, and add carrots and broccoli. Sauté for 10 minutes. Add sweet corn and bell peppers and cook for 5 minutes, stirring constantly. Finally, stir in mushrooms, and cook for 3-4 minutes.

Remove the vegetables, mix with rice, and set aside. Add the chicken to the pot and pour in 2 cups of water. Season with salt and pepper. Seal the lid and cook on High pressure for 7 minutes. Do a quick release. Open the lid, stir in rice and vegetables and serve warm sprinkled with Parmesan cheese.

Lime Bulgur Bowl

Serves: 2-4 | Ready in about: 30 minutes

Ingredients

1 tbsp olive oil
1 small onion, chopped
2 cloves garlic, minced

1 cup bulgur
2 ½ cups vegetable broth
1 tbsp lime juice

1 handful fresh parsley, roughly chopped
10 black olives to garnish
Salt and black pepper to taste

Directions

Heat oil on Sauté. Stir in garlic and onion and cook for 3-4 minutes until golden brown. Add in cilantro, bulgur, and salt. Place lime juice and broth into the cooker. Seal the lid and cook on High Pressure for 1 minute. Do a quick release. Add fresh parsley as you stir. Season with additional lime juice, salt, and pepper if desired. Serve in bowls topped with black olives.

Rich Louisiana Chicken with Quinoa

Serves: 2-4 | Ready in about: 20 minutes

Ingredients

2 tbsp olive oil	2 green bell peppers, deseeded and sliced	Salt to taste
4 chicken breasts, thinly sliced	1 cup dry rainbow quinoa	1 lemon, zested and juiced
1 tsp Creole seasoning	2 cups chicken broth	2 chives, chopped

Directions

Set your Instant Pot to Sauté. Heat the olive oil in the inner pot, season chicken with Creole seasoning, and fry with bell peppers until chicken is golden brown on both sides, and peppers soften, 5 minutes. Stir in quinoa, chicken broth, and salt.

Seal the lid, select Manual on High, and cook for 10 minutes. After cooking, perform quick pressure and select Sauté. Stir in lemon zest and lemon juice. Dish the meal into serving bowls and serve warm topped with chives.

Homemade Stuffed Mushrooms

Serves: 2-4 | Ready in about: 45 minutes

Ingredients

4 portobello mushrooms, stems and gills removed

2 tbsp melted butter	¼ cup black olives, pitted and chopped	Salt and black pepper to taste
1 cup brown rice, cooked	1 green bell pepper, seeded and diced	1 tbsp minced fresh cilantro
1 tomato, seed removed and chopped	½ cup feta cheese, crumbled	1 cup vegetable broth

Directions

Brush the mushrooms with butter. Arrange the mushrooms in a single layer in an oiled baking pan. In a bowl, mix the rice, tomato, olives, bell pepper, feta cheese, salt, and black pepper. Spoon the rice mixture into the mushrooms. Pour in the broth, seal the lid and cook on High Pressure for 10 minutes. Do a quick release. Garnish with fresh cilantro and serve immediately.

Cilantro Chicken with Rice Noodles

Serves: 2-4 | Ready in about: 30 minutes

Ingredients

4 chicken breasts	Salt and black pepper to taste	1 tbsp chopped peanuts to garnish
¾ cup chicken broth	5 oz rice noodles	1 tsp chopped cilantro to garnish
1 cup peanut sauce	1 cup green beans, trimmed and halved	

Directions

In theinner pot, add chicken, broth, peanut sauce, and salt. Seal the lid, select Manual/Pressure Cook on High, and set time to 12 minutes. After cooking, perform a quick pressure release. In a bowl, pour rice noodles and top with 2 cups water.

Allow sitting for 4 minutes. Strain noodles through a colander and divide between plates. Select Sauté and add green beans. Cook for 3 minutes and season. Top with chicken and sauce, garnish with peanuts, and cilantro and serve.

Colorful Bean & Quinoa Bowl

Serves: 2-4 | Ready in about: 30 minutes

Ingredients

1 tsp olive oil	1 tsp ground cumin	1 cup organic tri-color quinoa, rinsed
1 green bell pepper, diced	½ tsp salt	1 cup red salsa
1 onion, diced	14 oz canned pinto beans, drained	1 cup vegetable broth

Directions

Warm oil on Sauté. Add red onion and green bell pepper as you stir. Add salt and cumin, and cook for 7-8 minutes until fragrant. To the vegetable mixture, add quinoa, broth, salsa, and pinto beans. Seal the lid and cook on High Pressure for 12 minutes. Do a quick pressure release. Use a fork to fluff the quinoa. Divide between serving bowls and serve.

Smoky Chicken Pilaf

Serves: 2-4 | Ready in about: 50 minutes

Ingredients

2 tbsp olive oil
½ lb boneless chicken thighs, skin on
1 leek, chopped
1 cup rice, rinsed

Salt and black pepper to serve
¼ tsp ground smoked paprika
¼ tsp ground coriander
1 bay leaf

2 cups chicken stock
1 carrot, chopped
1 celery stick, chopped
2 garlic cloves, minced

Directions

Set your Instant Pot to Sauté and heat the olive oil. Cook chicken for 5 minutes per side or until golden brown; reserve. Put in leek, carrot, celery, and garlic and cook for 3 minutes. Stir in the rice, salt, black pepper, cumin, paprika, coriander, and bay leaf. Cook for 2 minutes. Pour in the stock and add stir. Return the chicken.

Seal the lid, select Manual, and set the cooking time to 15 minutes on High. When done, perform a natural pressure release for 10 minutes. Unlock the lid and remove the bay leaf. Fluff the rice with a fork and serve.

Bacon Chicken with Beans

Serves: 2-4 | Ready in about: 45 minutes

Ingredients

1 tbsp olive oil
4 slices bacon, crumbled
4 boneless, skinless chicken thighs
1 onion, diced
2 garlic cloves, minced
1 tbsp tomato paste

½ tsp oregano
1 tsp ground cumin
1 tsp chili powder
½ tsp cayenne pepper
1 (14.5-oz) can whole tomatoes
1 cup chicken broth

1 tsp salt
1 cup cooked corn
1 red bell pepper, chopped
15 oz red kidney beans, drained
1 cup shredded Monterey Jack cheese
1 tbsp chopped cilantro

Directions

Warm the olive oil in your Instant Pot on Sauté. Sear the chicken for 3 minutes for each side until browned. Set the chicken on a plate. In the same oil, fry bacon until crispy, about 5 minutes; set aside. Add in onion and cook for 2 to 3 minutes until fragrant. Stir in garlic, oregano, cayenne, cumin, tomato paste, bell pepper, and chili and cook for 30 more seconds.

Pour the chicken broth, salt, and tomatoes and bring to a boil. Take back the chicken and bacon to the pot and ensure it is submerged in the braising liquid. Seal the lid and cook on High Pressure for 15 minutes. Release the pressure quickly. Pour the beans in the pot, press Sauté, and bring the liquid to a boil. Cook for 10 minutes. Serve topped with cheese and cilantro.

Zesty Turkey Risotto

Serves: 2-4 | Ready in about: 40 minutes

Ingredients

2 boneless turkey breasts, cut into strips
2 lemons, zested and juiced
1 tbsp dried oregano
2 garlic cloves, minced

1½ tbsp olive oil
1 onion, diced
2 cups chicken broth
1 cup arborio rice, rinsed

Salt and black pepper to taste
¼ cup chopped fresh parsley, or to taste
Lemon slices for garnish

Directions

In a Ziploc bag, mix turkey, oregano, sea salt, garlic, juice and zest of two lemons. Marinate for 10 minutes. Warm the oil in your Instant Pot on Sauté. Add onion and cook for 3 minutes. Add rice and chicken broth and season with pepper and salt.

Empty the ziploc having the chicken and marinade into the pot. Seal the lid and cook on High Pressure for 12 minutes. Release the pressure quickly. Divide the rice and turkey between serving bowls; garnish with lemon slices and parsley.

Middle Easters Chicken with Couscous

Serves: 2-4 | Ready in about: 40 minutes

Ingredients

4 chicken thighs
2 tbsp za'atar mix
1 tbsp ground sumac
Salt and black pepper to taste

2 tbsp butter
2 cups chicken stock, divided
1 onion, chopped
1 garlic clove, minced

1 cup couscous
Juice from 1 lemon
2 tbsp fresh parsley, chopped

Directions

Season the chicken with salt, sumac, za'atar, and pepper. Melt butter in your Instant Pot on Sauté and sear the chicken in batches for 5 minutes per batch until lightly browned. Set aside. Into the cooker, add ¼ cup chicken stock to deglaze the bottom, scrape the bottom to get rid of any browned bits of food. Add in garlic and onion and cook for 3 minutes until soft.

Add in the remaining chicken stock, lemon juice, couscous, and chicken. Seal the lid and cook on High Pressure for 5 minutes. Naturally release the pressure for 10 minutes. Garnish with parsley and serve.

Yummy Pilaf with Roasted Bell Peppers

Serves: 2-4 | Ready in about: 25 minutes

Ingredients

2 tbsp olive oil

1 garlic clove, minced

1 cup vegetable stock

¼ cup lemon juice

1 tsp grated lemon zest

½ cup rice

Salt and black pepper to taste

6 oz roasted bell peppers

Directions

Warm half of the oil in your Instant Pot on Sauté and cook garlic until soft, about 1 minute. Stir in stock, lemon juice, lemon zest, salt, pepper, and rice. Seal the lid and cook on High Pressure for 20 minutes. Do a natural pressure release for 10 minutes. In a bowl, toss peppers with the remaining oil, salt, and pepper. Pour over the rice and serve.

Parsley Jasmine Rice

Serves: 2-4 | Ready in about: 25 minutes

Ingredients

½ cup jasmine rice

Salt and black pepper to taste

2 tbsp parsley, chopped

Directions

Place the rice and 1 cup of water in your Instant Pot. Season with salt and pepper. Seal the lid and cook for 15 minutes on High Pressure. Release pressure naturally for 10 minutes. Use a fork to fluff the rice. Top with parsley before serving.

Easy Zucchini Boats

Serves: 2-4 | Ready in about: 20 minutes

Ingredients

2 small zucchini, halved lengthwise

½ cup cooked rice

½ cup canned white beans, drained

½ cup chopped tomatoes

½ cup chopped toasted cashew nuts

½ cup grated Parmesan cheese

2 tbsp melted butter

Salt and black pepper to taste

Directions

Pour 1 cup of water in the instant pot and insert a trivet. Scoop out the pulp of zucchini and chop roughly. In a bowl, mix the zucchini pulp, rice, tomatoes, cashew nuts, ¼ cup of Parmesan, 1 tbsp of melted butter, salt, and black pepper.

Fill the zucchini boats with the mixture, and arrange the stuffed boats in a single layer on the trivet. Seal the lid and cook for 15 minutes on Steam on High. Do a quick release and serve.

Thai Chicken Curry Rice

Serves: 2-4 | Ready in about: 35 minutes

Ingredients

4 chicken thighs

Salt and black pepper to taste

1 tbsp olive oil

1 medium carrot, julienned

1 red bell pepper, thinly sliced

2 tbsp red curry paste

1 garlic clove, minced

1 tsp ginger paste

1 cup basmati rice

2 cups chicken broth

2 tbsp chopped cilantro to garnish

1 lime, cut into wedges

Directions

Set your Instant Pot to Sauté. Heat the olive oil in the inner pot, season chicken with salt and black pepper, and sear in oil until golden brown on both sides, 6 minutes. Place on a plate and set aside. Add carrots and bell pepper to oil and cook until softened, 4 minutes. Stir in curry paste, garlic, and ginger; sauté for 1 minute.

Add rice and broth and stir. Arrange chicken on top. Seal the lid, select Manual on High, and set the cooking time to 10 minutes. After cooking, do a natural pressure release for 10 minutes. Garnish with cilantro and lime wedges and serve.

Effortless Mexican Rice

Serves: 2-4 | Ready in about: 30 minutes

Ingredients

3 tbsp olive oil
1 small onion, chopped
2 garlic cloves, minced
1 serrano pepper, chopped

1 cup bomba rice
⅓ cup red salsa
¼ cup tomato sauce
½ cup vegetable broth

1 tsp Mexican seasoning mix
16 oz canned pinto beans, drained
1 tsp salt
1 tbsp chopped fresh parsley

Directions

Warm the olive oil in your Instant Pot on Sauté. Cook onion, garlic, and serrano pepper for 2 minutes, stirring occasionally until fragrant. Stir in rice, salsa, tomato sauce, vegetable broth, Mexican seasoning, beans, and salt. Seal the lid and cook on High Pressure for 10 minutes. Do a natural pressure release for 10 minutes. Sprinkle with fresh parsley and serve.

Yummy Kidney Bean & Spinach Stew

Serves: 2-4 | Ready in about: 45 minutes

Ingredients

2 tbsp olive oil
1 onion, chopped
2 cloves garlic, minced
1 carrot, chopped

1 cup celery, chopped
4 cups vegetable broth
1 cup white kidney beans, soaked
1 tsp dried thyme

1 tsp dried rosemary
1 bay leaf
1 cup spinach, torn into pieces
Salt and black pepper to taste

Directions

Warm the olive oil in your Instant Pot on Sauté. Stir in celery, carrot, garlic, and onion and cook for 5 minutes until tender. Add broth, bay leaf, thyme, rosemary, beans, and salt. Seal the lid and cook for 30 minutes on High Pressure. Quick-release the pressure and stir in spinach. Allow sitting for 2 to 4 minutes until the spinach wilts, and season with pepper and salt.

Basmati Rice & Beef Dinner

Serves: 2-4 | Ready in about: 40 minutes

Ingredients

¼ cup yogurt
2 cloves garlic, smashed
1 tbsp olive oil
1 lime, juiced
Salt and black pepper to taste
2 lb beef stew meat, cubed

1 tbsp garam masala
1 tbsp fresh ginger, grated
1 ½ tsp smoked paprika
1 tsp ground cumin
¼ tsp cayenne pepper
3 tbsp butter

1 onion, chopped
1 (14-oz) can puréed tomatoes
½ cup beef broth
1 cup basmati rice, rinsed
½ cup heavy cream
½ bunch fresh cilantro, chopped

Directions

In a bowl, mix garlic, lime juice, olive oil, pepper, salt, and yogurt. Stir in the beef. In a different bowl, mix paprika, garam masala, cumin, ginger, and cayenne pepper. Melt butter in your Instant Pot on Sauté. Stir-fry the onion for 7 to 9 minutes. Sprinkle spice mixture over onion and cook for about 30 seconds. Add in the beef-yogurt mixture. Sauté for 3 to 4 minutes until meat is slightly cooked. Mix in broth and puréed tomatoes. Set trivet over beef in the cooker's inner pot.

In an oven-proof bowl, mix 1 ¼ cups water and rice. Set the bowl onto the trivet. Seal the lid and cook on High Pressure for 10 minutes. Release pressure quickly. Remove the oven-proof bowl and the trivet. Add pepper, salt, and heavy cream into beef mixture and stir. Fluff the rice and divide it between serving plates. Top with beef and garnish with cilantro to serve.

Chili Chicken & Rice

Serves: 2-4 | Ready in about: 35 minutes

Ingredients

½ tsp cayenne pepper
1 tsp garlic powder
1 ½ tsp paprika
½ tsp chili pepper
½ tsp dried basil
¼ tsp red pepper flakes

1 tsp lemon juice
2 tbsp olive oil
1 lb chicken thighs
1 link andouille sausages, sliced
1 jalapeño pepper, deseeded and diced
1 yellow onion, diced

2 celery stalks, diced
1 cup basmati rice
2 cups chicken broth
Salt and black pepper to taste
2 tbsp scallions, chopped
2 tbsp chopped parsley

Directions

In a medium bowl, combine cayenne pepper, salt, garlic powder, paprika, chili pepper, basil, pepper flakes, lemon juice, and 1 tbsp oil and mix. Place in chicken, coat it in the marinade, cover with plastic wrap, and chill in the fridge for 1 hour.

Set your Instant Pot to Sauté. Heat the remaining oil in the inner pot. Remove chicken from marinade and sear in oil on both sides until golden brown, 6 minutes. Place on a plate and set aside. Brown sausages in the pot for 5 minutes and spoon to the side of chicken. To the pot, add jalapeño pepper, onion, and celery and sauté until softened, 3 minutes.

Stir in rice, chicken broth, salt, and pepper. Place chicken and sausages on top. Seal the lid, select Manual/Pressure Cook on High, and set time to 5 minutes. Allow sitting (covered) for 10 minutes and then perform a quick pressure release to let out remaining steam. Unlock the lid, stir rice, and spoon into serving plates. Garnish with scallions and parsley and serve.

Chicken with Asparagus & Jasmine Rice

Serves: 2-4 | Ready in about: 40 minutes

Ingredients

1 tbsp olive oil	2 garlic cloves, minced	1 cup asparagus, chopped
4 chicken breasts	1 cup jasmine rice	1 tbsp parsley for garnish
1 tsp garlic salt	1 lemon, zested and juiced	Black pepper to taste
½ cup onion, finely diced	2 ¼ cups chicken broth	Lemon slices to garnish

Directions

Set your Instant Pot to Sauté. Heat the olive oil in the inner pot. Season the chicken with garlic salt and black pepper and sear it on both sides until golden brown, about 6 minutes. Place on a plate and set aside.

Add onion to the pot and cook until softened, 3 minutes. Stir in garlic for 30 seconds. Stir in rice and cook until translucent, 2 minutes. Add lemon zest, lemon juice, chicken broth, asparagus, salt, pepper, and place chicken on top.

Seal the lid, select Manual/Pressure Cook mode on High, and set the cooking time to 5 minutes. After cooking, perform natural pressure release for 15 minutes, then quick pressure release to let out the remaining steam. Unlock the lid, fluff rice, and plate. Garnish with parsley and lemon slices; serve warm.

Roasted with Feta & Rice

Serves: 2-4 | Ready in about: 30 minutes

Ingredients

2 cups vegetable broth	Salt and black pepper to taste	2 tsp arrowroot starch
1 lb butternut squash, peeled and sliced	1 cup feta cheese, cubed	1 cup jasmine rice, cooked
2 tbsp melted butter, divided	1 tbsp coconut aminos	

Directions

Pour the rice and broth in your Instant Pot and stir to combine. In a bowl, toss butternut squash with 1 tbsp of melted butter and season with salt and black pepper. In another bowl, mix the remaining butter, water, and coconut aminos.

Toss in feta and arrowroot starch. Transfer to a greased baking dish. Lay a trivet over the rice and place the baking dish on the trivet. Seal the lid and cook on High for 15 minutes. Do a quick pressure release. Serve with squash and feta.

Vegetable & Shrimp Risotto

Serves: 2-4 | Ready in about: 1 hour 15 minutes

Ingredients

1 tbsp avocado oil	1 cup rice, rinsed and drained	16 shrimp, cleaned and deveined
1 lb asparagus, trimmed and chopped	1¼ cups chicken broth	Salt and black pepper to taste
1 cup spinach, chopped	¾ cup coconut milk	¾ cup Parmesan cheese, shredded
1½ cups mushrooms, sliced	1 tbsp coconut oil	

Directions

Warm the oil in your Instant Pot on Sauté. Add spinach, mushrooms, and asparagus, and sauté for 10 minutes. Add rice, coconut milk, and chicken broth to the pot as you stir. Seal the lid, press Manual, and cook for 40 minutes on High Pressure.

Do a quick release, open the lid, and put the rice on a serving plate. Take back the empty pot to the cooker, add coconut oil, and press Sauté. Add shrimp and cook each side taking 4 minutes until cooked through and turns pink. Set shrimp over rice, add pepper and salt. Top with Parmesan cheese. Serve.

Tortiglioni with Turkey Strips

Serves: 2 | Ready in about: 35 minutes

Ingredients

1 tsp chili powder
¼ tsp salt
½ tsp cumin
½ tsp onion powder
½ tsp garlic powder
¼ tsp thyme

½ lb turkey breast, cut into strips
½ tbsp olive oil
½ red onion, cut into wedges
1 garlic clove, minced
1 cup chicken broth
⅓ cup salsa

5 oz tortiglioni
½ red bell pepper, chopped diagonally
½ yellow bell pepper, chopped diagonally
⅓ cup shredded Gouda cheese
¼ cup sour cream
2 tbsp chopped parsley

Directions

In a bowl, mix chili powder, cumin, garlic powder, onion powder, salt, and oregano. Reserve 1 tsp of seasoning. Coat turkey with the remaining seasoning. Warm oil in your Instant Pot on Sauté. Add in turkey strips and sauté for 4 to 5 minutes until browned. Place the turkey in a bowl. Sauté the onion and garlic for 1 minute in the cooker until soft. Press Cancel.

Mix in salsa, broth, and scrape the bottom of any brown bits. Into the broth mixture, stir in tortiglioni, and cover with bell peppers and chicken. Seal the lid and cook for 5 minutes on High Pressure. Do a quick pressure release. Sprinkle with gouda cheese and reserved seasoning and stir. Divide into plates and top with sour cream. Add parsley for garnishing and serve.

Classic Shrimp Lo Mein

Serves: 2 | Ready in about: 20 minutes

Ingredients

1 tbsp sesame oil
1 lb shrimp, peeled and deveined
½ cup diced onion
2 cloves garlic, minced

1 cup carrots, cut into strips
1 cup green beans, washed
2 cups vegetable stock
3 tbsp soy sauce

2 tbsp rice wine vinegar
10 oz lo mein egg noodles
½ tsp toasted sesame seeds
Sea salt and black pepper to taste

Directions

Warm oil in your Instant Pot on Sauté. Stir-fry the shrimp for 5 minutes. Remove to a plate and set aside. Add garlic and onion to the pot and cook for 3 minutes until fragrant. Mix in soy sauce, carrots, stock, beans, and rice wine vinegar.

Add noodles into the mixture and ensure they are covered. Season with pepper and salt. Seal the lid and cook on High Pressure for 5 minutes. Release the pressure quickly. Serve the lo mein in plates, add the shrimp and sprinkle with sesame.

Cheesy Tagliatelle

Serves: 2 | Ready in about: 15 minutes

Ingredients

1 ½ tbsp goat's cheese, chopped
1 ½ tbsp grated Pecorino cheese
2 tbsp grated Parmesan

½ cup heavy cream
2 tbsp grated gouda cheese
2 tbsp butter, softened

½ tbsp Italian seasoning mix
⅓ cup vegetable broth
⅓ lb tagliatelle

Directions

In a bowl, mix goat cheese, pecorino, Parmesan, and heavy cream. Stir in Italian seasoning. Transfer to your instant pot. Stir in the broth and butter. Seal the lid and cook on High Pressure for 4 minutes. Do a quick release. Drop the tagliatelle in boiling water of the pot and cook for 6 minutes. Stir in the tagliatelle. Top with gouda and let simmer for 10 minutes on Sauté.

Garganelli with Mushrooms & Gruyere Cheese

Serves: 2-4 | Ready in about: 10 minutes

Ingredients

8 oz garganelli
1½ tsp salt
1 large egg

8 oz gruyère cheese, shredded
1 recipe sautéed mushrooms
2 tbsp chopped fresh cilantro

3 tbsp sour cream
3 tbsp melted butter
3 tbsp grated Cheddar cheese

Directions

Put the garganelli in your Instant Pot and cover with water. Add in butter and salt. Seal the lid and cook on High Pressure for 4 minutes. Do a quick pressure release. In a bowl, Whisk egg, Gruyère cheese, and sour cream. Stir in garganelli to melt the cheese and add the mushrooms. Serve hot sprinkled with cheddar cheese.

Chicken with Rotini & Spinach

Serves: 2-4 | Ready in about: 30 minutes

Ingredients

2 tbsp butter
4 chicken breasts, cut into cubes
Salt and black pepper to taste
1 small yellow onion, diced

4 cups sliced white mushrooms
1 garlic clove, minced
1 lb rotini pasta
1 cup chicken broth

1 tsp chopped oregano
4 cups chopped baby spinach
½ cup crumbled goat cheese

Directions

Set your Instant Pot to Sauté and adjust to medium heat. Melt butter in the inner pot, season chicken with salt and black pepper, and sear in oil until golden brown, 4 minutes. Place on a plate and set aside. Add onion and mushrooms in the pot and cook until softened, 4 minutes. Stir in garlic, allow to release fragrant for 30 seconds. Return the chicken to the pot.

Stir in rotini, chicken broth, and oregano. Seal the lid, select Manual on High, and set the cooking time to 3 minutes. After cooking, do a natural pressure release for 10 minutes, then a quick pressure release to let out remaining steam.

Select Sauté and unlock the lid. Stir in spinach, allow wilting, and mix in goat cheese until adequately incorporated. Adjust taste with salt and black pepper and serve warm.

Kale & Rigatoni with Tomato Sauce

Serves: 2 | Ready in about: 15 minutes

Ingredients

½ lb rigatoni pasta
5 oz canned tomato sauce
1 garlic clove, minced

½ tsp chili flakes
½ tsp salt
½ tbsp extra-virgin olive oil

2 tbsp fresh basil, minced
½ cup kale, chopped
2 tbsp cup Parmesan cheese

Directions

Add tomato sauce, salt, pasta, chili flakes, and garlic powder and mix well. Cover with water. Seal lid and cook for 5 minutes on Low Pressure. Release the pressure quickly. Stir in kale until wilted. Plate the pasta and top with the Parmesan cheese and basil. Drizzle olive oil over the pasta. Serve.

Pesto Minestrone with Pasta

Serves: 2-4 | Ready in about: 15 minutes

Ingredients

3 tbsp olive oil
1 onion, diced
1 celery stalk, diced
1 large carrot, peeled and diced
14 oz canned chopped tomatoes

4 oz rigatoni
1 cup chopped zucchini
1 bay leaf
1 tsp mixed herbs
¼ tsp cayenne pepper

½ tsp salt
¼ cup grated Pecorino Romano cheese
1 garlic clove, minced
⅓ cup olive-oil based pesto

Directions

Heat oil in your Instant Pot on Sauté and cook onion, celery, garlic, and carrot for 3 minutes, stirring occasionally until the vegetables are softened. Stir in rigatoni, tomatoes, 3 cups water, zucchini, bay leaf, herbs, cayenne, and salt.

Seal the lid and cook on High for 4 minutes. Do a natural pressure release for 10 minutes. Adjust the taste of the soup with salt and pepper and remove the bay leaf. Ladle the soup into bowls and drizzle the pesto over. Serve with the garlic toasts.

Chili Mac & Cheese

Serves: 2 | Ready in about: 15 minutes

Ingredients

4 oz macaroni
1 ¼ cups cold water
1 egg

½ tbsp chipotle chili powder
1 tbsp butter
½ cup milk

1 cup sharp cheddar cheese, grated
1 cup Pecorino Romano cheese, grated

Directions

Add salt, water, and macaroni. Seal the lid and cook for 4 minutes on High Pressure. Take a bowl and beat egg, chipotle chili powder, and black pepper to mix well. Release the pressure quickly. Add butter to the pasta and stir until melts. Stir in milk and egg mixture. Pour in Pecorino Romano and cheddar cheeses until melted. Season to taste and serve.

Linguine with Squash & Parmesan

Serves: 2-4 | Ready in about: 45 minutes

Ingredients

1 cup flour

2 tsp salt

2 eggs

1 cup seasoned breadcrumbs

½ cup grated Parmesan cheese

1 yellow squash, peeled and sliced

1 lb linguine, cut in half

24 oz canned tomato sauce

2 tbsp olive oil

1 cup shredded mozzarella cheese

2 tbsp minced fresh basil

Directions

Put the linguine in your Instant Pot and cover with salted. Seal the lid and cook on High Pressure for 5 minutes. Combine the flour and salt in a bowl. In another bowl, whisk the eggs and 2 tbsp of water. In a third bowl, mix the breadcrumbs and mozzarella cheese. Coat squash slices in the flour. Shake off excess flour, dip in the eggs, and dredge in the breadcrumbs.

Quickly release the pressure. Remove linguine to a serving bowl and mix in the tomato sauce and sprinkle with fresh basil. Heat oil on Sauté and fry breaded squash until crispy. Serve the squash topped mozzarella with the linguine on the side.

Homemade Stuffed Shells

Serves: 2 | Ready in about: 1 hour

Ingredients

½ cup onion, chopped

½ cup carrot, chopped

1 garlic clove, minced

2 tbsp olive oil

10 oz canned tomatoes, crushed

4 oz jumbo shell pasta

1 cup ricotta cheese, crumbled

½ cup feta cheese, crumbled

1 cup spinach, chopped

¼ cup grated Pecorino Romano cheese

1 tbsp chopped fresh chives

½ tbsp chopped fresh dill

Salt and black pepper to taste

½ cup shredded cheddar cheese

Directions

Warm 1 tbsp of olive oil on Sauté. Add in onion, carrot, and garlic, and cook for 5 minutes until tender. Stir in tomatoes and cook for another 10 minutes; set aside. Wipe the pot with a damp cloth, add pasta, and cover with enough water. Seal the lid and cook for 5 minutes on High Pressure. Do a quick release and drain the pasta. Lightly grease olive oil to a baking sheet.

In a bowl, combine feta and ricotta cheese. Add in spinach, Pecorino Romano cheese, dill, and chives, and stir well. Adjust the seasonings. Using a spoon, fill the shells with the mixture. Spread 4 cups tomato sauce on the baking sheet. Place the stuffed shells over with seam-sides down and sprinkle cheddar cheese atop. Use aluminum foil to cover the baking dish.

Pour 1 cup of water in the pot and insert a trivet. Lower the baking dish onto the trivet. Seal the lid and cook for 15 minutes on High Pressure. Do a quick release. Take away the foil. Place the shells to serving plates and top with tomato sauce to serve.

Tofu & Chili Rice Noodles

Serves: 2 | Ready in about: 20 minutes

Ingredients

¼ cup soy sauce

1 tbsp brown sugar

1 tbsp rice vinegar

½ tbsp sweet chili sauce

1 tbsp sesame oil

1 tsp fresh minced garlic

6 oz extra firm tofu, pressed and cubed

3 oz rice noodles

2 tbsp chopped fresh chives, for garnish

Directions

Heat the oil in your Instant Pot on Sauté and fry the tofu for 5 minutes until golden brown. Set aside. To the pot, add 1 cup water, garlic, olive oil, vinegar, sugar, soy sauce, and chili sauce and mix well until smooth. Stir in rice noodles.

Seal the lid and cook on High Pressure for 3 minutes. Release the pressure quickly. Split the noodles between bowls. Top with fried tofu and sprinkle with fresh chives before serving.

Vegan Sloppy Joes

Serves: 2 | Ready in about: 45 minutes

Ingredients

½ cup pearl barley, rinsed

½ cup green onion, chopped

1 clove garlic, minced

½ cup tomato sauce

1 tbsp brown sugar

1 tbsp Worcestershire sauce

½ tsp Dijon mustard

⅓ tsp smoked paprika

⅓ tsp chili powder

2 brioche buns

Dill Pickles for garnish

Directions

In the pot, mix Worcestershire sauce, 1 cup water, onion, garlic, brown sugar, barley, tomato sauce, and spices. Seal the lid and cook for 25 minutes on High Pressure. Release the pressure quickly. Press Sauté and cook until the mixture becomes thick. Transfer the sloppy joe mixture to the brioche buns and top with dill pickles.

Basil & Ricotta Pasta

Serves: 2 | Ready in about: 15 minutes

Ingredients

1 tbsp olive oil
½ onion, chopped
2 garlic cloves, minced
½ tsp red pepper flakes

2 cups dried fusilli
10 oz can tomato sauce
3/4 cup tomatoes, halved
2 tbsp basil leaves

½ tsp salt
½ cup Ricotta cheese, crumbled
½ tbsp chopped fresh basil

Directions

Warm the olive oil in your Instant Pot on Sauté. Add in red pepper flakes, garlic, and onion and cook for 3 minutes. Mix in fusilli, tomatoes, half of the basil leaves, 1 cup water, tomato sauce, and salt. Seal the lid, and cook on High Pressure for 4 minutes. Release the pressure quickly. Transfer the pasta to a platter and top with ricotta and remaining chopped basil.

Beef with Cheddar & Pasta

Serves: 2 | Ready in about: 20 minutes

Ingredients

3 oz ground beef
⅓ lb fettuccine pasta
⅓ cup cheddar cheese, shredded

⅓ cup fresh spinach, torn
½ small onion, chopped
1 cup tomatoes, diced

1 tbsp butter
Salt and black pepper to taste

Directions

Melt butter on Sauté. Stir-fry beef and onion for 5 minutes. Add pasta. Pour water enough to cover and season with salt and pepper. Cook on High Pressure for 5 minutes. Do a quick release. Press Sauté and stir in tomato and spinach. Cook for 5 minutes. Top with cheddar cheese to serve.

Chicken Parmigiana with Rigatoni

Serves: 2-4 | Ready in about: 40 minutes

Ingredients

4 chicken thighs, boneless and cubed
5 cups tomato pasta sauce
1 cup chicken broth

Salt and black pepper to taste
¼ tsp red chili flakes
1 tsp garlic powder

10 oz rigatoni
1 cup grated Parmesan cheese
2 cups grated mozzarella cheese

Directions

Add chicken to your Instant Pot. Top with pasta sauce, chicken broth, salt, black pepper, red chili flakes, and garlic powder. Seal the lid, select Manual/Pressure Cook on High, and set the cooking time to 12 minutes. After cooking, perform a quick pressure release. Stir in rigatoni. Seal the lid again, select Manual on High, and set the cooking time for 5 minutes. After cooking, perform a quick pressure release. Stir in Parmesan cheese to melt. Top with mozzarella and serve warm.

Basil Linguine with Cherry Tomato

Serves: 2-4 | Ready in about: 30 minutes

Ingredients

2 tbsp olive oil
1 small onion, diced
2 garlic cloves, minced
1 cup cherry tomatoes, halved

1 ½ cups vegetable stock
¼ cup julienned basil leaves
Salt and black pepper to taste
¼ tsp red chili flakes

1 lb linguine noodles, halved
1 tbsp fresh basil leaves, chopped
½ cup Parmigiano cheese, grated

Directions

Warm oil in your Instant Pot on Sauté. Cook onion, garlic, and cherry tomatoes for 5 minutes. Add in stock, salt, red chili flakes, and pepper and mix. Add linguine to the tomato mixture until covered. Seal the lid and cook on High Pressure for 5 minutes. Naturally release the pressure for 10 minutes. Stir the mixture. Top with basil and Parmigiano cheese and serve.

Cheesy Macaroni with Chicken & Bacon

Serves: 2-4 | Ready in about: 35 minutes

Ingredients

4 bacon slices, chopped
2 tbsp olive oil
4 chicken breasts

1 tbsp ranch dressing mix
16 oz macaroni
3 cups chicken broth

Salt and black pepper to taste
4 oz cream cheese, softened
1 cup grated Monterey Jack cheese

Directions

Set your Instant Pot to Sauté and adjust to medium heat. Cook bacon in the inner pot until brown and crispy. Remove onto a plate and set aside. Heat olive oil in bacon fat, season chicken with ranch dressing mix, and sear in oil until golden, 5 minutes. Return bacon to pot and top with macaroni and chicken broth. Season with salt and pepper.

Seal the lid, select Manual/Pressure Cook on High, and set the cooking time to 6 minutes. After cooking, perform a quick pressure release to let out remaining steam, and unlock the lid. Select Sauté and mix in cream cheese and Monterey Jack cheese until melted, 3 minutes. Dish food and serve warm.

Spinach & Pork Spaghetti

Serves: 2-4 | Ready in about: 35 minutes

Ingredients

2 tbsp olive oil
½ onion, chopped
1 garlic clove, minced
1 lb pork sausage meat

1 (14-oz) can diced tomatoes, drained
½ cup sun-dried tomatoes
1 tbsp dried oregano
1 teaspoon Italian seasoning

1 fresh jalapeño pepper, seeded, minced
1 tsp salt
8 oz dried spaghetti, halved
1 cup spinach

Directions

Warm oil in your Instant Pot on Sauté. Add in onion and garlic and cook for 2 minutes. Stir in sausage and jalapeño and cook for 5 minutes. Add in 2 cups water, sun-dried tomatoes, Italian seasoning, oregano, tomatoes, and salt with the chicken.

Mix spaghetti and press to submerge into the sauce. Seal the lid and cook on High Pressure for 9 minutes. Release the pressure quickly. Stir in spinach, seal the lid again, and simmer on Keep Warm for 5 minutes until spinach is wilted.

Enchilada Beef with Pasta Shells

Serves: 2-4 | Ready in about: 35 minutes

Ingredients

2 tbsp olive oil
1 lb ground beef
16 oz pasta shells
15 oz tomato sauce

15-oz can black beans, drained
15-oz canned corn, drained
10 oz red enchilada sauce
4 oz diced green chiles

1 cup shredded mozzarella cheese
Salt and black pepper to taste
Finely chopped parsley for garnish

Directions

Heat the olive oil in your Instant Pot on Sauté. Add ground beef and cook for 7 minutes until it starts to brown. Mix in pasta, tomato sauce, enchilada sauce, black beans, corn, green chiles, and enough water to cover and stir to coat.

Seal the lid and cook on High Pressure for 4 minutes. Do a quick pressure release. Mix in mozzarella cheese until melted; add black pepper and salt. Garnish with parsley and serve.

Sausage & Spinach Rigatoni

Serves: 2-4 | Ready in about: 45 minutes

Ingredients

1 tbsp butter
½ cup diced red bell pepper
1 onion, chopped
3 cups vegetable broth

¼ cup tomato purée
4 sausage links, chopped
½ cup milk
2 tsp chili powder

Salt and ground black pepper to taste
12 oz rigatoni pasta
1 cup baby spinach
½ cup Parmesan cheese

Directions

Warm butter on Sauté. Add red bell pepper, onion, and sausage, and cook for 5 minutes. Mix in broth, chili, tomato paste, salt, and pepper. Stir in rigatoni pasta. Seal the lid and cook on High Pressure for 12 minutes. Naturally release pressure for 20 minutes. Stir in spinach and let simmer until wilted. Sprinkle with Parmesan cheese and serve.

SALADS & EGGS

Creamy Frittata with Kale

Serves: 2 | Ready in about: 20 minutes

Ingredients

4 large eggs
1 tbsp heavy cream

¼ tsp grated nutmeg
Salt and black pepper to taste

½ cup kale, chopped
¼ cup grated Parmesan cheese

Directions

In a bowl, beat eggs, nutmeg, pepper, salt, and cream until smooth. Stir in Parmesan cheese and kale. Gease a cake pan with cooking spra. Wrap aluminum foil around the outside of the pan to cover fully. Place egg mixture into the prepared pan.

Pour in 1 cup of water, set a steamer rack over the water. Gently lay the pan onto the rack. Seal the lid and cook for 10 minutes on High Pressure. Release the pressure quickly. Serve sliced in wedges.

Chili Deviled Eggs

Serves: 2 | Ready in about: 20 minutes

Ingredients

4 large eggs
1 tbsp cream cheese

1 tbsp mayonnaise
Salt and black pepper to taste

1/8 tsp chili powder

Directions

Add 1 cup of water in your Instant Pot, insert a steamer basket, and lay the eggs inside. Seal the lid and cook on High Pressure for 5 minutes. Release the pressure quickly. Drop eggs into an ice bath to cool for 5 minutes. Peel eggs and halve them.

Remove the yolks to a bowl and use a fork to mash. Stir in cream cheese and mayonnaise. Add pepper and salt for seasoning. Spoon yolk mixture onto egg white halves. Serve.

Easy Homemade Omelet

Serves: 2 | Ready in about: 20 minutes

Ingredients

2 red bell peppers, chopped
4 eggs

2 tbsp olive oil
2 garlic cloves, crushed

1 tsp Italian seasoning mix

Directions

Grease in your Instant Pot with oil. Stir-fry the peppers for 2-3 minutes on each side or until lightly charred. Set aside. Add garlic to the pot and stir-fry for 2-3 minutes until soft. Whisk the eggs in a bowl. Season with Italian seasoning.

Pour the mixture into the pot and cook for 2-3 minutes or until the eggs are set. Using a spatula, loosen the edges and gently slide onto a plate. Add grilled peppers and fold over. Serve hot.

Spanish Omelet

Serves: 2 | Ready in about: 45 minutes

Ingredients

1 tbsp butter, melted
4 oz frozen hash browns, defrosted
6 large eggs

Salt and black pepper to taste
1 tsp tomato paste
¼ cup milk

¼ cup diced yellow onion
1 garlic clove, minced
4 oz grated cheddar cheese

Directions

Grease a ramekin with butter and spread hash browns at the bottom. In a bowl, whisk eggs, salt, and black pepper until frothy. In another bowl, smoothly combine tomato paste with milk and mix into eggs, onion, and garlic. Pour mixture on top of hash browns. Add 1 cup of water to the inner pot, fit in a trivet, and place the ramekin on top.

Seal the lid, select Manual/Pressure Cook on High, and set the cooking time to 15 minutes. After cooking, perform natural pressure release for 10 minutes, then a quick pressure release to let out the remaining steam.

Unlock the lid and remove the ramekin. Sprinkle with cheddar cheese and place ramekin back on top of the trivet. Cover with the lid, without locking, to melt the cheese for a minute. Once melted, slice, and serve.

Garam Masala Eggs

Serves: 2 | Ready in about: 30 minutes

Ingredients

4 eggs, whole
Ice bath
3 tsp ghee
¼ tsp fennel seeds
4 cloves

1 tbsp cinnamon powder
2 long, red chilies, halved
1-star anise
1 white onion, finely chopped
2 large tomatoes, finely chopped

¼ tsp garam masala
¼ tsp turmeric powder
½ tsp chili powder
Salt and black pepper to taste
2 tbsp chopped cilantro leaves

Directions

Place the eggs in your Instant Pot and cover with water. Seal the lid, select Manual on High, and cook for 5 minutes. After cooking, perform a quick pressure release. Transfer eggs to an ice bath. Peel cooled eggs, cut in halves, and set aside.

Discard the water from the inner pot and wipe clean with paper towels. Select Sauté and melt half of the ghee. Stir-fry fennel seeds, cloves, cinnamon, red chilies, and star anise for 3 minutes or until fragrant. Add half of the onion and tomatoes and sauté until softened, 5 minutes. Spoon mixture into a blender and process on low speed until smooth paste forms. Set aside.

Melt remaining ghee in the inner pot and sauté remaining onions until softened. Add the tomato paste, garam masala, turmeric powder, chili powder, and salt. Mix and cook for 3 minutes. Add eggs to coat in sauce, making sure not to break them. Allow heating for 1 to 2 minutes and spoon masala with eggs over bed rice. Garnish with cilantro and serve for lunch.

Mustardy Egg Salad

Serves: 2 | Ready in about: 30 minutes

Ingredients

2 eggs
1 tbsp crème frâiche

1 spring onion, minced
¼ tbsp curry paste

1 tsp Dijon mustard
Salt and black pepper to taste

Directions

Grease a cake pan with cooking spray. Carefully crack in the eggs. To your Instant Pot, add 1 cup of water and insert a trivet. Set the pan with the eggs on a trivet. Seal the lid and cook for 5 minutes on High Pressure. Do a quick release.

Drain any water from the eggs. Loosen the eggs on the edges with a knife. Transfer to a cutting board and chop into smaller sizes. Transfer the chopped eggs to a bowl. Add in onion, mustard, salt, crème frâiche, curry powder, and pepper. Serve.

Potato Salad from the North

Serves: 2 | Ready in about: 20 minutes

Ingredients

2 slices smoked bacon, chopped
1 tbsp apple cider vinegar
1 tbsp sugar

½ tsp mustard
Salt and black pepper to taste
1 red potato, peeled and quartered

½ red onion, chopped
1 tbsp parsley, chopped

Directions

Set your Instant Pot to Sauté and brown the bacon for 2 minutes per side; reserve. In a bowl, mix sugar, salt, mustard, vinegar, 2 tbsp of water, and black pepper. In the pot, add potato, chopped bacon, and onion and top with the vinegar mixture.

Seal the lid and cook for 6 minutes on High Pressure. Release pressure naturally for 10 minutes. Place on serving plate and add fresh parsley for garnishing.

Egg Caprese Breakfast

Serves: 2 | Ready in about: 15 minutes

Ingredients

2 thin slices ham
2 tbsp shredded mozzarella cheese

2 cherry tomatoes, halved
1 tsp dried basil

Salt and black pepper to taste

Directions

Pour 1 cup of water in your Instant Pot and fit in a trivet. Line 2 medium ramekins with a slice of ham each, crack in an egg into each one. Top with mozzarella cheese, basil, and tomatoes on top. Season with salt, black pepper, and cover with foil.

Place ramekins on the trivet. Seal the lid, select Manual/Pressure Cook on High, and set the cooking time to 3 minutes. After cooking, perform a quick pressure release to let out steam. Unlock the lid, remove bowls, and serve immediately.

Spinach Egg Bites

Serves: 2 | Ready in about: 30 minutes

Ingredients

5 bacon slices, chopped

4 large eggs

¼ cup coconut cream

¼ cup chopped spinach

¾ cup grated Parmesan cheese

Salt and black pepper to taste

Directions

Set your Instant Pot to Sauté and adjust to medium heat. Add in bacon pieces and fry until brown and crispy, 5 minutes. Transfer to a paper towel-lined plate to drain grease and set aside. Clean inner pot and return to base.

In a medium bowl, beat eggs with coconut cream and fold in spinach, Parmesan cheese, salt, and black pepper. Fill a silicone muffin tray (two-thirds way up) with the mixture, cover with aluminum foil, and set aside.

Pour 1 cup water into the pot, fit in a trivet, and place muffin tray on top. Seal the lid, select Manual/on High, and set time to 10 minutes. After cooking, perform a natural pressure release for 10 minutes. Unlock the lid, remove, and uncover muffin mold. Invert tray onto a plate to release egg bites and serve with hot sauce or butter.

Egg Breakfast Burritos

Serves: 2 | Ready in about: 25 minutes

Ingredients

4 eggs

½ cup heavy cream

Salt and black pepper to taste

1 red bell pepper, deseeded and diced

1 onion, diced

2 tbsp chopped chives

¾ cup chopped turkey ham

2 whole-wheat tortillas

¾ cup grated Monterey Jack cheese

Directions

In a bowl, whisk eggs with heavy cream, salt, and pepper. Mix in bell pepper, onion, chives, and ham. Transfer mixture to a large ramekin and cover with aluminum foil. Pour 1 cup water into the inner pot, fit in a trivet, and place the ramekin on top.

Seal the lid, select Manual/Pressure Cook on High, and set time to 10 minutes. After cooking, perform natural pressure release for 10 minutes. Unlock the lid, remove ramekin and stir eggs until broken into small pieces. Lay tortilla wraps on a clean, flat surface, divide eggs on top, and sprinkle with cheese. Roll and slice wraps into halves. Serve immediately.

Cheesy Shakshuka

Serves: 2 | Ready in about: 15 minutes

Ingredients

1 cup tomato passata

¼ tsp coriander powder

½ tsp smoked paprika

¼ tsp cumin powder

¼ tsp red pepper flakes

1 garlic clove, minced

Salt and black pepper to taste

4 large eggs, cracked into a bowl

2 tbsp crumbled goat cheese

Directions

Grease a large ramekin with cooking spray. Set aside. In a medium bowl, mix passata, coriander, paprika, cumin, red pepper flakes, garlic, salt, and black pepper. Spread mixture in the ramekin and create a hole for the eggs at the center. Pour eggs onto passata bed, scatter goat cheese on top, and season with salt and black pepper.

Pour 1 cup water into the inner pot, fit in a trivet, and place the ramekin on top. Seal the lid, select Manual/Pressure Cook on High, and set time to 2 minutes. After cooking, perform a quick pressure release. Serve eggs for breakfast.

Turkish Baked Eggs

Serves: 2 | Ready in about: 25 minutes

Ingredients

2 tbsp olive oil

1 onion, finely chopped

1 red bell pepper, deseeded and chopped

1 green bell pepper, deseeded and chopped

4 garlic cloves, minced

2 cups chopped tomatoes

2 scallions, chopped

4 large eggs

Salt and black pepper to taste

Directions

Set your Instant Pot to Sauté. Heat olive oil and sauté onion, garlic, and bell peppers for 4 minutes. Mix in tomatoes and scallions and cook for 10 minutes, stirring frequently until the sauce thickens. Transfer to a greased baking dish.

Create 4 holes in the sauce and pour an egg in each one. Season with salt and pepper. Pour 1 cup water into the inner pot, fit in a trivet, and place baking dish on top. Seal the lid, select Manual, and cook for 3 minutes. Perform a quick pressure. Serve.

Easy Potato Salad

Serves: 2 | Ready in about: 30 minutes

Ingredients

3 small potatoes, peeled
2 tbsp Greek yogurt
2 tbsp light mayonnaise

1 garlic clove, minced
1 tsp lemon zest
1 tbsp dill, chopped

½ small red onion, sliced
Salt and black pepper to taste

Directions

Place the potatoes, salt, and 1 cup of water in your Instant Pot. Seal the lid, select Steam, and cook for 10 minutes on High. When done, perform a natural pressure release for 10 minutes. Drain the potatoes and let them cool before slicing. Mix the remaining ingredients, except for the dill, and add it to the chopped potatoes, toss to coat. Serve sprinkled with dill.

Broccoli Scrambled Eggs

Serves: 2 | Ready in about: 20 minutes

Ingredients

2 tsp olive oil
½ cup finely chopped broccoli
1 orange bell pepper, diced

1 garlic clove, minced
4 large eggs
3 tbsp milk

¼ cup crumbled goat cheese
½ tsp dried oregano
Salt and black pepper to taste

Directions

Set your Instant Pot to Sauté. Heat the olive oil and sauté broccoli and bell pepper until softened, 4 minutes. Add garlic and keep cooking until fragrant, 1 minute. Beat the eggs with milk and pour mixture onto the vegetables. Using a spatula, begin scrambling the eggs immediately until set and soft, 2 minutes. Press Cancel and mix in goat cheese, oregano, salt, and black pepper until well-combined. Transfer scrambled eggs to serving plates and serve warm.

Leek & Poached Eggs

Serves: 2 | Ready in about: 15 minutes

Ingredients

3/4 cup leeks, chopped
4 eggs
1 ½ tbsp oil

½ tbsp butter
1 tsp mustard seeds
½ tbsp dried rosemary

¼ tsp chili flakes
¼ tsp salt

Directions

Heat oil on Sauté and add mustard seeds. Stir-fry for 2-3 minutes. Add leeks and butter. Cook for 5 minutes, stirring occasionally. Crack eggs and season with dried rosemary, chili flakes, and salt. Cook until set, about 4 minutes. Press Cancel and serve immediately.

Cheesy Egg Scramble

Serves: 2 | Ready in about: 20 minutes

Ingredients

1 tbsp butter
1 large yellow onion, sliced
1 tsp Worcestershire sauce

½ tsp chopped rosemary
4 large eggs
3 tbsp milk

¼ cup shredded Gruyère cheese
Salt and black pepper to taste

Directions

Melt butter in your Instant Pot on Sauté. Stir-fry onion until caramelized, 15 minutes. Season with Worcestershire sauce and rosemary. Beat eggs with milk and pour them into onion mixture. Scramble until eggs solidify. Add in Gruyere cheese and stir the mixture until cheese melts. Season with salt and pepper. Plate the eggs and serve immediately.

Cheddar Baked Eggs

Serves: 2 | Ready in about: 15 minutes

Ingredients

½ cup diced smoked kielbasa sausages
½ cup frozen hash brown potatoes

¼ cup shredded cheddar cheese
4 large eggs, cracked into a bowl

1 tbsp chopped scallions
Salt and black pepper to taste

Directions

Grease a large ramekin with cooking spray and lay in ingredients in this order: sausages, hash browns, and cheddar cheese. Create a hole in the center and pour in eggs. Scatter scallions on top and season with salt and pepper.

Pour 1 cup water into the inner pot and fit in a trivet. Place the ramekin on trivet. Seal the lid, select Manual on High, and set time to 2 minutes. When done, perform quick pressure release and unlock the lid. Carefully remove ramekin and serve.

Asparagus Baked Eggs

Serves: 2 | Ready in about: 15 minutes

Ingredients

½ cup finely chopped broccoli
½ cup chopped asparagus
½ cup finely chopped spinach
½ tsp onion powder
½ tsp garlic powder
4 large eggs, beaten
¼ cup crumbled ricotta cheese
1 tbsp chopped scallions
Salt and black pepper to taste

Directions

Grease a ramekin with cooking spray. Lay ingredients in the following way: broccoli, asparagus, and spinach. Sprinkle with onion and garlic powders and create a hole in the center of the greens. Pour over the eggs and top with ricotta cheese; season.

Pour 1 cup water in your Instant Pot, fit in a trivet, and place the ramekin on top. Seal the lid, select Manual/Pressure Cook on High, and set the cooking time to 5 minutes. After cooking, perform a quick pressure release to let out steam and unlock the lid. Carefully remove ramekin and serve eggs, scattered with scallions.

Mushroom Omelet with Fresh Mozzarella Cheese

Serves: 2 | Ready in about: 25 minutes

Ingredients

4 eggs
½ cup fresh mozzarella cheese, cubed
¼ cup milk
1 cup button mushrooms
1 large onion, finely chopped
1 tsp dried oregano
¼ tsp sea salt
2 tbsp olive oil
2 tbsp fresh parsley, chopped

Directions

Grease your Instant Pot with oil. Stir-fry onions for a few minutes, until translucent. Stir in oregano and button mushrooms. Cook for 5-6 minutes, stirring occasionally. Crack the eggs into a bowl, and mix with cheese and milk.

Remove the mushrooms from the pot; set aside. Pour the egg mixture in the pot and cook for 2 minutes, stirring constantly, on Sauté. Serve with button mushrooms and topped with fresh parsley.

Korean Steamed Egg Custard

Serves: 2 | Ready in about: 25 minutes

Ingredients

4 large eggs
2 tbsp sesame oil
¾ tsp fish sauce
2 chopped green onions

Directions

Beat eggs in a bowl. Mix in fish sauce, 1 green onion, and 1 cup of water. Pour mixture into a ramekin and cover with foil. Pour 1 cup water in the pot and fit in a trivet. Put the ramekin on the trivet.

Seal the lid, select Manual/Pressure Cook on Low, and set time to 7 minutes. After cooking, perform natural pressure release for 10 minutes. Unlock the lid, carefully remove ramekin, top with remaining green onion. Drizzle with sesame oil to serve.

Stuffed Avocado Bake

Serves: 2 | Ready in about: 30 minutes

Ingredients

1 avocado, halved
2 eggs
3 tbsp butter, melted
1 tsp dry oregano
½ tsp salt

Directions

Grease a baking dish with butter, and place the avocado halves in it. Crack an egg into each avocado half. Season with salt and oregano. Add 1 ½ cups of water and place the trivet inside the pot. Lower the baking dish on top. Seal the lid and cook on High Pressure for 10 minutes. When done, do a quick release and plate. Serve immediately.

Scrambled Eggs a la "Caprese"

Serves: 2 | Ready in about: 25 minutes

Ingredients

4 eggs

½ cup fresh mozzarella cheese

1 cup button mushrooms, sliced

1 large tomato, chopped

2 spring onions, chopped

¼ cup milk

2 tbsp olive oil

½ tsp salt

Directions

Grease the pot with oil and set on Sauté. Stir-fry the onions for 3 minutes, or until translucent. Add tomatoes and mushrooms. Cook until liquid evaporates for 5-6 minutes. Meanwhile, Whisk eggs, cheese, milk, and salt. Pour into the pot and stir. Cook for 2 minutes or until set.

Nut & Beef Steak Salad

Serves: 2-4 | Ready in about: 60 minutes

Ingredients

1 lb rib-eye steak, boneless

4 oz fresh arugula

1 large tomato, sliced

¼ cup fresh goat's cheese

4 almonds

4 walnuts

4 hazelnuts

3 tbsp olive oil

2 cups beef broth

2 tbsp red wine vinegar

1 tbsp Italian seasoning mix

Directions

Whisk together vinegar, Italian mix, and olive oil. Brush each steak with this mixture and place it in your Instant Pot. Pour in the broth and seal the lid. Cook on Meat/Stew for 25 minutes on High Pressure. Release the pressure naturally for about 10 minutes, and remove the steaks along with the broth. Grease the inner pot with oil and hit Sauté.

Brown the steaks on both sides for 5-6 minutes. Remove from the pot and chill for 5 minutes before slicing. In a bowl, mix arugula, tomato, cheese, almonds, walnuts, and hazelnuts. Top with steaks and drizzle with wine mixture.

Scramble with Cranberries

Serves: 2 | Ready in about: 10 minutes

Ingredients

4 large eggs, beaten

¼ tsp cranberry extract, sugar-free

2 tbsp butter

¼ tsp salt

1 tbsp skim milk

4-5 cranberries, to garnish

Directions

In a bowl, whisk eggs, cranberry extract, salt, and milk. Melt butter on Sauté. Pour the egg mixture and pull the eggs across the pot with a spatula. Do not stir constantly. Cook for 2 minutes, or until thickened and no visible liquid egg lumps. When done, press Cancel and transfer to a serving plate. Garnish with cranberries and serve.

Spicy Poached Eggs with Mushrooms

Serves: 2 | Ready in about: 25 minutes

Ingredients

6 oz button mushrooms, halved lengthwise

½ cup fresh arugula

2 eggs

2 tbsp olive oil

1 tsp red chili flakes

Directions

Melt butter your Instant Pot on Sauté. Add mushrooms and cook for 4-5 minutes until soft. Stir in arugula. Cook for one minute. Crack the eggs and cook until set – for 2 minutes. Season with chili flakes. Press Cancel and serve.

Sunday-Morning Spinach Egg

Serves: 2 | Ready in about: 20 minutes

Ingredients

6 oz spinach, chopped

2 eggs

3 tbsp oil

½ tsp garlic powder

¼ tsp dried oregano

¼ tsp dried rosemary

½ tsp sea salt, divided

4 Kalamata olives, pitted

¼ red bell pepper, chopped

Directions

Heat the oil your Instant Pot on Sauté and add chopped spinach. Season with salt and garlic powder. Give it a good stir and cook for 5 minutes, until soft. Crack eggs and season with oregano, rosemary, and salt. Cook until completely set for about 5 more minutes. Transfer to a serving plate and serve with Kalamata olives or chopped red bell peppers.

Spinach Hard-Boiled Eggs with Nuts

Serves: 2-4 | Ready in about: 25 minutes

Ingredients

1 lb spinach, rinsed, chopped	1 tbsp almonds, crushed	½ tsp chili flakes
3 tbsp olive oil	1 tbsp peanuts, crushed	½ tsp sea salt
1 tbsp butter	4 eggs	

Directions

Pour 1 ½ cups of water into the inner pot and insert a steamer basket. Place the eggs onto the basket. Seal the lid and cook on High Pressure for 5 minutes. Do a quick release. Remove the eggs to an ice bath. Wipe the pot clean, and heat oil on Sauté. Add spinach and cook for 2-3 minutes, stirring occasionally.

Stir in 1 tbsp of butter and season with salt and chili flakes. Mix well and cook for 1 more minute. Sprinkle with nuts. Peel and slice each egg in half, lengthwise. Transfer to a serving plate. Pour over the spinach mixture and serve.

Vegetable Frittata with Cheddar & Ricotta

Serves: 2-4 | Ready in about: 30 minutes

Ingredients

4 eggs	3 cherry tomatoes, halved	½ tsp salt
8 oz spinach, finely chopped	¼ cup red bell pepper, chopped	¼ tsp black pepper
½ cup cheddar cheese	1 cup chopped broccoli, pre-cooked	¼ tsp dried oregano
½ cup fresh ricotta cheese	4 tbsp olive oil	½ cup fresh celery leaves, finely chopped

Directions

Heat olive oil in your Instant Pot on Sauté. Add spinach and cook for 5 minutes, stirring occasionally. Stir in tomatoes, peppers, and broccoli. Cook for 3-4 more minutes. In a bowl, whisk 2 eggs, cheddar and ricotta cheeses.

Pour in the pot and cook for 2 more minutes. Then, crack the remaining 2 eggs and cook for another 5 minutes. When done, do a quick release. Serve immediately with chopped celery leaves.

Sausage Egg Scramble

Serves: 2 | Ready in about: 15 minutes

Ingredients

½ lb Italian sausages, casing removed	4 large eggs	Salt and black pepper to taste
½ cup finely chopped kale	3 tbsp milk	A pinch of red pepper flakes

Directions

Set your Instant Pot to Sauté. Add in sausages and cook with frequent stirring while breaking into small pieces until brown, 5 minutes. Top with kale and cook until wilted, 3 minutes. Beat the eggs with milk. Pour onto kale mixture and scramble until eggs solidify, 1 minute. Season the eggs with salt, black pepper, and red chili flakes. Plate and serve.

Scrambled Eggs with Beef & Cheese

Serves: 2 | Ready in about: 25 minutes

Ingredients

4 oz lean ground beef	¼ cup skim milk	1 tbsp tomato paste
½ onion, chopped	¼ cup ricotta cheese, crumbled	½ tsp sea salt
4 eggs	¼ tsp garlic powder	1 ½ tbsp olive oil

Directions

Heat the olive oil in your Instant Pot on Sauté. Stir-fry the onion for 4 minutes until translucent. Add beef and tomato paste. Cook for 5 minutes, stirring twice. Whisk the eggs, milk, ricotta cheese, garlic, and salt. Pour the mixture into the pot and stir slowly with a wooden spatula. Cook until slightly underdone. Remove from the heat and serve.

Mushroom & Chicken Salad

Serves: 2-4 | Ready in about: 60 minutes

Ingredients

2 chicken drumsticks
3 cups chicken broth
6 oz button mushrooms, whole
1 tomato, roughly chopped

2 oz lettuce
1 cup Kalamata olives, pitted
1 cucumber, chopped
2 tbsp olive oil

1 tbsp Dijon mustard
¼ cup white wine
1 tsp lemon juice
1 tbsp Italian seasoning mix

Directions

In a bowl, mix mustard, 2 tbsp olive oil, Italian mix, wine, and salt. Stir well and brush the meat. Wrap in aluminum foil and refrigerate for 30 minutes. Place the vegetables in a serving bowl. Add mushrooms and stir well. Set aside.

Remove the drumsticks from the fridge and transfer to the pot. Pour in the broth and seal the lid. Cook on Poultry mode for 15 minutes on High Pressure. Do a quick release and remove the drumsticks. Preheat a non-stick grill pan over high heat. Brown the drumsticks for 6-7 minutes, turning once. Serve with the salad.

Spring Onion & Steamed Eggs

Serve: 2 | Ready in about: 10 minutes

Ingredients

4 eggs
1 tbsp spring onions, chopped

¼ tsp garlic powder
Salt and black pepper to taste

Directions

In a bowl, whisk eggs and ½ cup water. Add the remaining ingredients and stir well. Transfer the mixture to a heat-proof bowl. Add 1 cup of water in your Instant Pot. Set the steamer tray and place the bowl on top. Seal the lid and cook on High Pressure for 5 minutes. Do a quick release. Serve warm.

Chili Hard-Boiled Eggs

Serves: 2-4 | Ready in about: 25 minutes

Ingredients

1 cup water
4 large eggs

Salt and black pepper to taste
A pinch of chili powder

Directions

In the pot, add 1 cup water and place a trivet. Lay your eggs on top. Seal the lid and cook for 5 minutes on High Pressure. Do a natural release for 10 minutes. Transfer the eggs to ice-cold water to cool. Peel and season with paprika, salt, and pepper.

Tuna & Egg Salad with Olives

Serves: 2-4 | Ready in about: 15 minutes

Ingredients

1 lb potatoes, quartered
3 tbsp melted butter
Salt and pepper to taste

6 pickles, chopped
2 tbsp red wine vinegar
½ cup pimento-stuffed green olives

½ cup chopped roasted red peppers
10 oz canned tuna, drained
2 eggs

Directions

Pour 1 cup of water into your Instant Pot and add potatoes. Place a trivet over the potatoes. Lay the eggs on the trivet. Seal the lid and cook for 8 minutes on High Pressure. Do a quick release. Drain and remove potatoes to a bowl.

Transfer the eggs to a bowl filled with ice water. Drizzle melted butter over the potatoes and season with salt and pepper. Peel and chop the chilled eggs. Add pickles, eggs, peppers, tuna, vinegar to the potatoes and mix to coat. Serve topped with olives.

Broccoli & Cauli Superpower Salad

Serves: 2-4 | Ready in about: 15 minutes

Ingredients

1 lb cauliflower florets
1 lb broccoli, into florets

3 garlic cloves, crushed
¼ tbsp olive oil

1 tsp salt
1 tbsp dry rosemary, crushed

Directions

Cut the veggies into bite-sized pieces and place them in the pot. Add olive oil and 1 cup of water. Season with salt, garlic, and rosemary. Seal the lid. Cook on High Pressure for 3 minutes. When ready, do a quick release. Serve.

Easy Mediterranean Omelet

Serves: 2-4 | Ready in about: 30 minutes

Ingredients

1 lb tomatoes, peeled, roughly diced	1 cup cottage cheese	1 tbsp Italian seasoning mix
1 tbsp tomato paste	4 eggs	¼ cup fresh parsley, chopped
1 tsp brown sugar	3 tbsp olive oil	¼ tsp salt

Directions

Grease the inner pot with oil. Press Sauté and add tomatoes, sugar, Italian seasoning, parsley, and salt. Give it a good stir and cook for 15 minutes or until the tomatoes soften. Stir occasionally.

Whisk eggs and cheese. Pour the mixture into the pot and stir well. Cook for 3 minutes. Serve immediately.

Swiss Chard Omelet

Serves: 2 | Ready in about: 25 minutes

Ingredients

1 cup spinach, chopped	4 eggs	½ tsp sea salt
1 cup Swiss chard, chopped	2 tbsp olive oil	¼ tsp red pepper flakes

Directions

Heat the olive oil in your Instant Pot on Sauté. Stir-fry the greens for 5 minutes; set aside. Whisk the eggs, salt, and red pepper flakes. Pour the mixture in the pot. Spread the eggs evenly and cook for 3-4 minutes on Sauté. With a spatula, ease around the edges and slide to a serving plate. Add greens and fold it over in half. Serve.

Cheesy Omelet Cups

Serves: 2 | Ready in about: 10 minutes

Ingredients

4 eggs	½ small onion, finely chopped	Salt and black pepper, to serve
½ cup cheddar cheese, crumbled	½ tsp Italian seasoning mix	2 tbsp heavy cream

Directions

In a bowl, mix eggs, salt, pepper, and heavy cream. Whisk until well combined and add the remaining ingredients. Add 1 cup of water and lay the steam rack. Lower the ramekins on the steam rack and seal the lid. Cook on High Pressure for 6 minutes. When ready, do a quick release. Serve hot.

Fast Soft-Boiled Eggs

Serves: 2-4 | Ready in about: 15 minutes

Ingredients

4 large eggs	Salt and black pepper to taste

Directions

To the pot, add 1 cup water and place a rack. Put eggs on it. Seal lid, press Steam, and cook for 3 minutes on High. Do a quick release. Cool completely in an ice bath. Peel the eggs and Season with salt and pepper before serving.

MORNING RECIPES

Vanilla Carrot Cake Oatmeal

Serves: 2 | Ready in about: 20 minutes

Ingredients

2 cups milk
1 cup old fashioned rolled oats
1 cup shredded carrots

2 tbsp maple syrup
1 tsp cinnamon
¼ tsp ground ginger

1 tsp vanilla extract
¼ cup chopped dates
¼ cup chopped pecans

Directions

Pour milk, oats, carrots, maple syrup, cinnamon, ginger, and vanilla extract into your Instant Pot. Seal the lid, select Manual on High, and set the cooking time to 3 minutes. After cooking, perform natural pressure release for 10 minutes. Unlock lid, stir in dates and pecans, and spoon oatmeal into bowls. Serve.

Breakfast Mix

Serves: 2 | Ready in about: 15 minutes

Ingredients

2 bacon slices, chopped
3 ham slices, chopped
½ cup chicken broth

1 cup frozen peas
1 tsp garlic powder
1 tsp onion powder

Salt and black pepper to taste
1 tbsp chopped parsley

Directions

Set your Instant Pot to Sauté and adjust to medium heat. Add bacon and cook until brown and crispy, 5 minutes. Mix in ham and heat through, 1 minute. Top with chicken broth, frozen peas, garlic powder, onion powder, salt, and black pepper.

Seal the lid, select Manual/Pressure Cook mode on High, and set the cooking time to 1 minute. After cooking, do a quick pressure release to let out steam, and unlock the lid. Dish food, garnish with parsley, and serve warm.

Maple Pumpkin Steel-Cut Oatmeal

Serves: 2 | Ready in about: 25 minutes

Ingredients

1 tbsp butter
2 cups steel-cut oats

¼ tsp cinnamon
1 cup pumpkin puree

3 tbsp maple syrup
½ cup pumpkin seeds, toasted

Directions

Melt butter in your Instant Pot on Sauté. Add in cinnamon, oats, pumpkin puree, and 3 cups water. Seal the lid, select Porridge and cook for 10 minutes on High Pressure to get a few bite oats or for 14 minutes to form oats that are soft. Do a quick release. Open the lid and stir in maple syrup. Top with pumpkin seeds and serve.

Easy Beef Sandwiches

Serves: 2 | Ready in about: 50 minutes

Ingredients

½ lb beef roast
½ tbsp olive oil
¼ onion, chopped

1 garlic clove, minced
2 tbsp dry red wine
½ cup beef broth stock

¼ tsp dried oregano
4 slices Fontina cheese
2 split hoagie rolls

Directions

Season the beef with salt and pepper. Warm oil your Instant Pot on Sauté and brown the beef for 2 to 3 minutes per side. Set aside on a plate. Add onion and cook for 3 minutes, until translucent. Stir in garlic and cook for one minute until soft. Add red wine to deglaze. Scrape the cooking surface to remove any brown sections of the food using a wooden spoon's flat edge.

Mix in beef broth and take back the juices and beef to your cooker. Over the meat, scatter some oregano. Seal the lid and cook on High Pressure for 30 minutes. Release the pressure naturally for 10 minutes.

Preheat a broiler. Transfer the beef to a cutting board and slice. Roll the beef and top with onions. Each sandwich should be topped with 2 slices of the fontina cheese. Place the sandwiches under the broiler for 2-3 minutes until the cheese melts.

Coffee Steel-Cut Oatmeal

Serves: 2-4 | Ready in about: 20 minutes

Ingredients

3 ½ cups milk
½ cup raw peanuts
1 cup steel-cut oats
¼ cup agave syrup

1 tsp coffee
1 ½ tsp ground ginger
1 ¼ tsp ground cinnamon
½ tsp salt

¼ tsp ground allspice
¼ tsp ground cardamom
1 tsp vanilla extract

Directions

In a blender, puree peanuts and milk to obtain a smooth consistency. Transfer to your Instant Pot. Add in agave syrup, oats, ginger, allspice, cinnamon, salt, cardamom, tea leaves, and cloves, and mix well. Seal the lid and cook on High Pressure for 12 minutes. Let pressure to release naturally on completing the cooking cycle. Add in vanilla and stir well before serving.

Almond Steel-Cut Oatmeal

Serves: 2 | Ready in about: 20 minutes

Ingredients

1 tsp olive oil

1 cup steel-cut oats

¾ cup almond milk

Directions

Warm шге двсэе oil your Instant Pot on Sauté until foaming. Add oats and cook as you stir until soft and toasted. Press Cancel. Add milk and 1 ½ water and stir. Seal the lid and Press Porridge. Cook for 12 minutes on High Pressure. Set steam vent to Venting to release the pressure quickly. Open the lid. Add oats as you stir to mix any extra liquid. Serve.

Coconut Porridge

Serves: 2 | Ready in about: 20 minutes

Ingredients

1 cup rye flakes
A pinch of salt

1 ¼ cups coconut milk
1 tsp vanilla extract

2 tbsp maple syrup
¾ cup frozen black currants

Directions

In your Instant Pot, combine rye flakes, salt, coconut milk, water, vanilla, and maple syrup. Seal the lid, select Manual/Pressure Cook on High, and set time to 5 minutes. After cooking, perform natural pressure release for 10 minutes. Stir and spoon the porridge onto serving bowls. Top with black currants and serve warm.

Cherry Oatmeal

Serves: 2 |Ready in about: 20 minutes

Ingredients

2 cups milk
1 cup old fashioned rolled oats

3 tbsp maple syrup
½ cup dried cherries

Greek yogurt for topping
¼ cup chopped walnuts

Directions

Pour milk, oats, maple syrup, and cherries in your Instant Pot. Seal the lid, select Manual/Pressure Cook on High, and set the cooking time to 3 minutes. After cooking, perform natural pressure release for 10 minutes. Unlock the lid, stir, and spoon oatmeal into serving bowls. Top with Greek yogurt and walnuts and serve warm.

Easy Oatmeal Bowls with Raspberries

Serves: 2 | Ready in about: 20 minutes

Ingredients

1 cup steel-cut oats
1 ½ cups milk

2 tbsp honey
½ tsp vanilla extract

Fresh raspberries, for topping
Toasted Brazil nuts, for topping

Directions

Add the oats, milk, honey, and vanilla extract into your Instant Pot. Seal the lid, select Manual, and set the cooking time to 6 minutes on High. When done, perform a quick pressure release to let out the steam. Unlock the lid and stir the oatmeal. Divide between serving bowls and top with raspberries and toasted Brazil nuts to serve.

Super-Fast Pomegranate Porridge

Serves: 2 | Ready in about: 5 minutes

Ingredients:

1 cup oats

1 cup pomegranate juice

1 cup water

1 tbsp pomegranate molasses

Sea salt to taste

Directions:

Place water, oats, salt, and pomegranate juice in your Instant Pot. Stir and seal the lid. Select Porridge and cook for 3 minutes on High pressure. Once ready, do a quick pressure release. Stir in the pomegranate molasses. Serve immediately.

Mushroom & Cheese Oatmeal

Serves: 2 | Ready in about: 35 minutes

Ingredients

1 tbsp butter

1 cup sliced cremini mushrooms

1 garlic clove, minced

Salt and black pepper to taste

1 cup chopped baby kale

1 cup old fashioned rolled oats

2 cups vegetable broth

¼ tsp red pepper flakes

¼ cup crumbled feta cheese

Directions

Set your Instant Pot to Sauté. Melt butter in the pot and sauté mushrooms until slightly softened, 4 to 5 minutes. Stir in garlic, salt, and pepper. Cook until fragrant, 3 minutes. Mix in kale to wilt; stir in oats, vegetable broth, and red pepper flakes.

Seal the lid, select Manual on High, and cook for 3 minutes. After cooking, perform natural pressure release for 10 minutes. Stir and adjust taste with salt and black pepper. Dish oatmeal into serving bowls and top with feta cheese. Serve warm.

Raspberry Yogurt

Makes: 6-8 serves | Ready in about: 23 hours 20 minutes

Ingredients

¼ cup Greek yogurt containing active cultures

1 lb hulled and halved raspberries

1 cup sugar

3 tbsp gelatin

1 tbsp fresh orange juice

8 cups milk

Directions

In a bowl, mash raspberries with a potato masher. Add sugar and stir well to dissolve; let soak for 30 minutes at room temperature. Add in orange juice and gelatin and mix well until dissolved. Remove the mixture, place it in a sealable container, close, and sit for 12 to 24 hours at room temperature before placing it in a refrigerator.

Into the cooker, add milk, and close the lid. The steam vent should be set to Venting then to Sealing. Select Yogurt until "Boil" is displayed on the readings. When complete, there will be a display of "Yogurt" on the screen.

Open the lid and using a food thermometer to ensure the milk temperature is at least 185°F. Transfer the steel pot to a wire rack and allow cool for 30 minutes until the milk has reached 110°F.

In a bowl, mix ½ cup warm milk and yogurt. Transfer the mixture to the remaining warm milk and stir without having to scrape the steel pot's bottom. Take the pot back to the base and seal the lid. Select Yogurt mode and cook for 8 hours. Allow the yogurt to chill in a refrigerator for 1-2 hours. Transfer the chilled yogurt to a large bowl and stir in raspberries.

Chicken Sandwiches with BBQ Sauce

Serves: 2-4 | Ready in about: 45 minutes

Ingredients

4 chicken thighs, boneless and skinless

Salt to taste

2 cups barbecue sauce

1 onion, minced

2 garlic cloves, minced

1 tbsp lemon juice

1 tbsp mayonnaise

1½ cups iceberg lettuce, shredded

4 burger buns

Directions

Season the chicken with salt and place in your Instant Pot. Add in garlic, onion, and barbeque sauce. Coat the chicken by turning in the sauce. Seal the lid and cook on High Pressure for 15 minutes. Do a quick release. Use 2 forks to shred the chicken and mix it into the sauce. Press Sauté and simmer for 15 minutes to thicken the sauce until desired consistency.

In a bowl, mix lemon juice, mayonnaise, and salt; toss lettuce into the mixture to coat. Separate the chicken in equal parts to match the sandwich buns; apply lettuce for topping and complete the sandwiches.

Chickpea & Avocado Burritos

Serves: 2 | Ready in about: 30 minutes

Ingredients

1 tbsp coconut oil
1 medium red onion, finely chopped
1 red bell pepper, deseeded and chopped
1 garlic clove, minced
1 tsp cumin powder

1 ½ cups canned chickpeas, drained
½ cup vegetable broth
Salt and black pepper to taste
3 corn tortillas
1 large avocado, pitted and chopped

½ cup shredded red cabbage
3 tbsp chopped cilantro
3 tbsp tomato salsa
½ cup sour cream

Directions

Set your Instant Pot to Sauté and adjust to medium heat. Heat coconut oil in the pot and sauté onion and bell pepper until softened, 4 minutes. Add garlic, cumin, and cook for 1 minute or until fragrant. Mix in chickpeas, heat through for 1 minute, and pour in vegetable broth; Season. Seal the lid, select Manual on High, and set the cooking time to 8 minutes.

After cooking, perform natural pressure release for 10 minutes. Unlock the lid, stir, and adjust taste with salt and black pepper. Turn Instant Pot off. Lay tortillas on a flat surface and divide chickpea filling at the center. Top with avocados, cabbage, cilantro, salsa, and sour cream. Wrap, tuck ends, and slice in halves. Serve for lunch.

Tofu Scramble with Black Beans

Serves: 2 | Ready in about: 25 minutes

Ingredients

1 cup canned black beans
2 cups vegetable broth
1 tbsp ghee
1 small red onion, finely chopped

3 garlic cloves, minced
3 tomatoes, chopped
1 (14 oz) extra-firm tofu, crumbled
1 tsp smoked paprika

1 tsp turmeric powder
1 tsp cumin powder
Salt and black pepper to taste

Directions

Pour beans and vegetable broth in your Instant Pot. Seal the lid, select Manual on High, and cook for 10 minutes. After cooking, perform a quick pressure release. Transfer the beans to a bowl. Drain excess liquid and wipe the inner pot clean.

Select Sauté. Melt the ghee and sauté onion, garlic, and tomatoes until softened, 4 minutes. Crumble tofu into pan and cook for 5 minutes. Season with paprika, turmeric, cumin, salt, and black pepper. Cook for 1 minute. Add black beans, stir, and allow heating for 3 minutes. Dish scramble and enjoy for breakfast.

Scallion & Corn Oatmeal

Serves: 2 | Ready in about: 25 minutes

Ingredients

2 cups vegetable broth
2 tbsp soy sauce
1 cup old fashioned rolled oats

1 tsp hot sauce
1 cup fresh corn kernels
4 scallions, sliced and divided

Salt and black pepper to taste
½ tsp black sesame seeds for garnishing

Directions

Pour broth, soy sauce, oats, hot sauce, corn, and half of the scallions in your Instant Pot. Seal the lid, select Manual on High, and set the cooking time to 3 minutes. After cooking, perform natural pressure release for 10 minutes, then a quick pressure.

Unlock the lid, season with salt and black pepper, stir and spoon oatmeal into serving bowls. Garnish with sesame seeds and remaining scallions. Serve with sunny side eggs.

Peanut Butter Oatmeal with Strawberries

Serves: 2 | Ready in about: 20 minutes

Ingredients

1 cup old-fashioned rolled oats
2 cups milk

2 tbsp strawberry jam
3 tbsp peanut butter

¼ cup fresh strawberries to serve
2 tbsp chopped roasted peanuts

Directions

Pour oats and milk in your Instant Pot. Stir in jam and peanut butter until well mixed. Seal the lid, select Manual/Pressure Cook on High, and set the cooking time to 3 minutes. After cooking, perform natural pressure release for 10 minutes. Unlock the lid, stir, and spoon oatmeal into serving bowls. Top with strawberries, peanuts, and serve.

Black Beans with Cotija Cheese

Serves: 2 | Ready in about: 25 minutes

Ingredients

1 tsp olive oil
1 large white onion, chopped
1 tsp grated garlic

1 cup dried black beans, soaked
2 cups vegetable broth
1 tsp Mexican seasoning

2 tbsp chopped cilantro
Salt to taste
½ cup Cotija cheese, grated

Directions

Set your Instant Pot to Sauté. Heat the olive oil and sauté onion and garlic until softened, 3 minutes. Add beans, broth, Mexican seasoning, and salt. Seal the lid, select Manual on High, and set the cooking time to 12 minutes. After cooking, perform a quick pressure release. Unlock the lid. Spoon beans into plates, top with Cotija cheese and cilantro, and serve.

Lentil-Arugula Pancake

Serves: 2 | Ready in about: 45 minutes

Ingredients

1 cup split yellow lentils, soaked
2 garlic cloves, whole
½ tsp smoked paprika

1 pinch turmeric
¼ tsp coriander powder
¼ tsp cumin powder

¼ tsp salt
3 eggs, beaten
2 cups chopped arugula

Directions

Line a cake pan with parchment paper and grease with cooking spray. In a blender, process lentils, garlic, paprika, turmeric, coriander, cumin, salt, eggs, and 1/3 cup of water until smooth.

Pour mixture into the cake pan and mix arugula through the batter. Cover with foil. Pour remaining water into the pot, fit in a trivet, and place cake pan on top. Seal the lid, select Manual on High, and cook for 35 minutes.

After cooking, do a quick pressure release and unlock the lid. Carefully remove the pan, take off the foil, and release pancake onto a plate. Slice and serve with yogurt.

Walnut & Banana Oat Cups

Serves: 2 | Ready in about: 25 minutes

Ingredients

½ cup steel-cut oats
1 banana, mashed

1 ½ cups water
1 tsp sugar

1 tbsp walnuts, chopped

Directions

Spread the banana onto the bottom of your Instant Pot. Pour the water, steel-cut oats, and sugar over the banana. Seal the lid, select Manual/Pressure Cook mode, and cook for 6 minutes on High.

When done, perform a natural pressure release for 10 minutes, then a quick pressure release to let out the remaining steam. Unlock the lid and stir the oatmeal. Divide between cups. Top with walnuts and serve.

Navy Beans with Mushrooms & Spinach

Serves: 2 | Ready in about: 35 minutes

Ingredients

1 tbsp olive oil
1 medium white onion, diced
1 lb white button mushrooms, quartered

½ lb butternut squash, chopped
Salt and black pepper to taste
1 cup chopped tomatoes

2 cups chicken broth
2 cups baby spinach
1 (15 oz) can navy beans, drained

Directions

Heat olive oil in your Instant Pot on Sauté. Cook onion, mushrooms, and squash for 6 minutes. Season with salt and pepper and cook for 1 minute. Stir in tomato and broth. Seal the lid, select Manual on High, and set the cooking time to 3 minutes.

After cooking, perform natural pressure release for 10 minutes, and then quick pressure to release steam, and unlock the lid. Press Sauté, add spinach, navy beans, and allow spinach to wilt, 3 minutes. Adjust taste with salt and black pepper and serve.

DESSERTS

Fresh Strawberry Cheesecake

Makes: 6-8 serves | Ready in about: 50 minutes + cooling time

Ingredients

4 oz graham crackers, crushed
3 tbsp butter, melted
1 lb mascarpone cheese, softened

¾ cup sugar
¼ cup sour cream, at room temperature
2 eggs

1 tsp vanilla extract
1 tbsp lemon juice
1 cup strawberries, halved

Directions

In a bowl, mix crushed crackers with butter. Press the crumbs into the bottom of a springform pan in an even layer; set in the freezer. In a stand mixer, beat sugar, mascarpone cheese, and sour cream for 3 minutes until a fluffy and smooth mixture forms. Scrape the bowl's sides and add eggs, lemon juice, and vanilla. Carry on to beat the mixture until you obtain a consistent color and all ingredients are completely combined. Pour filling over crust.

Into the Instant Pot, add 1 cup water and insert a trivet. Place the springform pan on the trivet. Seal the lid, press Cake, and cook for 40 minutes on High Pressure. Release the pressure quickly. Let cool the cheesecake. Top with strawberries and serve.

Walnut Chocolate Brownies

Serves: 2 | Ready in about: 40 minutes

Ingredients

1 egg
2 tbsp granulated sugar
2 tbsp olive oil

2 tbsp flour
2 tbsp dark chocolate chips
2 tbsp chopped walnuts

⅓ tbsp milk
¼ tsp baking powder
⅓ tbsp vanilla extract

Directions

Add 1 cup water and set steamer rack into your Instant Pot. In a bowl, beat egg and sugar until smooth. Stir in oil, milk, baking powder, chocolate chips, flour, walnuts, and vanilla. Transfer the batter to a greased baking pan. Spread it into an even layer. Seal the lid, press Cake, and cook for 20 minutes on High. Release the pressure quickly. Let brownie cool before cutting.

Party-Style Cranberry Cheesecake

Makes: 6-8 serves | Ready in about: 50 minutes + cooling time

Ingredients

1 cup coarsely crumbled cookies
2 tbsp butter, melted
1 cup mascarpone cheese, softened

½ cup sugar
2 tbsp sour cream
½ tsp vanilla extract

2 eggs, beaten
⅓ cup dried cranberries

Directions

In a bowl, combine butter and crushed cookies. Press firmly to the bottom and about ⅓ of the way up the sides of a cake pan; freeze. In a separate bowl, beat mascarpone and sugar until smooth. Whisk in eggs, vanilla, and sour cream. Stir in cranberries. Spread the mixture over the crust. Add 1 cup water in your Instant Pot and insert a trivet. Place the cake on the trivet. Seal the lid, press Cake, and cook on High Pressure for 40 minutes. Release the pressure quickly. Serve the cake cooled.

Apple Crisp with Oat Topping

Serves: 2-4 | Ready in about: 30 minutes

Ingredients

½ cup oat flour
½ cup old-fashioned rolled oats
½ cup sugar

¼ cup olive oil
4 apples, peeled, cored, and halved
2 tbsp arrowroot powder

1 tsp ground cinnamon
¼ tsp ground nutmeg
2 tbsp tsp vanilla paste

Directions

In a bowl, combine sugar, oat flour, oats, and olive oil and mix to form coarse crumbs. Ladle the apples into the Instant Pot. Mix ½ cup water with arrowroot powder in a bowl. Stir in nutmeg, cinnamon, and vanilla. Toss in the apples to coat. Apply oat topping to the apples. Seal the lid and cook on High Pressure for 10 minutes. Release the pressure quickly. Serve cold.

Homemade Cherry Cake

Makes: 4-6 serves | Ready in about: 30 minutes

Ingredients

1 cup flour	½ tsp salt	3 eggs
1 tsp baking powder	1 tsp cherry extract	¼ cup cocoa powder
½ cup sugar	3 tbsp butter, softened	¼ cup heavy cream

Directions

Mix all dry ingredients except cocoa in a bowl. Beat in eggs, one at the time for one minute. Add in sour cream, sugar, butter, and cherry extract. Continue to beat until well mixed. Divide the mixture in half and add cocoa powder in one-half of the mixture. Pour the light batter into a greased baking dish. Drizzle with cocoa dough to create a nice marble pattern.

Pour 1 cup water and insert a trivet in your Instant Pot. Lower the baking dish on top of the trivet. Seal the lid and cook for 20 minutes on High Pressure. Release the pressure naturally for 10 minutes. Let it cool for a while and transfer to a serving plate.

Buckwheat Pancake with Yogurt & Berries

Serves: 2 | Ready in about: 15 minutes

Ingredients

3/4 cup buckwheat flour	1 cup milk	1 tsp vanilla sugar
1 tsp baking powder	1 egg	½ cup fresh berries

Directions

In a bowl, whisk milk and egg until foamy. Slowly add flour baking powder and continue beating combined. Spread the batter on a greased baking pan. Pour 1 cup water in your Instant Pot and insert a trivet. Lay the pan on the trivet. Seal the lid and cook for 5 minutes on High Pressure. Do a quick release. Top the pancake with berries and serve.

Winter Fruit Compote

Makes: 6-8 serves | Ready in about: 20 minutes

Ingredients

7 oz fresh cherries, pitted	3 large apples, peeled and chopped	1 tbsp cloves
7 oz plums, pitted	1 tbsp cornstarch	1 cup sugar
¼ cup raisins	1 tsp cinnamon, ground	1 lemon, juiced

Directions

Mix all ingredients with 3 cups water in the Instant Pot. Seal the lid and cook for 10 minutes on High. Release the pressure naturally for 10 minutes. Remove the clove and serve cooled.

Classic New York Cheesecake

Makes: 6-8 serves | Ready in about: 1 hour

Ingredients

1 cup graham crackers crumbs	2 cups cream cheese, softened	1 tsp vanilla extract
2 tbsp butter, melted	½ cup sugar	2 eggs, beaten

Directions

In a bowl, combine butter, 1 tsp of the sugar, and crackers. Press into the bottom and about ⅓ up the sides of a greased pan. Set the crust in the freezer. In a separate bowl, beat the remaining sugar, cream cheese, and vanilla until smooth. Whisk in eggs and stir until combined. Spread the filling on the chilled crust. Add 1 cup water in your Instant Pot and set a steam rack.

Place the pan on the rack. Seal the lid, press Cake and, cook for 40 minutes on High Pressure. Release the pressure quickly. Chill the cake. With a knife, run along the edges between the pan and cheesecake to remove it. Invert onto a plate and serve.

Yummy French Squash Pie

Makes: 6-8 serves | Ready in about: 30 minutes

Ingredients

15 oz mashed squash	½ tsp cinnamon, ground	½ cup granulated sugar
6 fl oz milk	3 large eggs	1 pack pâte brisée

Directions

Place squash puree in a bowl. Add milk, cinnamon, eggs, and sugar. Whisk until well incorporated. Gently place pate in a greased baking dish creating the edges with hands. Pour the squash mixture over and flatten the surface with a spatula.

Pour 1 cup of water in the pot and insert a trivet. Lay the baking dish on the trivet. Seal the lid, and cook for 25 minutes on High Pressure. Do a quick release. Transfer the pie to a serving platter. Refrigerate overnight before serving.

Vanilla Pumpkin Cake

Makes: 6-8 serves | Ready in about: 1 hour 30 minutes

Ingredients

3 eggs
½ cup sugar
1 cup flour
½ cup half-and-half

¼ cup olive oil
1 tsp baking powder
1 tsp ground cinnamon
1 cup packed shredded pumpkin

½ cup chopped walnuts
4 oz cream cheese, softened
8 tbsp butter
½ cup confectioners sugar

Directions

In a bowl, beat eggs with sugar until smooth. Mix in oil, flour, cinnamon, half-and-half, and baking powder. Fold in walnuts and pumpkin. Spread batter on a greased cake pan. Add 1 cup water in your Instant Pot and insert a steamer rack. Lay cake pan onto the trivet. Seal the lid, select Cake, and cook on High Pressure for 40 minutes. Release pressure quickly. In a bowl, beat cream cheese, confectioners' sugar, and butter. Keep in the fridge. Spread the frosting over the cooled cake and serve.

Cranberry Cheesecake with Greek Yogurt

Makes: 6-8 serves | Ready in about: 25 minutes +cooling time

Ingredients

2 lb Greek yogurt
2 cups sugar
4 eggs

2 tsp lemon zest
1 cheesecake crust
7 oz dried cranberries

2 tbsp cranberry jam
1 tsp vanilla extract
1 tsp cranberry extract

Directions

In a bowl, combine yogurt, sugar, and eggs. With a mixer, beat well on low until well-combined. Grease a springform pan with oil. Place in the crust and pour in the filling. Leave in the fridge for 30 minutes.

Combine cranberries, jam, lemon zest, vanilla, cranberry extract, and ¾ cup lukewarm water in the Instant Pot. Simmer for 15 minutes on Sauté. Remove to a bowl. Add in 1 cup water and a trivet. Remove the springform pan from the fridge and set it on the trivet. Pour cranberry topping over. Seal the lid and cook for 20 minutes on High. Do a quick release. Refrigerate.

Homemade Apple Pie

Makes: 6-8 serves | Ready in about: 30 minutes

Ingredients

2 lb apples, cubed
¼ cup sugar
¼ cup breadcrumbs

2 tsp cinnamon
3 tbsp freshly squeezed lemon juice
¼ tbsp oil

1 egg, beaten
¼ cup all-purpose flour
Pie dough

Directions

Mix the breadcrumbs, sugar, apples, and cinnamon in a bowl. On a floured surface, roll out the pie dough, making 2 circle-shaped crusts. Place one pie crust in a greased baking dish. Spoon the apple mixture on top and cover with the other crust.

Seal by crimping edges and brush with beaten egg. Pour 1 cup of water in the Instant Pot and lay the trivet. Lower the baking sheet on the trivet. Seal the lid, and cook on High Pressure for 20 minutes. Do a quick release and serve chilled.

Lemony Cinnamon Apples

Serves: 2 | Ready in about: 13 minutes

Ingredients

2 apples, peeled and cut into wedges

½ cup lemon juice

½ tsp cinnamon

Directions

Combine lemon juice and 1 cup water in your Instant Pot and insert a steaming basket. Add in the apples in. Seal the lid, select Pressure Cook, and cook for 3 minutes. Release the pressure quickly. Dust the apples with cinnamon and serve cooled.

Pumpkin Pudding with Apple Juice

Serves: 2-4 | Ready in about: 20 minutes

Ingredients

1 lb pumpkin, chopped

1 cup granulated sugar

½ cup cornstarch

4 cups apple juice, unsweetened

1 tsp cinnamon, ground

3-4 ground cloves

Directions

In a bowl, beat sugar and apple juice until sugar dissolves. Pour the mixture into the Instant Pot and stir in cornstarch, cinnamon, cloves, and pumpkin. Seal the lid and cook for 10 minutes on High. Do a quick release. Serve chilled.

Classic Crème Brûlée

Serves: 2-4 | Ready in about: 15 minutes

Ingredients

5 cups heavy cream

8 egg yolks

1 cup honey

4 tbsp sugar

1 vanilla extract

¼ tsp salt

Directions

In a bowl, combine heavy cream, yolks, vanilla, and honey. Beat well with an electric mixer. Split the mixture into 4 ramekins. Pour 1 cup water in the Instant Pot and insert a trivet. Lower the ramekins on the trivet. Seal the lid and cook for 10 minutes on High Pressure. Do a quick pressure release. Top the ramekins with sugar and burn it with a culinary torch. Serve chilled.

Catalan Dessert

Serves: 2 | Ready in about: 45 minutes + cooling time

Ingredients

2 egg yolks, room temperature

3 tsp sugar

1 cup milk

1 cinnamon stick

1 strip lemon peel

1 tbsp superfine sugar for topping

Directions

Warm the milk, cinnamon, and lemon peel in your Instant Pot on Sauté. Remove to a bowl and allow to infuse for 10 minutes. Then, drag the cinnamon and lemon peel. In a bowl, beat the eggs with the sugar until the sugar dissolves. Slowly add the egg mixture into the milk and gently stir until everything is well mixed. Divide the mixture between ramekins.

Pour 1 cup water in the pot and fit in a trivet. Place the ramekins on the trivet. Seal the lid. Cook on Manual for 20 minutes. Perform a quick pressure release. Let cool the dessert. Top with sugar. Place under the broiler to caramelize the sugar. Serve chilled.

Fresh Cottage Cheesecake

Makes: 6-8 serves | Ready in about: 35 minutes

Ingredients

10 oz cream cheese

¼ cup sugar

½ cup cottage cheese

1 lemon, zested and juiced

2 eggs, cracked into a bowl

1 tsp lemon extract

3 tbsp sour cream

10 strawberries, halved

Directions

Blend with an electric mixer, the cream cheese, quarter cup of sugar, cottage cheese, lemon zest, lemon juice, and lemon extract until a smooth consistency is formed. Add in the eggs. Fold in at low speed until fully incorporated. Spoon the mixture into a greased cake pan. Level the top with a spatula and cover with foil. Fit a trivet in the pot and pour in 1 cup water. Place the cake pan on the trivet. Seal the lid, select Manual at High, and set the cooking time to 15 minutes.

In a bowl, mix the sour cream and 1 tbsp of sugar. Once the timer has gone off, do a natural pressure release for 10 minutes. Use a spatula to spread the sour cream mixture on the warm cake. Let cool. Top with strawberries and serve.

Caramel Flan with Whipping Cream

Serves: 2-4 | Ready in about: 30 minutes

Ingredients

½ cup granulated sugar

4 tbsp caramel syrup

3 eggs

½ tsp vanilla extract

½ tbsp milk

5 oz whipping cream

Directions

Combine milk, whipping cream, and vanilla extract in your Instant Pot. Press Sauté and cook for 5 minutes or until small bubbles form. Set aside. Using an electric mixer, whisk the eggs and sugar.

Gradually add the cream mixture and whisk until well combined. Divide the caramel syrup between 4 ramekins. Fill with egg mixture and place them on top of the trivet.

Pour in 1 cup of water. Seal the lid, and cook for 15 minutes on High Pressure. Do a quick release. Remove the ramekins from the pot and cool completely before serving.

Delicious Tiramisu Cheesecake

Makes: 6-8 serves | Ready in about: 1 hour + chilling time

Ingredients

1 tbsp Kahlua liquor
1 ½ cups ladyfingers, crushed
1 tbsp granulated espresso
1 tbsp butter, melted

16 oz cream cheese, softened
8 oz mascarpone cheese, softened
2 tbsp powdered sugar
½ cup white sugar

1 tbsp cocoa powder
1 tsp vanilla extract
2 eggs

Directions

In a bowl, beat the cream cheese, mascarpone, and white sugar. Gradually beat in the eggs, powdered sugar, and vanilla. Combine the liquor, ladyfingers, espresso, and butter in another bowl.

Press the ladyfinger crust at the bottom of a greased baking dish. Pour the filling over. Cover the pan with a paper towel and then close it with aluminum foil.

Pour 1 cup of water in your pressure cooker and lower the trivet. Place the pan inside and seal the lid. Select Manual and set to 35 minutes at High. Wait for about 10 minutes before pressing Cancel and releasing the pressure quickly. Allow cooling completely before refrigerating the cheesecake for 4 hours.

Lemon Peach Pie

Makes: 6-8 serves | Ready in about: 50 minutes

Ingredients

1 cup fresh blueberries
1 peach, chopped
1 cup flour

2 large eggs
1 tsp baking powder
¼ cup butter, softened

¼ cup powdered stevia
¼ tsp vanilla extract
2 tsp freshly squeezed lemon juice

Directions

In a bowl, combine flour and baking powder. Mix well and set aside. In a separate bowl, combine eggs and powdered stevia. Using a hand mixer with a whisking attachment, beat the mixture for 2 minutes until light and fluffy. Transfer to a bowl.

Add butter, vanilla, and lemon juice. Gradually add the egg mixture, beating constantly. Transfer the mixture to a greased baking dish. Spread the batter evenly with a kitchen spatula. Arrange the fruit on top.

Pour 1 cup of water in your Instant Pot and insert the trivet. Place the pan on top. Seal the lid and cook for 30 minutes on High Pressure. Release the pressure quickly and let chill thoroughly before serving.

Strudel with Walnut & Pumpkin

Makes: 6-8 serves | Ready in about: 30 minutes

Ingredients

2 cups pumpkin puree
1 tsp vanilla extract
2 cups Greek yogurt

2 eggs, beaten
2 tbsp brown sugar
2 tbsp unsalted butter, softened

2 puff pastry sheets
1 cup walnuts, chopped

Directions

In a bowl, mix yogurt and vanilla until smooth; set aside. Cut each pastry sheet into 4-inch x 7-inch pieces and brush with some beaten eggs. Place approximately 2 tbsp of pumpkin puree and 2 tbsp of the yogurt mixture in the middle of each pastry and sprinkle with walnuts. Fold the sheets and brush with the remaining eggs. Cut the surface with a sharp knife.

Gently place each strudel into an oiled baking dish. Pour 1 cup of water in the pot and insert the trivet. Place the pan on top. Seal the lid and cook for 25 minutes on High Pressure. Release the pressure naturally for about 10 minutes. Let it chill for 10 minutes. Carefully Transfer the strudels to a serving plate.

Chocolate-Glazed Yogurt Cake

Makes: 4-6 serves | Ready in about: 35 minutes

Ingredients

3 cups yogurt	1 cup oil	7 oz dark chocolate
3 cups flour	2 tsp baking soda	10 tbsp milk
2 cups sugar	3 tbsp cocoa	5 oz butter

Directions

In a bowl, combine yogurt, flour, sugar, oil, baking soda, and cocoa. Beat well with an electric mixer. Transfer a mixture to a springform pan. Wrap the pan in foil. Insert a trivet in the Instant Pot. Pour in 1 cup water and place the pan on top. Seal the lid and cook for 30 minutes on High Pressure. Do a quick release, remove the springform pan, and unwrap. Chill well.

Meanwhile, melt the chocolate in a microwave. Transfer to a bowl and whisk in butter and milk. Beat well with a mixer and pour the mixture over the cake. Refrigerate for at least two hours before serving.

Squash Tart Oatmeal

Serves: 2-4 | Ready in about: 35 minutes

Ingredients

3 ½ cups coconut milk	½ cup sultanas, soaked	¾ tsp ground ginger
1 cup steel-cut oats	⅓ cup honey	½ tsp orange zest
1 cup shredded butternut squash	1 tsp ground cinnamon	¼ cup toasted walnuts, chopped

Directions

In your Instant Pot, mix sultanas, orange zest, ginger, milk, honey, squash, and oats. Seal the lid and cook on High Pressure for 12 minutes. Do a natural release for 10 minutes. Stir in sugar. Top with walnuts and serve.

Vanilla Fruity Cheesecake

Makes: 6-8 serves | Ready in about: 30 minutes

Ingredients

1 ½ cups graham cracker crust	1 tbsp fresh orange juice	¾ cup sugar
1 cup raspberries	3 eggs	1 tsp vanilla paste
3 cups cream cheese	½ stick butter, melted	1 tsp finely grated orange zest

Directions

Insert the tray into the pressure cooker, and add 1 ½ cups of water. Grease a springform. Mix in graham cracker crust with sugar and butter in a bowl. Press the mixture to form a crust at the bottom. Blend the raspberries and cream cheese with an electric mixer. Crack in the eggs and keep mixing until well combined. Mix in the remaining ingredients and stir.

Pour the mixture into the pan and cover with aluminium foil. Lay it on the tray. Select Pressure Cook and cook for 20 minutes at High. Once the cooking is complete, do a quick pressure release. Refrigerate the cheesecake for at least 2 hours.

Sweet Pie Cups with Fruits

Makes: 6-8 serves | Ready in about: 35 minutes + chilling time

Ingredients

2 cups + 2 tbsp flour	½ fresh peach, chopped	2 tbsp flour
¾ cup butter, softened	1 apple, chopped	½ tsp cinnamon
2 tbsp sugar	¼ cup dry cranberries, soaked	1 egg yolk, for brushing

Directions

Place 2 cups of the flour, butter, 1 tbsp sugar, and ½ cup ice water in a food processor and pulse until dough becomes crumbly. Remove to a lightly floured work surface. Divide among 4 equal pieces and wrap in plastic foil. Refrigerate for 1 hour.

Place apple, peach, cranberries, remaining flour, cinnamon, and remaining sugar in a bowl. Toss to combine and set aside. Roll each piece into 6-inch round discs. Add 2 tablespoons of the apple mixture at each disc's center and wrap to form small bowls. Brush each bowl with egg yolk and gently transfer to a greased baking dish.

Pour 1 cup water in the pot and insert a trivet. Place the pan on top. Seal the lid and cook for 25 minutes on Manual. Release the pressure quickly. Serve. chilled

RECIPE INDEX

Made in United States
Troutdale, OR
12/13/2024

26420148R00091